鼓 舞

gǔ wǔ

for secondary Mandarin Chinese

Hannah Hui-Chen Hua

Kwun Shun Shih   Yan Wang

Teacher Pack

OXFORD

MW01260056

UNIVERSITY PRESS

Great Clarendon Street, Oxford, OX2 6DP, United Kingdom

Oxford University Press is a department of the University of Oxford.
It furthers the University's objective of excellence in research,
scholarship, and education by publishing worldwide. Oxford is a
registered trade mark of Oxford University Press in the UK and in
certain other countries

© Oxford University Press 2017

The moral rights of the authors have been asserted.

First published in 2017

All rights reserved. No part of this publication may be reproduced,
stored in a retrieval system, or transmitted, in any form or by any
means, without the prior permission in writing of Oxford University
Press, or as expressly permitted by law, by licence or under terms
agreed with the appropriate reprographics rights organization.
Enquiries concerning reproduction outside the scope of the above
should be sent to the Rights Department, Oxford University Press, at
the address above.

You must not circulate this work in any other form and you must
impose this same condition on any acquirer.

British Library Cataloguing in Publication Data
Data available

978-0-19-840835-2

10 9 8 7 6 5 4

Paper used in the production of this book is a natural, recyclable
product made from wood grown in sustainable forests.
The manufacturing process conforms to the environmental
regulations of the country of origin.

Printed in Great Britain

Contents

About this book

Gǔ Wǔ for Secondary Mandarin Chinese is a thematic course which will build students' confidence and ability in all of the key language skills – reading, writing, speaking, and listening. Written by an international team of expert teachers and examiners, the skills-based approach is suitable for a range of international curricula, including Cambridge IGCSE, IB DP *Ab Initio* and MYP Language Acquisition (Phases 1-3).

This Teacher Book and CD will assist you in delivering the content of the Gǔ Wǔ Student Book. It is mapped exactly to the structure of the Student Book and provides sample answers and guidance for all activities. Homework and assessment suggestions are provided for each lesson and are differentiated for ability level and curriculum, allowing flexible teaching for all of your learners. These icons will help you identify differentiated content:

MYP Material tailored to the MYP specification

DP Material tailored to the Ab Initio specification

Ideas to try with students who require more support

Ideas to try with students who require further challenge

The CD includes the following additional resources, to support you and your students:

– a detailed **scope and sequence chart,** showing how all of the key skills are covered throughout the Gǔ Wǔ course

– printable lists of all of the essential **vocabulary** and **glossary** terms from the Student Book

– a full suite a sample **examination-style papers** for IGCSE and *Ab Initio*

– **worksheets** to support the extra activities in the Teacher Book

– generic **language learning games** for you to use throughout the course

– **transcripts and audio recordings** for all of the Student Book listening activities

UNIT OBJECTIVES

- Share information about yourself and your family for a range of purposes.
- Discuss why people keep pets.

- Share your views on hobbies and interests.
- Discuss what you do in your leisure time.
- Discuss how people celebrate special occasions.

1.1 预习 Unit introduction

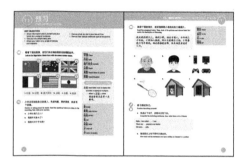

Prior knowledge

Students should be familiar with language basics such as numbers for age, height, birthdays; colours for hair, eyes and clothing; personal characteristics; family members; hobbies and interests.

Icebreaker activity

Students make their own Chinese business cards showing: name, date of birth, "I like ...", "I dislike ...", "I am ...". They should include the categories in Chinese. After making 3 or 4 copies, they introduce themselves to classmates and exchange cards. (Tell them that it is Chinese etiquette to offer and accept business cards with both hands.)

Students can report on the people they interview, using the information on their business cards.

Lesson activities

 **1** Reading

  Show one of the many videos on the internet teaching nationalities in Chinese. You can then ask: "你是哪国人?"

Note students' nationalities and teach them the names of the countries.

Answers

a. i **b.** iii **c.** vi **d.** iv **e.** v **f.** ii

Ensure students can state their own nationality.

Encourage students to learn the nationalities of everyone in the class. You could find recent news items about international events or sports and introduce additional nationalities for students to learn.

2 Listening

Point out to students that the purpose of this listening practice is to train them to hear numbers in context, such as ages, number of family members, height, etc.

Tell students to always read the questions and note down the question words before listening. Here, the question words are:

几口 (listen for a small number, normally below 10); 多大 (listen for an age); 吗 (listen out for a statement and give a Yes or No answer).

Transcript

a. 我叫小华。我的家里有四口人：爸爸、妈妈、哥哥和我。

b. 我的哥哥今年十八岁了，我十五岁。

c. 我的爸爸不高也不矮，但是我的妈妈很高，有一米七十。

Answers

a. 四口人 **b.** 十八岁 **c.** 很高，有一米七十

 **3** Reading

Before doing the activity, discuss with the class what each picture represents.

Answers

b, c, f

4 ✏️ ⭕ Writing and Speaking

Help students to pronounce and write their names in Chinese. Ensure they know the vocabulary for numbers so they can give their ages.

Sample answer for part a

你好，我叫心美，我今年十六岁。我家有四口人，爸爸，哥哥和我都很高，但是妈妈不高。我家有两只可爱的小狗，他们是我们最爱的宠物。

Further differentiation

🤲 Give students extra speaking and writing practice in making sentences in the first/second/third person, using 我/你/他/她. They can write short sentences introducing themselves, their friends and family.

📈 Encourage students to use 也, 很, 不, or the structure 又 ...... 又 ...... to expand their writing.

1.2 我自己 About myself

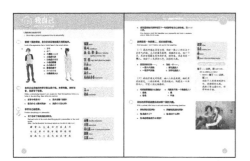

Icebreaker activity

Display pictures of celebrities, and get students to describe them, using the vocabulary in the Student Book. Ask:

谁最漂亮／帅气？　　　谁的鼻子最小／高？

谁有黑黑的长头发？　　谁有洁白的牙齿？

谁有金色的短发？　　　谁长得最高大？

谁有棕色的大眼睛？

Lesson activities

1 📖 Reading

Answers

a. ii, iv, vi, viii, x　**b.** i, iii, v, vii, ix

Ensure everyone can describe their own appearance.

📈 Ask students to imagine they are telling their grandmother about some new friends they made on holiday. They should describe how they looked and give their nationality and home town.

2 🔊 Listening

Tell students always to read the questions first, paying attention to the question words/phrases. Here, the listening focus is: a. number, b. country/nationality, c. reasoning (students should listen for the reason after 因为) and d. personality.

Transcript

a. 大家好。我的名字是志军。今年十五岁。

b. 我来自中国。

c. 因为爸爸的工作，我们全家搬来了英国。

d. 我很开心成为这个班级的学生。我是一个爱笑，爱说话的人。初次见面，请多关照。谢谢！

Answers

a. 十五岁　**b.** 中国　**c.** 因为爸爸的工作

d. 他是个爱笑，爱说话的人。

3 📖 ✏️ Reading and Writing

For part a, remind students that the Student Book word search contains additional vocabulary not given in the vocabulary box.

For part b, encourage students to give a supporting statement to go with each characteristic they have chosen.

Answers for part a

友善 (friendly), 开朗 (cheerful), 懒 (lazy), 马马虎虎 (careless), 聪明 (clever)

Sample answers for part b

A: 我的个性内向，所以我不喜欢去人多的地方。

B: 我的个性开朗外向，我喜欢热闹，结交新的朋友。

4 Reading

Remind students that the key words to look out for in the passage as they read are: a. 脸，b. 礼貌，c. 颜色，d. 热情

Answers

a. ii **b.** i **c.** i **d.** i

5 Speaking

Walk around the classroom and listen to students' conversations. Provide support where necessary.

Students can try to use transitional words such as 但是，所以，认为，即使 to make longer/more complex sentences.

If time permits, students can write out their answers. It is good to get students to speak first and then write about their discussion. Speaking imprints the knowledge and writing reinforces it.

Some students may need extra help with numbers, colours and physical features. Rather than writing from scratch, you may like to ask them to fill in the blanks using the passage below as an opportunity for reading practice.

请把下面的词语填入文章中的空格：

不　　又高又瘦　　也　　九年级　　头发　　褐

我叫李明，今年13岁，读 _____。我是意大利人，我的头发是黑色的，眼睛是 _____ 色的，我长得 _____ 高，只有150公分。我的好朋友叫丽娜，她 _____ 是13岁，她是瑞典人，她的 _____ 是金色的，眼睛是蓝色的。她长得 _____ 。

Assessment suggestion

Ask students to imagine that a friend has got lost on a school trip. It is important to give the police a detailed description of the person's appearance and character. It should include: name, age, height, appearance and characteristics.

Homework suggestion

Tell students they are standing for election as class representative on the school council (or equivalent) and need to create a candidate poster. They should describe their personality and say what they are passionate about. They need to make their poster stand out to win the election. Students will then have the opportunity to vote for the best poster.

1.3 个人信息 Personal information

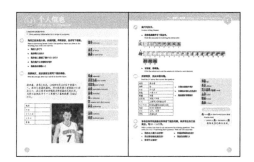

Lesson activities

1 Listening

Remind students to read the questions before listening and note the key words. Here they should listen out for: a. a number; b. her place of birth; c. another place she moved to; d. a time; e. family members.

Transcript

a. 大家好。我叫海伦。今年十五岁了。

b. 我是英国人，出生于伦敦。

c. 但是现在和家人一起住在中国的上海。

d. 我们是去年搬家到上海。我们都很喜欢住在上海。

e. 我们家有四口人：爸爸、妈妈、姐姐和我。

Answers

a. 十五岁   b. 英国的伦敦   c. 中国的上海

d. 去年   e. 爸爸、妈妈、姐姐和海伦。

Ask where students were born or currently live. Introduce the place names in Chinese if possible.

Going on a journey

This game reinforces the learning of place names in Chinese. Mark a large circle on the floor with city names dotted randomly inside. Students stand on a city each. When you call out "从 X 往 Y" the students standing on those cities change places. They will need to stay alert as the places they stand on will keep changing.

Language and culture

Students will recognise 哪里 as meaning "where". Explain that when said twice in response to a compliment (哪里哪里), it is an expression of modesty, meaning something like "Don't mention it. I don't deserve this praise." Modesty is greatly valued in Chinese society. Unless among very close friends, people never speak of their merits or strengths.

 ## 2 Reading

Take students through the form and tell them to use it as a guide for the reading. Help them to develop the habit of reading with a purpose. As the form asks for name, nationality, birthday, birthplace and height, encourage students to look for that information.

Answers

姓名	林书豪
国籍	美国
出生日期	1988年8月23日
出生地	美国加州
身高	1米91

 ## 3 Writing

For part a, the strokes animation on the MGDB online dictionary is useful for showing students the sequences of writing individual characters.

For part b, ask students to tell you what the radical is for each character. If they struggle to do so, write out some common radicals on the board as prompts.

Answers for part b

国：部首：口，笔画：8

籍：部首：竹，笔画：20

 ## 4 Reading

Ask students to read the questions first: a. is about height, b. is about birthplace, and c. is about hobbies. Tell them to bear these 3 points in mind when reading the form and look for the appropriate answers.

Answers

a. 日晴长得高。

b. 日晴是在中国广州市出生的。

c. 她的爱好是唱歌、跳舞。

 ## 5 Speaking and Writing

Walk around the classroom providing support to individual pairs as necessary. Remind students to make notes during the speaking part of the activity so they can use them for the CV.

You could give students a vocabulary list for dates, places, countries and hobbies.

Assessment suggestion

Tell students they are to take part in a TV interview activity. In pairs, they take it in turns to ask and answer questions about themselves and their families – either as themselves or as a celebrity. Give them time to prepare, then ask them to perform their interviews in front of the class.

Homework suggestion

Students write a report on the person they interviewed and on themselves, using the answers given in the interview.

Sample answer

我的生日是1999年12月18日，今年17岁，我是在法国的巴黎出生的。我以前在德国、意大利、西班牙住过。现在我住在英国的伦敦。

1.4 家庭成员 My family

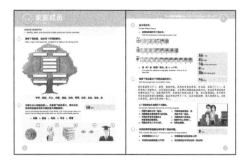

Icebreaker activity

In order to help students grasp complicated Chinese family relationship vocabulary, you could use pictures of a well-known family, perhaps from national life or from a television series, to introduce the names for each family member. Students should contribute any family vocabulary they know.

Language and culture

The Chinese language has a more complicated system for describing family relationships: relatives on the father's side of the family are referred to differently from those on the mother's side.

Lesson activities

  Reading

Ensure students have a firm grasp of relevant vocabulary by getting them to introduce their immediate and extended family, giving their names and ages.

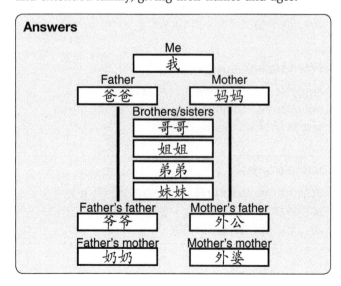

Answers

Me — 我
Father — 爸爸 Mother — 妈妈
Brothers/sisters — 哥哥 / 姐姐 / 弟弟 / 妹妹
Father's father — 爷爷 Mother's father — 外公
Father's mother — 奶奶 Mother's mother — 外婆

2  Listening

Students should identify the main points illustrated by each of the images, and listen out for the relevant vocabulary in Chinese to help them.

Transcript

a. 我是安娜，我今年十六岁，来自美国。我有金色的头发。

b. 我的爸爸是美国人。他很高，有两米高。他非常喜欢打篮球。

c. 我的妈妈是西班牙人，她长得不高也不矮。妈妈有很漂亮的绿色的眼睛。

d. 我们的爷爷和我们住在一起。爷爷喜欢安静，常常一个人看书。

e. 我有一个哥哥，他今年十八岁。我觉得哥哥很聪明。

Answers

a. ii **b.** i **c.** iv **d.** iii **e.** v

3 Writing

For part a, the strokes animation on the MGDB online dictionary is useful for showing students the sequences of writing individual characters.

For part b, remind students they can use vocabulary learned in other lessons as well as this one to help construct their answers.

Sample answer for part b
爸爸的工作很忙，经常忙得忘记吃饭。

 You could ask a few questions to give students practice in making sentences with 忙.

4 Reading

Ask students to pay attention to the key words in each statement to help them to work out the answers. Discuss with them what they think the key words are.

Answers

i, iii, v, viii

Who in your family ... ? survey

To give students additional practice in talking about their families, put them in pairs of similar ability and give them each a "Who in your family ... ?" worksheet from the CD-ROM. Students who need more support should use the table in the top half of the worksheet. Instruct students to use the sentence patterns:

谁(最)……

因为……

e.g. **Q:** 你家谁最能吃？　**A:** 我哥哥最能吃。

Q: 为什么？　**A:** 他每餐都吃五碗饭，他是个大饭桶。

It is good to build sentence pattern practice into classroom activities to reinforce grammar acquisition.

5 ◯ **Speaking**

Walk around the classroom providing support to individual pairs as necessary. Remind students to refer to Lesson 1.2 for vocabulary for people's personalities.

Sample answers

a. 我家有四个人：爸爸、妈妈、姐姐和我。

b. 我觉得我爸爸很内向，我妈妈很外向，我姐姐也很活泼，我跟爸爸一样，比较安静。

c. 我觉得妈妈比较严厉。

d. 我没有跟爷爷奶奶一起住，不过他们住在我们家附近。

Give students a list of vocabulary for numbers, family members and personal characteristics or direct them to the relevant flashcards on the Quizlet site for vocabulary practice.

Assessment suggestion

Ask students to think of a famous family from a book, a play or a period of history they have studied. They should write a paragraph saying what they have chosen and who the family members are.

Homework suggestions

1. Students create a small photo album to introduce their family members and label them in Chinese.

2. Students create an ideal imaginary family, choosing anyone from the past or present. They need to write a paragraph explaining who they have chosen and why.

1.5 我家的宠物 Pets in my family

Icebreaker activity

Ask students whether they have pets at home, what they are, their names, likes and dislikes.

Lesson activities

1 📖 **Reading**

Before the activity, get the class to practise saying the animal names in Chinese out loud. To help students remember the pronunciations, explain that for some animal names, such as 猫 and 马, the pronunciation is similar to the sound the animal makes.

This activity is an opportunity to introduce measure words. Go through 只, 条 and 匹 with the class.

Answers

a: **a.** ii **b.** v **c.** vi **d.** iii **e.** i **f.** vii **g.** iv

b: **i** 狗被称为人类的好朋友。
ii 猫喜欢抓老鼠。
iii 老鼠又小又毛茸茸的。
iv 马儿又高大又跑得快。
v 小鸟的叫声很好听，有时候像唱歌一样。
vi 金鱼喜欢生活在水里，看上去非常漂亮。

 Ask students to identify which words from part b are descriptions of appearance and which are descriptions of temperament.

Measure words activity

Divide students into groups of 3–4 and give each group a "Measure-word dice" template (on the CD-ROM). This features the 6 most common measure words: 个, 位, 只, 条, 张, 杯. Ask students to make up the dice and throw it to each other. When they catch it, they need to make a sentence with the measure word on top of the dice.

Give students a dice with additional measure words. (You may change the measure words on the dice using the template in the worksheet folder.) Here are some suggestions for alternatives: 本, 件, 支, 把, 座, 匹, 双

Language and culture

Remind students that measure words are important in Chinese grammar. Students need to know that different measure words are used depending on the category to which the thing being counted belongs (e.g. people, animals, cars, and so on).

2  Listening

Remind students to read the questions first and pick out the key words, so they know what information to listen for. Ask what they think the key words are in each case.

a. 小明／为什么／没有宠物；**b.** 丽青爷爷／鸟；
c. 约翰／地方／动物；**d.** 海伦／宠物；**e.** 阿里／猫／以后

 Accept shorter answers as long as they include the key information.

Transcript

a. 小明：我是小明。我家在城市的中心，房子不大，所以我们家没有养宠物。

b. 丽青：我是丽青。我们住在上海，爷爷养了两只会说话的鸟，可有意思了！

c. 约翰：我是约翰。我家后面有个农场，我和弟弟各自都有一匹马。

d. 海伦：我是海伦。我们家客厅的鱼缸里有很多漂亮的小鱼。

e. 阿里：我是阿里。以前我们家里养了一只棕色的猫，可是有一天猫离开了家以后就再也没有回来。我希望以后再养一只猫。

Answers

a. 因为他家在城市的中心，房子不大，所以没有养宠物。

b. 爷爷养了两只会说话的鸟。

c. 约翰家后面有个农场，他养了一匹马。

d. 漂亮的小鱼。

e. 阿里以前的猫不见了，他希望以后再养一只猫。

 Show students Lesson 19 (Talking about pets, 1.10–2.20 minutes) of CCTV's *Growing up with Chinese*. Before they watch it, ask students to listen out for what pets Lan Lan and her friends have (Lan Lan: a dog; male student: a dog and two turtles; female student: no pets but she would like to have a cat).

3  Reading

Remind students to read the questions carefully and look out for key words as they read.

 You could give students the following words to help them form their answers: a. 一开始／日晴／礼物; b. 上个月／聚餐／爷爷生气; c. 鸟／为什么.

Answers

a. 一开始日晴想给爷爷买一部新的智能手机，可以上网。

b. 因为大家都在玩手机。

c. 因为每天早上爷爷可以提着鸟笼子去公园玩，既锻炼了身体，还会觉得心情好。

4  Speaking

Walk around the classroom providing support to individual pairs as necessary.

 You may need to give students a list of vocabulary for places, descriptions for places, descriptions for pets and their temperaments.

Sample answers

a. 我和家人住在一个小村庄里。

b. 我觉得那么多人喜欢养狗或养猫是因为这些宠物是人们的好朋友，使人的生活更开心。

c. 我一定会养宠物，我特别喜欢小狗，因为我觉得小狗忠诚可爱。

Assessment suggestion

 Ask students to research how animals changed from being useful on the farm to being household pets, and write a report.

Homework suggestion

Students design a robot pet for an exhibition about the future. They should include the following:

a. What does it look like? How big is it?

b. What can it do? How can it improve our life?

c. What makes this pet stand out?

1.6 我的兴趣和爱好
My interests and hobbies

Icebreaker activity

Students take it in turns to mime hobbies while the rest of the class guesses the activity.

Lesson activities

1  Reading

Answers

a. vii **b.** i **c.** vi **d.** iii **e.** iv **f.** viii **g.** v **h.** ii

After students have completed Activity 1, ask them questions (using words like 什么, 多久, 去哪儿, 跟谁) to enable them to use the new vocabulary to construct sentences.

2  Reading and Speaking

Do this as a group activity by writing each part of the sentence onto a separate card and ask students to put the cards in the right order. To extend the activity, make some new cards to replace parts of the sentence.

Answers

a. 他的爱好是看电视。

b. 她有很多兴趣。

c. 我除了喜欢写作还喜欢摄影。

3 Reading

 To motivate students before the reading activity, you could show them a video clip from a popular TV programme in China, "中国好声音" (*The Voice of China*). Ask questions about the contestants, such as their age and where they come from.

Show students how to approach the reading comprehension. As always, they should read the questions first. Tell students to pay attention to the question words and the verbs before or after them.

a. This is a "What" question so students should look out for the things that come after "学". However, they should note that this question specifies the time: "at primary school age".

b. This is a "When" question. They need to look out for the time phrase, which links with the verb "唱歌".

c. This is a "Why" question. They should listen for the reason after "因为", which is associated with "唱歌".

d. This is another "What" question for a different time period, "去年冬天".

Answers

a. 她跟着姐姐一起学了跳舞。

b. 中学一年级的时候因为看了《中国好声音》，小寒喜欢上了唱歌。

c. 因为有同学说小寒唱得不好听，她就很少唱歌了。

d. 去年冬天，小寒在日本学会了滑雪。

4 Writing

List-writing should be a straightforward activity for most students, but if anyone struggles, remind them to refer to the vocabulary covered in Activity 1.

Sample answer

我喜欢看书、滑雪、看电影、旅行、听古典音乐。

5 Listening

Help students to develop the habit of reading all the answer options to each question. All the pictures show interests and hobbies so that's what students should expect to hear about. Encourage them to take notes while listening so that they can match hobbies with people.

Remind students to write down the Chinese or pinyin for each picture first. This will make the listening and matching easier.

Transcript

我的名字是丽青。我和家人住在上海，家里一共有六口人：爷爷、奶奶、爸爸、妈妈、弟弟和我。

我的爸爸喜欢去美丽的地方拍照片。

妈妈特别爱唱歌。

弟弟呢，最喜欢打游戏机。

我不喜欢玩游戏，我的爱好是画画，美术老师说我画画画得不错。

爷爷喜欢安静地看书，奶奶这几年爱上了跳舞，晚饭以后经常去公园和她的朋友们跳舞。

Answers

a. ii **b.** v **c.** iii **d.** iv **e.** i **f.** vi

Language and culture

Chinese names indicate parents' best wishes for their children. There are always meanings behind Chinese names, such as strong, beautiful, brave or intelligent. If you got a Chinese phonetic translation for your English name, it won't be a proper Chinese one because it wouldn't have a meaning behind it. Think of a quality you would like to have and give yourself a name to reflect the quality.

It is Chinese custom to write one's surname before one's given name, some Chinese people prefer to use this format even when writing their names in English. One example is Xi Jinping, the current President of the People's Republic of China.

Assessment suggestion

Students give a brief talk on their hobbies, when and where they do them, and with whom.

 Students could include: how they came to choose their hobbies, how they develop their skills and any high-profile people in their area of interest.

Homework suggestion

Tell students that researching into family history is very popular. Family names can be a guide to occupations or to the area where the family

originated. Ask them to research the origin of their own family name and write a paragraph about it.

 Students carry out a research project on 10 Chinese family names and write a short report.

1.7 周末计划 Weekend activities

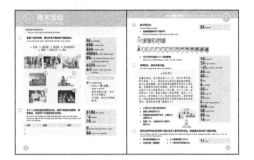

Icebreaker activity

Ask the class what they like to do at the weekend and create a list on the board. Students write down the various activities and indicate which ones they take part in. Rank them in order of popularity. Tell students they will need this information later.

1  Reading

The above warm-up activity should help students to complete this reading activity with relative ease.

Answers

a. v **b.** ii **c.** vii **d.** iii **e.** vi **f.** i **g.** iv

 Ask students to talk about the activity in each of the pictures, adding their own details.

In groups of 3 or 4, students ask each other about their weekend activities, for instance:

你喜欢 _____ 吗? 　　多久去 _____?
你跟谁一起 _____? 　　做了什么?
在哪儿 _____? 　　你觉得如何?
怎么去的?

Afterwards, ask each group to present a spoken or written report about one member's weekend activity.

Language and culture

Tell students that the order of Chinese language follows the order of Chinese philosophy: sky, earth and humans. The time phrase, related to the sun and moon in the sky, usually comes first; location is next and human activities come last.

2 Listening

Tell students to listen out for the time first, then the location and then the human activity.

Transcript

a. 这个周末天气很好，我要和朋友一起去爬山。

b. 这个星期六我打算和太太一起去看一场音乐剧。

c. 这个星期天我的先生和儿子要去湖边钓鱼。

d. 下个周末我想和女儿逛街。

e. 下个周末，我们一家人都去郊游。

Answers

人物	时间	活动
1	这个周末	和朋友去爬山
2	这个星期六	和太太去看音乐剧
3	这个星期天	先生和儿子要去湖边钓鱼
4	下周末	和女儿逛街
5	下个周末	一家人去郊游

3 Writing

For part a, the strokes animation on the MGDB online dictionary is useful for showing students the sequences of writing individual characters.

For part b, use the table below to help students to make sentences:

Time	Sentence pattern	Activities
这个周末	我打算 我想 我会 我要 我可能会	Suggest that students use some of the activities they have learned so far.

4 Reading

Offer students some guidance as to what to look for in each question: a. a reason – in the phrases after "因为"; b. something to learn – a subject, a language, an activity; c. an activity for fine weather; d. an activity for rainy days.

Answers

a. 因为周末不用上学，所以不用早起，可以多睡一会儿。

b. 心美最近在学跳舞。

c. 心美会约朋友一起去郊游，有时候去爬山，有时候去划船。

d. 如果下雨，心美会和朋友一起去城里的图书馆看书和上网或去朋友家里打游戏机。

5 Speaking

This activity involves making sentences in present, past and future tenses. You may use this chart to help students:

Time (tense needed)	Sentence pattern
周末 (present tense)	常常／通常
上个周末 (past tense)	了
下个周末 (future tense)	要／想

Walk around the classroom providing support to individual pairs if necessary.

Sample answers

a. 周末我常常跟家人看电影。

b. 上周末我去看了星际争霸战。

c. 我是跟爸爸和哥哥一起去的。

d. 下个周末我打算陪妈妈去看一部爱情片。

Assessment suggestion

Students write a short report on the class's weekend activities, indicating the most and least popular.

Homework suggestion

Students write a paragraph about how they and their family spent their free time last weekend.

1.8 周末计划 Planning for the weekend

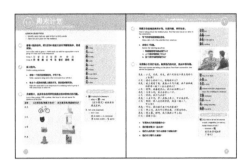

Lesson activities

1 Reading

Activities 1 and 2 can be carried out together. First, create 2 sets of flashcards. Divide students into 2 groups: group A are verbs and group B are nouns. Each student picks a card and has to find the person in the other group with the corresponding noun or verb.

Ask students to make up more phrases using the verbs from group A.

> **Answers**
>
> 听音乐， 看书， 写作， 玩游戏， 唱歌， 跳舞， 画画， 骑马， 爬山

2   Writing

Once the verb and noun students have been correctly paired up, ask each student pair to compose a sentence using their word compound and write it down.

> **Sample answers**
>
> a. 我的家人有许多不同的爱好，爸爸喜欢看书和听音乐。妈妈喜欢唱歌也喜欢画画。哥哥喜欢运动，他常常爬山和骑马。妹妹喜欢唱歌、跳舞和玩游戏。我最喜欢写作。
>
> b. 看电影， 爬树， 听收音机， 写信， 骑自行车

3 Speaking

Walk around the classroom providing support to individual pairs as necessary.

> You may need to give students vocabulary for weekend activities and remind them of the expressions for the past and future.

> **Sample answers**
>
> 马克上个周末去骑自行车了，下个周末他要去看电影。
>
> 小文上个周末去看戏了，下个周末她要写作。
>
> 日晴上个周末去购物了，下个周末她要去钓鱼。
>
> 阿里上个周末去露营了，下个周末他要去骑马。

At the weekend I will...
Students can practise the future tense and reinforce their grasp of activity vocabulary by playing "这个周末我要……". One student says what they will do at the weekend. The next repeats what the first said and adds another activity, and so on until the list gets too long!

4 Listening

For part a, students can jot down the activities they hear in pinyin, before writing them out in characters.

For part b, point out the key words in each question: a. 通常， b. 上个周末， c. 这个周末。

> **Transcript**
>
> 我周末的时候比较有空，会做一些有意思的活动。
>
> 通常周末我都会去图书馆上网和看书。但是上个周末我没有去图书馆，因为我的表哥结婚了，我去参加了他的婚礼。在婚礼上我吃了很多好吃的食物。
>
> 这个周末呢，星期六我会跟爸爸妈妈一起去爷爷家吃饭，星期天我们想去森林公园骑自行车。

> **Answers**
>
> a. 上网、看书、结婚、参加婚礼、骑自行车
>
> b. i 玛莉通常周末会去图书馆上网和看书。
>
>   ii 上个周末玛莉去参加了表哥的婚礼。
>
>   iii 星期六玛莉会跟爸爸妈妈一起去爷爷家吃饭，星期天他们打算去森林公园骑自行车。

5 Reading

You could use this chart to help students pick up key information in the reading passage.

Time (tense needed)	Sentence pattern
周末，暑假， 寒假， 放假的时候	常常／通常
上个周末， 上个月， 去年	了
下个周末， 下个月， 明年	要／想

> Prompt students to look out for the key point in each question: a. some activity; b. a place, how to get there; c. time of departure, reason for leaving; d. food to bring.

Answers

a. 开车去山里玩。

b. 爬大青山，开车去。

c. 八点半出发，因为早一点路上车少，可以快点到。

d. 水果、三明治和水。

If time allows, you can ask students these questions:

Present tense: 你周末通常都做什么?

Past tense: 你上个周末看了什么电影?

Future tense: 你下个月想去哪儿旅行?

Assessment suggestion

Students design and present a special weekend programme for visiting students from China.

 Students can talk about the advantages and disadvantages of various programme options.

Homework suggestion

Students write a paragraph about a proposed weekend away to celebrate a family member's birthday. They should say where they will go, where they will stay and what they propose to do.

1.9 特别的日子 Special occasions

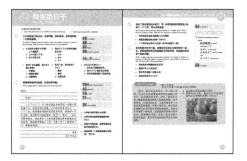

Icebreaker activity

You could begin by asking students about special occasions they celebrate at home, e.g. "你家庆祝哪些特别的日子? "

Sample answer: 我家庆祝每一个人的生日，还有爸爸妈妈的结婚纪念日。

Lesson activities

1 Listening

Remind students to read the questions first, so they know what to focus on when listening. If necessary, give them these focus points: a. day and dates; b. number of people; c. type of restaurant; d. an activity; e. a reason – they should listen for what comes after 因为.

Transcript

a. 上个星期五是我的生日。

b. 我请了六个同学来我的生日会庆祝生日。

c. 我们先在我家里吃了生日蛋糕，然后去了一家法国餐馆吃饭。

d. 吃完了饭还去了卡拉OK厅唱歌。

e. 那天我很高兴，因为大家玩儿得都很开心，而且那天我还收到了很多生日礼物。

Answers

a. i **b.** iii **c.** iii **d.** ii **e.** ii

2 Reading

Remind students to read the questions carefully so they know what to look out for: a. the date; b. activities; c. activities; d. a person and the reason.

Answers

a. 今年的中秋节是九月二十二日。

b. 家庭聚会

c. 一边赏月、聊天，一边吃月饼和烤肉。

d. 丽青有一个要去英国读大学的表姐特别想认识海伦，她想问海伦一些关于英国的事情。

Grammar focus: 快／快要／要……了

To practise the above grammar, each student writes 2 predictions on a card – one for a celebrity and one for him/herself. They then read out their predictions. Keep all the cards in a safe place. At the end of the term or of the academic year, read the predictions again. Everyone will be surprised how many have come true!

3  Writing

Remind students they are writing a letter to a friend, so the style and tone of their writing should be friendly and fairly informal.

You could give students 3 lists of vocabulary to help them with their writing: phrases to express thanks and gratitude; food; activities.

Sample answer:

张明你好，

非常感谢你上个礼拜邀请我跟你的家人一起过中秋节。你妈妈做的月饼真是可口极了。你爸爸讲的笑话让我非常开心。晚饭后，我们一起去散步，黑暗的天空上看到五光十色的烟火跳跃着，叫人难忘。

下个礼拜我们全家要去海边玩，你愿意跟我一起去度个周末吗？

王强

4 Speaking

Remind students that the conversation is about a future event, so they need to use the future tense. Walk around the classroom providing support as necessary.

Sample answer

A: 这个星期六是我的生日，我有两张音雷丁乐节 的门票，你有没有兴趣跟我一起去？

B: 好呀！我正想找你一起去呢！星期六早上几点出发呢？

A: 我想早点去，我们早上7点半出发吧。

B: 没问题，我7点在火车站等你。我们先坐火车再坐公车。

A: 好的，你知道谁会来表演吗？

B: 我听说Korn乐团要来唱歌，我很兴奋呢！

A: 太棒了！

B: 周六早上见。

Cultural spotlight

Apart from eggs, noodles are also a popular Chinese dish for birthdays and new year celebrations. As their shape indicates, noodles symbolise longevity. As such, it is important not to cut or break the noodles when cooking or serving them!

Assessment suggestion

Ask students to write an email to a friend, telling them about a special party they have just been to.

Homework suggestion

Students choose a special occasion and report how they celebrate it. Include information such as: Who decides what form the celebration will take? What food is eaten? What activities are there?

1.10 复习 Progress check

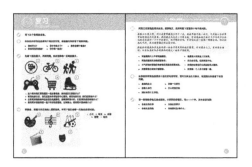

1  Writing

Answers

小狗、小猫、沙鼠、金鱼、兔子

Make a note of students who struggle with the words.

2  Speaking

You may need to remind students of basic vocabulary for nationalities, family members, numbers and places. Walk around the classroom and listen to students' conversations. Provide support as necessary.

 If some students struggle to remember key vocabulary, direct them to the relevant flashcard sets on Quizlet for further practice.

Sample answers

a. 我叫彼得。   d. 我现在住在新加坡。

b. 我今年十六岁。   e. 我跟外婆住在一起。

c. 我来自英国。

3 Writing

MYP The images could be used as a stimulus for further discussion or more detailed writing.

Answers

i. a   **ii.** f   **iii.** d   **iv.** c

4 🔊 Listening

Tell students they can make notes by jotting down the activities in pinyin as they listen to the recording.

Transcript

a. 我是小文。我每个星期三下午都会做运动。

b. 我是马克。我一般是星期二去看电影，因为那天的票是半价。

c. 我是米娜。我每周五晚上会去看戏剧。

d. 我是丽青。我喜欢画画，每个星期天我会去郊外画画。

e. 我是海伦。如果星期六天气不好，我喜欢在家里听音乐。

Answers

a. iv **b.** v **c.** i **d.** ii **e.** iii

5 📖 Reading

Remind students that they can work out what is true and what is false by using the context and some key words in the statements.

Prompt students to note down the key words in each statement before carrying out the activity.

Answers

a, c, f, g

6 ⭕ Speaking

Remind students of the vocabulary required for this activity: names, dates, places, time and activities. Walk around the classroom and listen to students' conversations, providing support as necessary.

Sample answers

a. 马克的生日快到了，他要举行生日聚会。

b. 生日聚会在星期六。

c. 生日聚会在马克家举行。

d. 聚会从下午一点开始。

e. 他们要先看电影，然后一起吃饭，玩游戏。

7 ✏️ Writing

Tell students this activity needs vocabulary for: names, appearance, personal characteristics, reasoning.

 You could give students vocabulary lists.

Sample answer

我的好朋友叫李大伟，他是马来西亚人，今年十七岁。他长得又高又帅，个性外向活泼。我很喜欢他，因为他很善良大方。

Further differentiation

Find and show students some pictures of famous people doing an activity (e.g. playing football, cycling, drawing, going to a film premiere, walking their dog in the park).

 Students can make simple sentences to describe what the person in the photo is doing, and what they may do next (students have to use their imagination here). The idea is to get students to practise making sentences using vocabulary they have learned in this unit, as well as writing about present and future events.

 Students can add extra detail in their writing by describing what the person looks like, whether or not they seem to be enjoying the activity, etc.

Assessment suggestion

Ask students to write a short paragraph on how they spend their free time. You could give them questions to answer as a basis for their writing. For example:

• 你有什么爱好?   • 在哪儿 _____? 怎么去的?

• 你跟谁一起 _____?   • 你觉得如何?

UNIT OBJECTIVES

● Describe and discuss different aspects of your school life.
● Share information about your home.
● Discuss the role digital technology plays in your daily life.

2.1 预习 Unit introduction

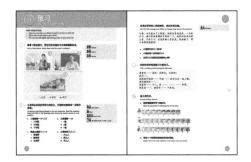

Prior knowledge

Students should have learned vocabulary for nationalities, family members, animals and places. They should be able to describe people's appearances, personalities, likes and dislikes. They should be able to use simple expressions of time to describe events in the present, past and future.

> **MYP Icebreaker activity**
>
> Show students some photos from your school website – for example, the head teacher, various members of staff, the science lab, sports centre, etc. Ask them:
>
> "他（她）是谁？"
>
> "这是什么地方？"

Lesson activities

1  Reading

You could warm up by asking students to describe the pictures using the vocabulary they already know. For example, ask the class the following questions about picture b: 她是哪国人？她的头发是什么颜色？她有几本书？她穿什么颜色的衣服？

> **Answers**
>
> **a.** i **b.** iii **c.** ii

2 Listening

Before playing the recording, ask students to read the questions and identify what is being asked for in each case.

> **Transcript**
>
> 亲爱的班主任李老师、同学们，大家好！我叫小明。
>
> 我很高兴来到十年级A班和大家一起上课。
>
> 我的爱好是玩电子游戏。我喜欢上学，但不喜欢考试。
>
> 我家有四口人。有爸爸、妈妈、哥哥和我。

> **Answers**
>
> **a.** iii **b.** i **c.** i **d.** ii

> ▶ **MYP** Show students the first minute or so of the "Family introductions" video from the BBC Real Chinese series (the video is entitled "The family"). Ask them:

- What do Chinese people call their wives (太太 or 爱人)/their fathers and mothers (父亲 for father and 母亲 for mother)/their sons? (儿子)

- For how many years did the young entrepreneur's parents try to persuade him to get married? (五年)

- How do you say "I am married" in Chinese? (我结婚了。)

In pairs, students could take it in turns to introduce themselves and ask their partners 4–5 questions, using the ideas and vocabulary from the listening activity and the video clip. Walk around the classroom listening to students' conversations. Provide support as necessary.

Language and culture

Whereas in the West, a person's marital status is considered personal (often private), it is not a social taboo for Chinese people to ask someone about their marital status, how many children they have, or even their monthly salary. Explain to students that they shouldn't be offended if their Chinese friends ask personal questions. They can always respond with an enigmatic smile!

3  Reading

Remind students to read the questions first and help them to identify the key words in each one: a. 多少个房间; b. 房间有什么; c. 什么时候再发短信.

Answers

a. 小明家有五个房间。

b. 每个房间都有不同的家具。

c. 他明天再发短信给心美。

4 Speaking

Walk around the classroom and listen to students' conversations. Provide support as necessary.

Sample answers

亲爱的陈老师、同学们，大家好！

我叫李大伟。

我很高兴来到十年级八班和大家一起上课。我的爱好是足球、网球和滑雪。

我家有四口人，有爸爸、妈妈、姐姐和我。

我住在伦敦，我家有四个房间。

 Students create an identity for a new student in a new school, and introduce themselves in that persona following the above format.

5 Writing

For part a, the strokes animation from the MGDB online dictionary is useful for showing students the sequences of writing individual characters.

For part b, remind students to use vocabulary not just from this lesson but from the previous unit to help them construct their sentences.

Sample answers for part b

教室，图书馆，老师，同学，班级，父母，家人，花园，房间，家具

Further differentiation

Write the following words on the board: 老师，同学，父母，家人，班级，花园，房间，教室，家具，图书馆.

 Ask students to separate the words into two groups: vocabulary relating to school and vocabulary relating to home life.

 Ask students to write a short paragraph using as many of these words as possible.

2.2 学校的不同学科 School subjects

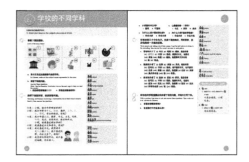

Lesson activities

1 Writing

Before the activity, point out that individual characters or their radicals can act as clues to what the word compounds mean. For example, we can deduce that 生物 means "biology" (study of living things) because the first character, 生, can be translated as "living", "life" or "growth", while the second character, 物, means "matter" or "thing".

Answers

a. i = 数学　　ii = 中文　　iii = 生物　iv = 音乐
　　v = 美术　　vi = 历史　　vii = 地理　viii = 政治
　　ix = 经济　x = 信息技术

Sample answers for part b

i. 我的学校有英文、数学、物理、化学、生物、美术、电脑、历史、地理等各种学科。

ii. 我现在读数学、物理、经济和英文。

2 Reading

Before getting students to read the text, go through the questions and highlight the key words in each that will help them find the answers: a. 喜欢中文; b. 喜欢哪一门学科; c. 不喜欢学化学; d. 不喜欢学地理.

> **Answers**
>
> **a.** i **b.** i **c.** i **d.** ii

Put students in pairs. Ask them to say which are their favourite and least favourite subjects and explain why. They will need to use this common sentence pattern: 我(不)喜欢……，因为……。

Walk around the room listening to the conversations and offering support as needed.

Encourage students to note down their reasons for use in a future activity.

 If students need help with giving reasons, you could show them the following table and ask them to choose one. Use this opportunity to go over some common stative verbs and adjectival stative verbs (see underlined characters).

我（不）喜欢	因为
数学	我觉得XX很好玩
中文	老师很帅
英语	老师很严厉
体育	太难
宗教	我听不懂
物理	上XX课的时候，我就打瞌睡
化学	上课很有趣
音乐	考试太难
	考试很简单

3 Listening

Remind students to read the questions before listening to the recording. Explain that in each case the person will first talk about what exam they took, then about which subjects they like and dislike, and finally what they think about one particular subject. Because there are multiple answer options, it might be helpful for students to first jot down the pinyin for the answer options.

Transcript

a. 苏菲昨天考了德语，她说考得很好。她喜欢中文，也喜欢地理。她觉得中文作业很容易。

b. 莉莉昨天考了化学。她说考得还可以。她不喜欢中文，也不喜欢美术。她觉得美术作业很难。

c. 志军昨天考了历史，他说考得不好。他喜欢中文，也喜欢政治。他觉得政治作业很容易。

> **Answers**
>
> **a.** 苏菲：iii; vi; viii; xi
>
> **b.** 莉莉：i; iv; ix; xii; xiii
>
> **c.** 志军：ii; v; vii; x; xiv

 To reinforce students' understanding of stative verbs, go through the transcript with students and ask them to highlight all the stative verbs.

 Show students the first 2 minutes of "Homework and courses", from the CCTV's *Growing up with Chinese*, Lesson 20. Ask them:

- 今天星期几?
- 麦克今天上学为什么迟到了?
- 小明今天有几堂体育课?
- 兰兰喜欢什么课? 不喜欢什么课?
- 兰兰邀请麦克和小明去她家做什么?

4 Speaking and Writing

Remind students to make notes while their partners speak – these will help with the writing part of the activity. Walk around the classroom and listen to students' conversations. Provide support as necessary.

 Students can refer to the table from Activity 2 for support for both speaking and writing.

> **Sample answers**
>
> 我喜欢中文、历史和数学。
>
> 我觉得中文作业很有意思。

Further differentiation

List-making is a typical writing task for those following the IGCSE syllabus. To reinforce students' knowledge of subject names, replay the audio recording from Activity 3, then ask students to:

 Make a list of 5 subjects mentioned.

 Make a list of 5 subjects and write a short sentence about each one.

Homework suggestions

1. Students write about their favourite and least favourite subjects, giving their reasoning, using 也 and 很.

2. Students write about the subjects they are studying. Have they chosen them because they enjoy them, because they would need them for a future career, or for some other reason?

2.3 学校设施和环境 My school facilities and environment

Lesson activities

1 Reading

Use the pictures to ask students questions about the facilities in your school before they carry out the reading activity. This will help to reinforce the vocabulary. For example:

学校有几间教室? 中文教室在哪儿? 图书馆在哪儿? 你常用什么学校设施?

Answers

a. vii **b.** iii **c.** vi **d.** v **e.** viii **f.** i **g.** iv **h.** ii

2 Reading

Explain to students that, to find the answers, they should look out for mentions of the storeys (一楼/二楼/三楼/四楼/五楼) throughout the passage and then find the facilities that follow each one.

 This is a good time to revise Chinese numbers.

Answers

a. 篮球场 **b.** 图书馆 **c.** 办公室 **d.** 教室 **e.** 食堂

3 Listening

Remind students to read the questions first and note the key words in each one to help them find the answers as they listen. Ask them what they think the key words are here (**a.** 看书, **b.** 运动, **c.** 为什么, 体育馆).

Transcript

小明: 我喜欢我们的校园, 你喜欢吗?

心美: 我也很喜欢。我最喜欢三楼的图书馆。我喜欢看书, 看书很有趣。

小明: 我对看书不感兴趣, 做运动有意思多了! 我最喜欢游泳, 你喜欢吗?

心美: 我喜欢游泳, 我更喜欢打篮球, 因为打篮球很好玩儿。我们先去游泳, 然后去体育馆打篮球, 好吗?

小明: 啊! 我忘了体育馆怎么走!

心美: 小明, 你忘了老师的话了吗? 它在四、五楼, 就在图书馆的上面。

小明: 知道了。谢谢! 啊! 心美对了, 我忘了老师叫我下课后去找她, 我不去体育馆了。心美, 办公室怎么走? 你能告诉我吗?

心美: 你真没意思。我才不告诉你呢!

Answers

a. ii **b.** ii **c.** 小明要去办公室找老师

Go through any vocabulary in the transcript with which students are unfamiliar: 忘了 (to have forgotten), 怎么走 (how to get to...), 上面 (above), 告诉 (to tell).

Language and culture

Students may not understand "你真没意思" in the recording. Explain that it translates roughly as "You're so useless!" It is an expression friends jokingly use to each other.

Speaking and writing

Remind students to make notes as their partners speak – they can use these to help in the writing part of the activity. Listen to students' conversations and provide support as necessary.

Sample answers

a. 我喜欢学校的网球场、游泳池和健身房，因为我很爱运动。

b. 我喜欢学校的社团和一些庆典活动。

c. 我不喜欢假期的时候还要来学校上课。

School open day

Put students in groups of 3 or 4. Ask each group to prepare and deliver a presentation to prospective parents and students on the school's open day. The presentation should cover: the basic facts about the school (number of students and staff); school facilities; courses provided; anything special that makes the school stand out to attract the prospective parents and students.

Listen to the groups and offer support as needed.

 After their presentation, students can produce a promotional poster for the school. (This could also be done as a homework activity.)

Homework suggestions

Students write answers to the following questions on "我的学校".

- 你的学校在哪里？
- 学校里有多少老师和学生？
- 你的学校有什么设备？
- 学校提供什么课程和活动？
- 你喜欢你的学校吗？为什么？

 Ask students to write an additional 50–100 characters on "是什么造就了好学校?" They should consider the following points:

- 学校设立的目的；
- 好学校应该追上科技的变化吗？
- 好学校应该满足人类的什么需要？

Sample writing

我的学校在英国南部的一个小镇。学校不大，有六十位老师和一千多个学生。我的学校很古老，有一百多年的历史。

学校提供很多学科，我们还有很多课外活动。我参加了游泳社和中国武术社团。我很喜欢我的学校，因为这里的老师很会教学，我的同学也都很友善。

2.4 你的考试成绩怎么样？ How did you do in your exams?

Icebreaker activity

Ask students to suggest adjectives in English to describe how people feel before taking an exam and adjectives to describe how they feel after an exam. Translate these into Chinese (e.g. 紧张、担心、忧虑、安心、满意、高兴) and get students to practise saying and writing them.

Lesson activities

Listening

Remind students to read the passage and answer options before listening to the recording. They should note the words or phrases immediately before each gap they are supposed to fill. These will help them to pay special attention to the answers they are about to hear.

Transcript

米娜今年要读八个学科，包括中文、英文、法语、经济、物理、音乐、美术和信息技术。

米娜最喜欢读中文。她在考试一星期前开始复习。

这次考试她取得了好成绩，她觉得很高兴。

因为她常常练习写汉字，所以她的中文成绩比上一次更好。

Answers

a. 中文 **b.** 法语 **c.** 中文 **d.** 复习

e. 考试 **f.** 练习

Put students into groups of 5. Give each group a copy of the "My transcripts" worksheet (on the CD-ROM). Each student should choose one academic transcript from the worksheet. Tell them that the pass mark is 60 and ask them to discuss the following questions, using information from the transcript they have chosen. They should give reasons for their answers where relevant.

- 你哪一科考得最好？为什么？
- 你哪一科考得最差？为什么？
- 你打算怎么做让下次考试能够进步？
- 你大学打算读什么方向？文科？理科还是艺术设计？为什么？

Go round the groups offering advice as needed.

2 Reading

DP In true-or-false exam questions, students are often expected to give reasons why statements are false, so you can extend this activity by asking them to do so here.

Answers

a. 对

b. 错 (苏菲考得最好。)

c. 对

d. 对

e. 错 (本杰明学习不用功。)

After the activity, you could ask students to change the first paragraph of the reading passage into negative statements by using 不 and 没. For example:

今天我很**不**高兴！因为在这次中文考试中，我得了五十分，成绩<u>没有</u>上次好，老师也说我<u>没有</u>进步。

 Ask students to rewrite the first paragraph of the reading passage using stative verbs of their own, so that it consists of negative statements. For example:

> 今天我很<u>伤心</u>！因为在这次中文考试中，我<u>不及格</u>，只得了五十分，成绩<u>比</u>上次<u>低了</u>很多。老师也说我<u>退步了</u>，要更用功。

3 Speaking

Either carry out this speaking activity as a group discussion or put students into pairs and ask them to discuss recent exams using the questions in the Student Book. Students should note down the answers they and their partners give for use in the next activity. Walk around the classroom and listen to students' conversations. Provide support as necessary.

Sample answers

a. 这次的数学考试很难。

b. 这次考试我只得了60分。

c. 我觉得自己的成绩很不好。

d. 我觉得考试压力很大。

e. 我觉得这次考试比上次难。

f. 我觉得班长读书最用功。

4 Writing

Students use their notes from Activity 3 to prepare a written report. Remind them to support all their statements with arguments and evidence.

Sample writing

这次的汉语考试我觉得很难，我只得了60分，刚好及格，我觉得这个成绩很不好。每次考试我的压力都很大，我总是很紧张，怕自己考不好。其实这次考试并没有比上次难，但是我太紧张，把很多汉字都写错了。我要向张杰学习，他每天都很用功，考试成绩总是最好。如果我天天练习写汉字，下次汉语考试的成绩一定更好。

5 Writing

For part a, the strokes animation from the MGDB online dictionary is useful for showing students the sequences of writing individual characters.

For part b, remind students to use vocabulary learned not just from this lesson but from previous units to help them construct their sentences.

Sample answer for part b

我觉得写汉字很难，因为笔画太多。

Homework suggestion

On the basis of their discussions during the academic transcript worksheet activity, ask students to write an email to their parents about their exam results and how they feel about them.

2.5 我的一天 My day at school

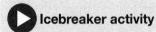

▶ Icebreaker activity

Since the focus of this session is on time and academic subjects, you could begin by finding and showing students an online video called *Xiao Long's and Xiao Hong's timetable*. Ask:

- 小红为什么不喜欢星期一？
- 小龙为什么喜欢星期三？
- 小龙为什么说星期五是黑色的星期五？
- 星期六他们有课吗？ 小红建议他们做什么？

Lesson activities

 Listening

Before the activity, review expressions of numbers and time in Chinese. Tell students to listen out for subjects and some school activities.

Transcript

志军: 玛莉，新学期又到了，今天是开学的第一天，你上什么课？

玛莉: 让我先看看课程表吧！早上八点二十分点名。第一节到第二节，我先上英文课，然后上经济课。下课后就是休息时间。休息后，在第三节和第四节，我先上数学课，然后上历史课。

午休之后的第一节是中文课，放学之前是两节的美术课。到了下午三点二十分就放学了。

志军: 你知道今年什么时候放暑假吗？

玛莉: 你这个人，就只想着放假！我们九月一号开学，到明年期末考试之后才放暑假！

志军: 明年？ 我希望明天就放暑假！

Answers

a. 点名　**b.** 经济　**c.** 中文　**d.** 放学

Draw students' attention to the words 今天 and 明年. Ask them if they know what 今 and 明 stand for, and ask them to give more examples of time expressions involving these two characters.

DP You could turn the listening transcript into a true-or-false activity. Write a number of statements based on the transcript, then ask students to explain why some are wrong.

2 Listening

Before carrying out the activity, go through the questions with the students and highlight the following words which will help them when listening out for the answers: a. 九月一日; b. 放暑假; c. 放学.

Answers

a. 九月一日是开学日。　　**b.** 期末考之后放暑假。

c. 下午三点二十分放学。

For more practice on dates, show students a calendar with some birthdays, medical appointments, parties and holidays marked. Ask them about the dates, times and durations of these events.

Alternatively, say to the class: "所有三月份出生的人/所有有两个兄弟姐妹的人/所有学九个学科的人……都站起来". Students who meet those criteria will have to stand up and answer a further question about themselves, e.g. "你三月哪一天出生？"

3  Reading

Before tackling the activity, analyse the elements of an email with the class. Ask students to point out the receiver (收件人); sender (发件人); subject (主题); form of address (称谓); main body of email (主体); greetings (祝语); signature (落款).

Answers

a. 小明迟到了。

b. 午休之后，玛莉上了中文课。

c. 因为本杰明觉得汉字很难写。

Language and culture

Back in Activity 3 in Lesson 2.3, students would have come across the phrase "你真没意思" ("You're so useless"). In the context of the email, however, 没意思 just means "boring".

4  Speaking

Walk around the classroom and listen to students' conversations. Provide support as necessary.

Sample answers

a. 早上点名之后我有数学课。

b. 放学之前我上体育课。

---

5  Writing

For part a, the strokes animation from the MGDB online dictionary is useful for showing students the sequences of writing individual characters.

For part b, ask students to write down their weekday timetable, including all their daily activities. They can then interview one another in pairs, and make notes on their partner's answers. Listen in on students' conversations and provide support as needed.

 Write out some key vocabulary on the board as prompt: 起床、刷牙、洗脸、吃早饭、上学、上第一堂课、吃午饭、放学、参加社团、回家、吃晚饭、听音乐、看电视、做功课、玩电脑游戏、上床睡觉.

Sample timetable for part b

时间	星期一	星期二	星期三	星期四	星期五
7:00–8:00	起床、刷牙、洗脸、吃早饭				
8:10	上学				
8:30–9:00	点名				
9:00–9:50	数学	法语	中文	数学	数学
10:00–10:50	数学	物理	生物	中文	化学
11:00–11:50	英文	物理	政治	物理	法语
12:00–12:50	午休				
13:00–13:50	历史	化学	经济	政治	美术
14:00–14:50	地理	化学	信息技术	自习	美术
15:00–15:50	音乐	体育	信息技术	体育	社团
16:00	放学				
16:30–18:00	做功课				游泳 (16:30–17:30)
18:15–19:15	吃晚饭				
19:30–20:30	看电视				
22:00	上床睡觉				

Assessment suggestion

Students create their ideal timetable. They decide how long each subject should be taught for and when, then write the information on the "My ideal timetable" worksheet (on the CD-ROM). This forms the basis for a presentation, with opportunities for other students to question them about their reasoning. You can record the students' presentations to assess their spoken language skills.

Homework suggestion

Using the notes made in Student Book Activity 5 (part b), students can write a brief summary outlining how the person they interviewed spends their time.

2.6 我的家 My home

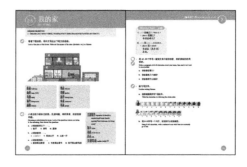

Icebreaker activity

Ask students to come up with some adjectives in English to describe their home (e.g. small, big, house, apartment, bungalow, new-build, old, made of bricks, made of wood, made of concrete) – and translate them into Chinese if they can. Write out any new words (e.g. 公寓、新建、用砖做、用木做、混凝土) on the board for students to copy and learn.

Lesson activities

1 Writing

Point out that individual parts of a character or its radical can sometimes act as clues to what the word compounds mean. For example: 饭 in 饭厅 contains the radical 饣, which is a simplified form of 食 (to eat). 饭 also means rice. A dining room is where one would eat!

You could do Activity 1 as a class activity. Assign letters to the rooms as follows: a. bedroom, b. toilet, c. dining room, d. study, e. living room, f. kitchen, g. balcony, h. garden, i. bathroom, j. garage. Say to students: "I am in Room A. What is it in Chinese?" Get students to say 卧室 together, and then they can write it down. Move on to the next room.

Answers				
a. 卧室	**b.** 厕所	**c.** 饭厅	**d.** 书房	**e.** 客厅
f. 厨房	**g.** 阳台	**h.** 花园	**i.** 浴室	**j.** 车库

 2 Listening

Prompt students to read the questions and note down key words before listening to the recording.

Transcript

小明: 心美，我搬新家了，新房子比以前大。

心美: 小明，你住在哪儿？

小明: 我住在长青街三号。

心美: 你的新房子有多少个房间？

小明: 有三个房间，还有一个饭厅和客厅，是人们常常说的三房两厅。我家地下还有一个车库，爸爸的车就停在那儿。

心美: 哇！你的家真的很大！考试快到了，今天放学后能来你家一起复习吗？

小明: 可以。我家还有一台大电视，也有一套大沙发，我们复习后可以坐在沙发上一起看卫星电视。

心美: 太好了。我最喜欢看电视！你的家人在哪儿？他们不在家吗？

小明: 爸爸在书房里边看书。妈妈在厨房里边煮饭。我们可以到客厅里边看电视。

心美: 好啊！放学见！

Answers

a. ii **b.** i **c.** ii

 DP Re-use the listening transcript here by turning it into a sentence-matching activity. Rephrase some of the sentences in the text, break each one into two chunks, then ask students to match up the correct chunks.

Language and culture

Show students the transcript from Activity 2. Ask them if they can spot any interjections in the dialogue (哇 and 啊). Explain that 哇 is an exclamation of wonder, while 啊 is an exclamation of surprise as well as confirmation.

 3 Writing and Speaking

Remind students to use adjectival stative verbs to describe their home and furniture.

 If students struggle to find words to embellish their writing, you can provide a list of adjectival stative verbs for them to choose from.

 Note: furniture is covered in more detail in the next lesson (2.7), so question c can be reserved for more-able students.

4 Writing

For part a, the strokes animation from the MGDB online dictionary is useful for showing students the sequences of writing individual characters.

For part b, remind students to use vocabulary learned in other lessons as well as this one in their answer.

Sample answer for part b

我每天都很晚睡觉，大概十二点以后才上床。

Assessment suggestion

Students write a paragraph about their home, answering some or all of the following questions:

- 你家在哪儿？
- 你家有多少房间？
- 你喜欢在家里做什么？为什么？

Homework suggestion

Students take on the role of an architect designing a home for a client – perhaps a celebrity. They should consider:

- Who will live there?
- Is it a house or an apartment?
- Where is it located?
- What is it made of? (You may have to provide vocabulary for building materials.)
- How many rooms does it have? What are they?
- Does it have any special features?

They then write a brief report on the property, including plans if they wish. This could form the basis of a class interview activity in a subsequent lesson.

2.7 我的房间 **My room**

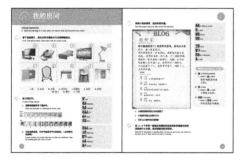

Icebreaker activity

Students suggest adjectives in English to describe their bedroom (e.g. comfortable, messy, cosy, small, big) and translate them into Chinese if they can. Write any new words (e.g. 舒适、乱) on the board.

Lesson activities

1  Reading

Go through the pictures and ask students which of the items they have in their own bedroom. Ask students to name items in their room which are not listed in the Student Book, as a way to extend their vocabulary.

Answers

a. iii **b.** ii **c.** i **d.** iv **e.** vi **f.** v **g.** ix **h.** x **i.** viii **j.** vii

2 ✏️ Writing

For part a, the strokes animation from the MGDB online dictionary is useful for showing students the sequences of writing individual characters.

For part b, remind students to use vocabulary learned in other lessons as well as this one to help construct their answers.

Sample writing

我住在英国，英国的夏天不热，人们不用空调。但是英国的冬天很冷，大家都会开暖气。

3  Reading

Prompt the class to study the questions carefully before reading Xiaoming's blog post so they know what to look out for.

Answers

1. 小明的房间里有一台电视机。
2. 小明的书桌上边有电脑、台灯和电话。
3. 小明房间的窗户特别大，小明常常开窗户，特别凉快，不用开空调。

Language and culture

Point out the term 没有 in one of the blog comments. Ask students what this means ("no" or "don't have"). Explain that sometimes the character 有 is needed but it is possible to omit it, e.g. 我没有钱; 我没空. Note, however, that 没(有) is used differently to 不.

4 ✏️ Writing

Students may find it helpful to ask themselves the following questions to guide their writing:

- Is their room large or small?

- What furniture do they have in their room?

- What do they like best about their room?

Sample writing

我的房间不大。里面有一个衣柜，一张床，还有一张书桌。书桌前面有一扇窗户，我喜欢可以看到花园里的花草。

Assessment suggestions

1. Students imagine that they have just moved to a new home. They should write about how they feel about living there, considering questions such as:

   - 你住在什么地方？

   - 你的房子是什么样子？跟旧房子有什么不同？

   - 你有朋友住在你家附近吗？

   - 有没有花园？

   - 你在家玩什么游戏？

2. Students imagine they are living in the year 2030. They should write about their home life (家庭生活), considering the following questions:

   - 你住在什么地方？地上？地底下？天空？海上？

   - 你的房子是什么样子？

   - 谁做饭和清扫屋子？怎么做？

   - 你在家玩什么游戏？

Homework suggestion

Ask students to imagine they are completely redecorating their bedroom. They should write to a Chinese friend about their plans. What colour will they paint it? What will be on the floor? What kind of pictures will they put on the walls? What new furniture will they buy and what gadgets will they have in their room?

2.8 开学前的准备 Getting ready for school

Icebreaker activity

Divide students into two groups. Students in one group take it in turns to take something from their bags (or point to an object in the classroom) for the other group to name and give the correct measure word for it.

Lesson activities

1 📖 Reading

Before doing the activity, ask students to look at the words below the pictures. Remind them that individual parts of a character or its radical can sometimes act as clues to what the word compounds mean. For example: 笔 is made of two parts: 竹 (bamboo) and 毛 (hair). Traditional Chinese brushes are made of bamboo and hair – so it makes sense for 笔 to be a word for writing implement!

Answers for part a

a. x **b.** iv **c.** viii **d.** ii **e.** vii **f.** vi **g.** v
h. iii **i.** ix **j.** i

Answers for part b

a. 一本词典	**b.** 一把尺子	**c.** 一支铅笔
d. 一块橡皮	**e.** 一本课本	**f.** 一本练习本
g. 一张纸	**h.** 一把剪刀	**i.** 一个卷笔刀
j. 一支钢笔		

2 🔊 Listening

Remind students to read the diary entry before listening to the recording. They should pay particular attention to the words immediately before the gaps, so that they know what to listen out for.

Transcript

妈妈：志军，新学期的文具，你都有了吗？等吃完饭以后，我们一起去买新文具，好吗？

志军：我先回房间，看一看我还有多少文具吧！

志军：妈妈，我还有很多文具。我有十支铅笔、八把尺子、五块橡皮、三个卷笔刀，让我看一看......还有四本练习本！

妈妈：那我们就不用买新文具了。明天开学了，你今晚十点钟之前就要上床睡觉，知道吗？

志军：知道了。

Answers

a. 吃完饭 **b.** 十 **c.** 八 **d.** 五 **e.** 三 **f.** 四
g. 上床睡觉

Students could play "I went to the shop and I bought ...", with each student repeating the items previous students have bought in preparation for the new school year and adding one of their own. This is a good way to reinforce measure words as well as vocabulary.

   Writing and Speaking

For part a, remind students to use the correct measure words for this activity.

For part b, students can use what they wrote in part a as a basis for their conversation. Listen to students' conversations and provide support as necessary.

Sample answer for part b

下星期一就要开学了，我到商场去买东西准备开学，我买了一支钢笔，一本中文词典，一块橡皮，还有很多本练习本和很多支铅笔。我想多多练习写中文字。我还买了一双运动鞋和很多件新衣服。新学期，我要更酷！

Assessment suggestions

Give students a scenario: The school is asking students for donations to a school in a refugee camp. They should write out a list of things they would like to donate. The list must include appropriate measure words.

 Students design a poster for a meeting to which students can bring their donations.

 Students write a paragraph in response to the question "为什么年轻人该拥受教育的权利？"

Homework suggestions

1. Ask students to write their own diary entry for the last day of the holidays and their preparations for the new school year. Remind them that since it is a personal diary they should adopt an informal and honest tone throughout, and remember to express personal feelings.

   Students can more or less copy the diary entry in Activity 2, but just replace the times and the objects to buy with their own suggestions.

2. **MYP** Students research into the differences between school life in China and in one western country. They should choose one aspect to compare in more detail – for example, the school timetable.

2.9 智能生活 Digital life

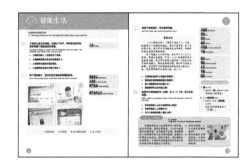

Lesson activities

1   **Listening**

Before the activity, ask students, in pairs, to compare and list some similarities and differences between letters and emails.

Now, turn students' attention to the four statements in Activity 1. Remind them to read the statements carefully first, so they will know what to listen out for in the recording.

 True-or-false exam questions often ask students to give reasons why the statements are true or false – you can ask students to do so here.

Transcript

小明：前几天，我给北京的朋友写信，他还没回复我。

心美：小明，现在哪有人写信?

小明：我喜欢写信，我觉得写信有意思多了。

心美：你可以给朋友发电邮，这比写信方便多了。我常常发电邮给外国的朋友。

小明：我知道。不过，我还是喜欢写信，写信比发电邮更有意思。

Answers

a. 错 (他写了信。)

b. 对

c. 错 (她常常发电邮给他们。)

d. 对

2  Reading

When faced with unfamiliar word compounds that contain multiple characters, remind students they can try to break up the word compound into character groups they recognise. For example, while 网络游戏 or 网上购物 may look daunting to begin with, students will have come across 游戏 (game) or 购物 (shopping), so they can assume that the terms mean "online game" and "online shopping".

Answers

a. iii **b.** ii **c.** iv **d.** i

3  Reading

Before reading the passage, ask students to go through the questions and highlight any key words they think will help them locate the answers (a. 以前, b. 现在, c. 连上网络的手机, d. 哪些事情).

Answers

a. 以前我们只能写信联络国外的朋友。

b. 现在我们可以用电脑收发电子邮件和国外的朋友联络。

c. 手机连上网络可以上社交网络给朋友发短信，不用打电话。

d. 在网络上可以听音乐、看电影、购物、玩游戏和使用网上银行业务。

After the activity, ask your students how digital technology has changed people's lives. Ask them to use 以前 and 现在 to make comparisons. For example:

以前	现在
以前人们写信。	现在人们发电邮。
以前人们用打字机。	现在人们用电脑。
以前人们用百科全书找资料。	现在人们用谷歌 (Google)。
以前人们玩棋盘游戏。	现在人们玩网络游戏。

 Students can also suggest some disadvantages of using digital technology.

Ask students to make a list of five things digital technology can't yet do. (List-making questions are a common feature of IGCSE papers.)

4 ✏️ Writing

Before students start on a writing task, it is always a good idea to get them to talk about the topic to consolidate their knowledge of the relevant vocabulary. Also ask them to name some features of an informal letter.

Sample writing

小明，你好!

我和家人很早就开始上网。妈妈常常在网上购物，处理网上银行业务。我会在社交网站跟国外的朋友聊天。我们喜欢上网，因为网络让我们的生活更方便也更有趣味。

下次再谈!

彼得

Cultural spotlight

This Cultural spotlight feature discusses the tradition of using messenger pigeons as a means of communication. Read the paragraph and go through any challenging vocabulary together as a class, such as 传递 (to deliver), 辨认 (to identify or recognise), 多方面 (multi-faceted), 驯化 (to tame or domesticate).

Assessment suggestions

1. Students prepare and deliver a presentation on one of four online activities: banking, communication, shopping and games. They should include their own experiences and their opinions.

2. Ask students to imagine they are living in 2030. They should write about their school life (学校生活), considering the following questions:

   * 你的学校在哪里?
   * 它是实体 (physical) 还是虚拟 (virtual) 学校?
   * 你的学校有什么设施?
   * 你怎么上课?
   * 你的学校有什么课外活动?

Homework suggestion

Students write about the role of the Internet in their lives, including both the benefits and the drawbacks.

2.10 复习 Progress check

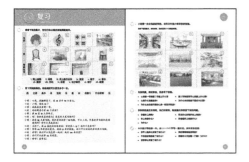

Lesson activities

1 Reading

Ask students to call out vocabulary on the topics of school, home and digital life. Encourage them to think of as many words as they can. Then use the reading activity as a revision exercise.

> **Answers:**
>
> **a.** ii   **b.** vi   **c.** vii   **d.** xii   **e.** v   **f.** ix
> **g.** iv   **h.** xi   **i.** x   **j.** iii   **k.** i   **l.** viii

2 Reading

This activity allows you to test students' understanding of various features of written Chinese, including question phrases, measure words, words of comparison, and expressions of time.

> **Answers:**
>
> **a.** 的   **b.** 比   **c.** 在哪儿   **d.** 多少   **e.** 的
> **f.** 有   **g.** 有   **h.** 台   **i.** 最   **j.** 在哪儿
> **k.** 在   **l.** 在   **m.** 什么时候   **n.** 之后

To give additional support, you could either fill in the blanks with pinyin and then ask students to find the correct Chinese, or write each word/phrase on a flashcard and ask students to work out which suits the context of the sentence best.

3 Listening

Before the listening activity, ask students simple questions about the pictures and help them to review the vocabulary for school facilities.

Remind students that it would be helpful to note down the names of these facilities in pinyin first, so they can listen out for mentions of them in the recording.

> **Transcript**
>
> 小　明: 老师好! 我很喜欢游泳, 请问学校有游泳池吗?
>
> 黄老师: 有, 学生们每个星期都上游泳课。
>
> 小　明: 我也喜欢踢足球。请问学校有足球场吗?
>
> 黄老师: 没有足球场, 学校有一个篮球场。
>
> 小　明: 学校有实验室吗?
>
> 黄老师: 有。学生可以在里边和老师一起做实验。
>
> 小　明: 请问学校有没有图书馆?
>
> 黄老师: 有。我们有一个很大的图书馆。你喜欢看中文书吗?
>
> 小　明: 我最喜欢看中文书。
>
> 黄老师: 太好了, 我就是学校的中文老师。以后我介绍几本中文书给你看。
>
> 小　明: 老师, 学生中午在哪里吃饭?
>
> 黄老师: 可以在学校食堂吃饭。
>
> 小　明: 谢谢老师的介绍。

Answers

游泳池 (d); 篮球场 (e); 实验室 (b); 图书馆 (a); 食堂 (g)

Sample answers

a. 我喜欢上网，我几乎天天上网。

b. 我在有Wi-Fi以后就几乎天天上网。

c. 我上网购物、跟朋友聊天、处理网上银行业务。

d. 我最喜欢上网跟朋友聊天。

e. 因为在网上跟朋友聊天非常方便。

 **4** 🔊 **Listening**

Remind students to find the key words in the questions. This will help them find the answers in the recording.

Transcript

本杰明: 心美，今天是开学的第一天，你要上什么课？

心　美: 让我先看看课程表吧！早上第一节到第二节，我先上英文课，然后上经济课。休息后，在第三节和第四节，我先上数学课，然后上历史课。

午休后的第一节是中文课，放学以前是两节的美术课。到了下午三点二十分就放学了。

本杰明: 心美，你喜欢中文课吗？

心　美: 我喜欢中文课，我觉得中文课很有趣。

本杰明: 我最不喜欢中文课，我觉得写汉字很难，学中文很没意思。

心　美: 多复习中文就会好。放学后我们一起回家好吗？

本杰明: 不行，我放学以后要去游泳。

心　美: 不要紧！

Answers

a. 心美第一节上英文课，第二节上经济课。

b. 心美第三节上数学课，第四节上历史课。

c. 她下午三点二十分放学。

d. 因为他觉得写中文很难。

e. 因为本杰明放学以后要去游泳。

5 💬 **Speaking**

Before the speaking activity, ask whether students have ever been to an internet café (网吧). Explain that in countries where internet is not available in individual households, young people may go to an internet café to check their emails, chat with friends, and socialise.

6 ✏️ **Writing**

Before the activity, get students to discuss the questions in pairs. This will help them to recap the vocabulary they've learned and to clarify their thinking. Remind students they are writing a diary entry – ask them to think about what tone the writing needs to be in.

Sample writing

今天是开学的第一天，我六点就起床，吃过早饭就坐上妈妈的车到学校去。点完名以后，我拿到新课程表。我很喜欢这个学期的课程表，因为每天下午都有体育课。午休的时候，我跟好朋友一起吃饭。今天我最喜欢的课是数学课，因为新的数学老师很有趣。放学以后我跟同学们一起踢足球，非常开心！

Further differentiation

Find a picture showing a family relaxing at home (for example, some people watching TV, one person playing on their tablet, and another talking on the phone).

 Ask students to describe what each person is doing in the picture.

 Ask students to describe how those people would feel and what they would say if their home suddenly suffered a loss of internet connection.

Assessment suggestion

 Ask students to make a 2-minute recording/video to introduce themselves. They should talk about their family, home and school. They should also discuss how they communicate with their friends using social media. You could compare these recordings with the presentations they made at the end of Lesson 2.5 to check students' progress. (You can even show students the videos from both lessons so they can see the progress they've made.)

食物、健康和健身
FOOD, HEALTH AND FITNESS

UNIT OBJECTIVES

- Describe and discuss different types of food and drink.
- Discuss your experiences of dining out.

- Describe the state of your physical health.
- Describe the state of your mental wellbeing.
- Discuss ways to live a healthy life.

3.1 预习 Unit introduction

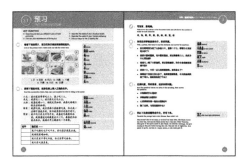

Prior knowledge

Students should be able to discuss personal information, including their home and school lives, both in speech and in writing.

Icebreaker activity

Carry out a Q&A to find out which country's cuisine is most popular with the class. Say out loud the following one by one (中国菜, 印度菜, 日本菜, 英国菜, 法国菜, etc.) and note down the number of people who choose it as their favourite.

Lesson activities

 **Reading**

Go through the vocabulary item by item. Ask if students can work out what each term means by looking at the radicals of the characters or by breaking down the character components. For example, the 艹 (grass) radical for 蔬菜 suggests it is to do with plants; the 虫 (insect) radical in 虾 suggests it is not to do with mammals; the 鸟 component in 鸡 suggests it's a bird.

Answers

a. iv **b.** v **c.** vi **d.** i **e.** ii **f.** viii **g.** iii **h.** vii

 **Reading**

Before the activity, introduce the following frequency words to students:

常常, 很少, 天天, 每天早上. Ask students what they eat and drink daily, and what they rarely eat or drink. They must include the frequency words in their answers.

Answers

阿里	我不吃猪肉也不吃牛肉。我吃很多蔬菜水果。
大海	我特别爱喝咖啡。
小文	我们家里不常吃米饭，但是经常吃面条。
丽青	我们家里吃很多鱼。

Writing

Explain that radicals are the basic elements in Chinese characters. The majority of the 214 radicals are pictographic, indicating the meaning of each word. Encourage students to learn radicals to help them to recognise and learn new vocabulary.

 汉字的动画 is an online animation that helps students to learn radicals and 36 Chinese characters in 10 minutes.

Show students some new vocabulary and ask them to spot the radicals.

Answers

字	部首	笔画	字	部首	笔画
鸡	鸟	7	茶	艹	9
海	氵	10	病	疒	10
鲜	鱼	14	疼	疒	10
虾	虫	9	运	辶	7
菜	艹	11	动	力	6

   汉字书院 (Hanzi House) has produced many online animated clips that look at radicals in more detail. Ask students to choose one of the videos. In small groups, they can give a presentation about their chosen radical.

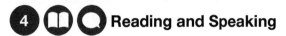

4 📖 🗣 Reading and Speaking

Go through the essential vocabulary with students before tackling this activity. Listen to students' conversations and provide support as necessary.

Sample answers

a. 哥哥吃了太多海鲜。 **b.** 她不爱吃蔬菜，也不喜欢运动。 **c.** 他晚上喝了三杯咖啡。
d. 弟弟牙疼。 **e.** 鸡汤。

5 🔊 Listening

This is a good opportunity to review sports-related vocabulary and sentence patterns.

sports vocabulary: 篮球、游泳、跑步、足球、骑自行车

sentence patterns: 长得、每个星期三（每个星期......）、常常 ...... 一起、除了...... 还

Transcript

a. 我是大海。我长得很高，我喜欢的运动是篮球。

b. 我叫米娜。我每个星期三的下午去学校里的游泳馆游泳。

c. 我的名字是心美，星期六我常常和我的好朋友小明一起去公园里跑步。

d. 我的同学马克热爱足球。除了足球，他还喜欢骑自行车。

Answers

a. 大海喜欢篮球。 **b.** 星期三。

c. 和她的好朋友。 **d.** 他还喜欢骑自行车。

6 ✏ Writing

Remind students that, when translating, they need to pay attention to the Chinese sentence order: time followed by place, then human action.

Sample translation

妈妈不喜欢吃肉，所以我们不常吃肉。她每天喝花茶，因为她觉得花茶好喝。每个星期四她到运动中心打网球，星期六早上她到公园跑步。她吃很多的蔬菜，做很多运动。她的个性很开朗，所以她很少生病。

Further differentiation

Give each student a copy of the worksheet "Food and drink questionnaire" (on the CD-ROM). In pairs, students take turns to ask and answer the questions.

 Students aren't expected to give reasons for their answers.

 Students should give reasons for their answers and write them out.

3.2 一日三餐 Three meals a day

Lesson activities

1 ✏ Writing

Look at the picture with the class. Ask students to make a sentence adding an adjective to a food/drink, e.g. 我喜欢喝咖啡 → 我喜欢喝黑咖啡。

Point out that many Chinese words are loan words. Say the following slowly and see if students can work out what they are: 三明治, 热狗, 可乐, 咖喱, 柠檬, 汉堡, 慕斯, 派, 巧克力.

Answers

a. 热狗	**b.** 蛋糕	**c.** 三明治	**d.** 饼干
e. 薯片	**f.** 果汁	**g.** 可乐	**h.** 草莓

2 📖 Reading

For part a, read out the list of food and drink items with the class to help them work out the pinyin.

For part b, remind students it may be easier to sort the food items they do recognise first before tackling the ones they aren't sure of. Some students may not be familiar with Chinese breakfast items – you may want to show them pictures on the internet when explaining what they are.

b. Answers

中式早餐	西式早餐	饮料
鸡蛋 jī dàn, eggs	牛奶 niú nǎi, milk	果汁 guǒ zhī, juice
面条 miàn tiáo, noodles	面包 miàn bāo, bread	热巧克力 rè qiǎo kè lì, hot chocolate
粥 zhōu, Chinese porridge	黄油面包 huáng yóu miàn bāo, bread with butter	奶茶 nǎi chá, tea (with milk)
鸡蛋饼 jī dàn bǐng, Chinese omelette	蛋糕 dàn gāo, cake	
包子 bāo zi, steamed buns	咖啡 kā fēi, coffee	
	鸡蛋 jī dàn, eggs	
	麦片 mài piàn, oatmeal	
	水果 shuǐ guǒ, fruit	

Food memory game

This game reinforces knowledge of food-related vocabulary. Ask one student what they had for breakfast this morning:

你早餐通常吃什么？你今天早餐吃了什么？

After the student has responded, ask a second student, who should repeat the first student's answer before giving their own answer. Subsequent students say what the others ate before adding their own breakfast item to the list.

 **Listening**

Tell students to read the questions first and identify the key words to help them to find the answers. They should listen out for: a. food, b. what the person eats and drinks, c. food items, d. food and drinks, e. rice porridge or buns; an opinion.

In the recording, students will hear 水果 (shuǐ guǒ) to be pronounced as shuí guǒ. Take this opportunity to explain the "tone sandhi" rules regarding the third tone.

Transcript

a. 我是小文。我们家一般吃中餐，所以早饭我通常吃两个大馒头，喝一碗粥。

b. 我是日晴，有时候我吃中式早餐，有时候吃西式早餐。今天早上我除了吃了三片面包，一些水果，还喝了果汁。

c. 我是海伦，我早餐吃得很少，一般就喝一杯咖啡吃一块蛋糕。

d. 我是汤姆，我刚刚去了日本旅游。在日本的时候我吃了很多健康的日式早餐。日式早餐有生鱼片，还包括绿茶。

e. 我是马克。现在在上海。我住的酒店里既有中式早餐，也有西式早餐。今天我尝了菜包子，我觉得菜包子好吃又健康。

Answers

a. 两个大馒头，喝一碗粥。

b. 她今天吃了三片面包，一些水果，还喝了果汁。

c. 一块蛋糕。　**d.** 生鱼片，饮料有绿茶。

e. 他尝了菜包子。

 Discuss eating habits around the world with the students. You could show a short video on ordering a meal from the BBC *Real Chinese* series. Play students the clip on breakfast and lunch, pausing the video so students can hear the Chinese. Students then interview one another in pairs about their breakfast habits. Here are some questions for them to ask:

你喜欢吃什么？　　　　你不喜欢吃什么？

中国人早餐喜欢吃什么？　你早餐喜欢吃什么？

中式早餐和西式早餐有什么不同？

 Play students the clip about lunch again and write unfamiliar vocabulary on the board. Ask:

中国人午餐喜欢吃什么？　你午餐喜欢吃什么？

4 ✎ **Writing**

Break each sentence into smaller segments. Ask students to reorder the segments so they follow sentence patterns in the Chinese language before translating them into Chinese. For example:

a. I often ate English breakfast / when I lived in the UK.
　→ When I lived … / I often ate …

b. I often have … / for breakfast.
　→ For breakfast / I often have …
　→ I / for breakfast / often have …

Sample answers

a. 当我住在英国的时候，我通常吃英式早餐。

b. 我早餐通常吃面包喝果汁。

5 📖 **Reading**

True-and-false activities are typical IB questions. Help students to note the key words/phrases in each statement and the corresponding sentences in the text. Compare them to judge whether the statement is true or false. For example:

a. 小文常常很晚起床，没有时间吃早饭。

b. 小文中午吃的饭是自己带的。

c. 马克觉得早餐要吃得好。

d. 马克中午常常买学校食堂的三明治。

Answers

a. 对   **b.** 错（在学校食堂里买午餐。）

c. 错（晚餐通常是中餐。）   **d.** 对

e. 对   **f.** 错（他自己带三明治。）

g. 错（他今天想吃烤牛肉。）   **h.** 对

Assessment suggestion

Ask students to list 3 starchy foods and write a sentence to say which they eat most often in their household.

Homework suggestion

Tell students they are hosting a cultural exchange foreign student in their home for a week. They need to design a weekly menu for their exchange student.

3.3 外出就餐 Dining out

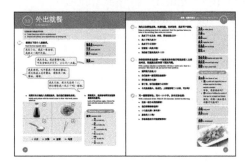

Icebreaker activity

In pairs, students interview one another, using the "Special restaurant" worksheet from the CD-ROM.

Lesson activities

1 📖 **Reading**

For part a, make sure students know what each picture represents before matching it to the correct person.

For part b, refresh students' memories of measure words (量词). Remind them the importance of learning the correct measure word for each object, action or event. Chinese measure words are similar to the English use of classifiers, e.g. a <u>piece</u> of cake (一<u>块</u>蛋糕) or a <u>pair</u> of shoes (一<u>双</u>鞋).

Answers

a. iii   **b.** i   **c.** iv   **d.** ii

b. 一瓶酱油，一碗牛肉面，一勺盐，一双筷子

 Students choose the most suitable measure words for:

a. 可乐（一瓶）   **b.** 粥 （一碗）

c. 咖啡（一杯／一壶）   **d.** 茶 （一杯／一壶）

e. 刀／叉 （一把）

2 🔊 **Listening**

Before the activity, help students to identify the key words in the questions. For question a. 主食 literally means "main meal"; however, it is different from what is meant by a main dish in western restaurants. 主食 refers to all the carbohydrates/staple food accompanying the meat and vegetable dishes, such as rice (米饭), noodles (面条), potatoes (土豆), spring onion pancakes (葱油饼), etc. For b. they should listen for dishes. For c. they should listen for drinks: in a Chinese restaurant, coffee is unlikely, but soft drinks and teas will be offered. For d. they should listen for the cost of the meal. For e. they should listen for a sum of money again: the tip.

 Write the key vocabulary on the board for students who may need a reminder.

Transcript

服务员： 您好，请问您们几位客人？

海伦: 就我一位。还有，请给我一份菜单。

服务员： 好的。这边请。您要点什么菜？

海伦: 我不吃肉，我是素食者。请问这里的素食有哪些？

服务员： 您可以要一盘西兰花，一份香辣豆腐和一碗米饭。今天我们店里免费提供酸辣汤，您也可以来一份。

海伦: 好的，就这些吧! 您们这儿有免费的花茶吗？

服务员： 有的，您要来一壶吗？

海伦: 是的，谢谢!

服务员： 不客气! 请问您是用刀叉还是筷子？

海伦: 我会用筷子，就筷子吧。谢谢。

服务员： 好的。您稍等。

旁白: 四十分钟后，海伦吃完了饭。

海伦: 服务员，请给我账单，谢谢。

服务员： 一共是七十元。谢谢。

海伦: 这是七十元，还有这十元是给你的小费。

服务员： 谢谢，欢迎下次再来。

Answers

a. 一碗米饭 b. 一盘西兰花、一份香辣豆腐、一碗米饭和一份酸辣汤 c. 一壶花茶

d. 一共七十元 e. 小费十元

 For more practice with food and restaurant vocabulary, you may like to show students the clip on "Eating fast food" from CNTV's *Growing up with Chinese* series and ask them questions about what the friends wanted to eat, what they ordered, how much they spent and what they did next.

 Language and culture

Show students "In the restaurant" from the BBC *Real Chinese* site to introduce Chinese dining culture.

Tell students that if they are invited out to a restaurant by a Chinese host, they must leave the ordering to the host. The host will usually ask the guests for their food preferences.

Point out that Chinese people get to know one another through eating together before any serious business cooperation. It's important for students to know this if they ever need to do business with the Chinese!

  Speaking

Walk around the room and listen to the students' conversations. Provide support to students as necessary.

Sample answers

a. 四位 b. 绿茶

c. 我們要点烤鸭、东坡肉、高僧排骨、龙井虾仁

d. 一瓶橙汁，一瓶蕃茄汁 e. 可以

  Writing

Show students a sample restaurant review. Ask them to play the role of a food critic and write a review on a restaurant they have been to.

Sample writing

每次我去北京都爱到大董烤鸭店吃烤鸭，餐厅的布置很优雅，服务员很友好。除了烤鸭之外，他们的菜和海鲜也非常新鲜可口。因为每次都是朋友请客，所以我没有付过钱，但是我想一定很贵。 如果你去北京，一定要去大董烤鸭店。

 Students can refer to the notes made on the "Special restaurant" worksheet to help them with this writing activity.

Homework suggestion

Students design a poster for the opening of a new restaurant specialising in Szechuan food (四川菜). They should do some research on Szechuan food (e.g. what are the most popular or common dishes) and include them as part of the restaurant's opening-night menu.

3.4 世界各地的美食 Food from around the world

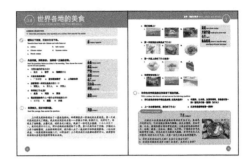

  Icebreaker activity

Show students one of the following *American Kids Try* videos online:

Episode 1: Breakfasts from Around the World

Episode 2: School Lunches from Around the World

Episode 3: Dinners from Around the World

Ask them which cuisine(s) they would most like to try, and why.

Lesson activities

  Writing

Discuss the multiple meanings of 菜 (cài) with students.

1. 菜 means "greens" or "vegetables". For example, 弟弟不喜欢吃菜。

2. 菜 can also mean "dishes"/"courses". For example, 那道菜很好吃。

3. 菜 can also mean "cuisines". You add a country name or a place name in front and it becomes that nation's or that place's cuisine. For example, 法国菜、四川菜。

4. 菜 also means "type" (this is a colloquialism). For example, 他不是我的菜。

Answers

a. 菜   b. 美味的菜   c. 中国菜
d. 日本菜   e. 法国菜

Explain to students that 美食 and 料理 are other common words for "cuisine", for example, 日本料理.

Ask students to state their preferred cuisine and give some example dishes. You may need to help them with the names of dishes. For example:

我喜欢吃四川菜，例如辣子鸡丁和麻婆豆腐。

 Ask students to give reasons for their preferences. For example: 我喜欢吃四川菜，例如辣子鸡丁和麻婆豆腐，因为我特别喜欢辣椒和花椒。

2 🔊 Listening

Ask students to go through the questions and identify the key words in each one:

a. 为什么？ The question is asking for a reason. Encourage students to look at the 3 options: 生日、春节 and 结婚 and listen out for one of them in the listening activity.

b. 在哪里？ Help students to look at the 3 options and the differences in the different type of cuisines.

c. 多少客人？ They can delete option 2, which is only for 50 people. Many Chinese restaurants can accommodate hundreds of guests.

d. 喝了什么汤？ Students should listen out for the word right before 汤.

e. 什么甜点？ They should listen for the dessert (likely to be near the end of the recording).

Transcript

朋友结婚了。结婚宴会在一家酒店的广东菜馆里举行。

去结婚宴会的客人很多，听说有两百人。不过没关系，这家广东菜馆很大，经理说餐厅一共有五百个座位。

餐桌上的饭菜各式各样，有烤肉，有海鲜，有鱼，有素菜，好看又好吃，大家都很喜欢。爷爷因为吃素，开胃餐只喝了菜汤。

我呢，因为好吃的东西太多了，吃得很饱，所以最后酒店给每位客人的甜点 --- 冰淇淋 --- 我都没有吃。

Answers

a. iii   b. i   c. iii   d. iii   e. i

---

3 📖 Reading

Before reading the passage, ask students to look at the pictures in the answer options and write down the

Chinese or pinyin for each one. This will make it easier for them to look for the key words in the passage itself.

Answers

a. i   **b.** ii   **c.** iii   **d.** iii

 **4** **Speaking**

Walk around the classroom listening to the conversations and providing support as necessary. Then select a few pairs to give a presentation about each other's answers.

Sample answers

a. 我们家常吃中餐。

b. 我最喜欢中国菜的烤鸭，皮脆味香，色泽红润，肉质肥而不腻，好看又好吃！

c. 我们吃了北京烤鸭，好好吃喔!

d. 法国菜

Cultural spotlight

Go through any unfamiliar vocabulary and expressions with students (e.g. 豆制品, 热气腾腾, 来年红红火火). Show students more pictures of Chinese hotpot.

Homework suggestion

Give students the worksheets "Three-cup chicken" and "Three-cup tofu" from the CD-ROM. Using the English translation as reference, they should find as many Chinese verbs as they can to do with ways of preparing and cooking a meal (for example, chopping, boiling, frying, baking).

3.5 健康状况 My health

 Icebreaker

Revise body parts vocabulary by showing the class one of the many videos on the internet of the song "Heads, shoulders, knees and toes" in Chinese.

Lesson activities

 **1** **Writing**

This is a simple labelling activity.

Answers

a. 眼睛   **b.** 耳朵   **c.** 鼻子   **d.** 口   **e.** 手   **f.** 手指

g. 腿   **h.** 脚

To reinforce learning, carry out this activity: Divide students into two groups. Each group takes turns describing a person in their own group. The other group then tries to guess the identity of that person. Ask students to mention as many body parts as possible in their description (nothing rude though!).

2 **Reading**

Before carrying out the activity, ask students to practise combining the body parts with 疼、痛、红、痒、发炎 and 受伤 to make up various ailments. This will help them to become familiar with the vocabulary.

Answers

a. vii   **b.** i   **c.** viii   **d.** ix   **e.** v

f. vi   **g.** x   **h.** ii   **i.** iii   **j.** iv

3 **Reading**

Remind students to read the questions first and highlight the key words in each one to help them look for the answers in the passage.

Answers

a. 吃了海鲜(对海鲜过敏)   **b.** 请假半天

c. 忘了穿暖和的衣服

 Ask students to write an article on health advice for various illness for the school magazine.

 **Listening**

Before listening to the recording, go through the questions with the students to highlight the key words so they know what to listen out for: a. 几岁开始喜欢跑步, b. 饮食, c. 为什么没有跑步, d. 下次运动会, e. 希望有什么样的成绩.

Transcript

记者： 杰西卡，你是什么时候开始喜欢跑步的？

杰西卡： 我七岁那年开始跟爸爸一起去公园跑步，然后慢慢地就喜欢上了。

记者： 除跑步以外，你是怎样保持健康的？

杰西卡： 我十分注意饮食，我每天都会吃大量的水果、蔬菜和少量的肉食。

记者： 听说你最近得好好休息，为什么？

杰西卡： 两个星期前，我的脚受伤了，所以这两个星期都没有跑步，等脚好了再参加训练。

记者： 祝你的脚早点儿好。

杰西卡： 谢谢。

记者： 你下一次比赛将会是什么时候？

杰西卡： 两个月后我会参加大学生运动会，希望在运动会上得第一名。

记者： 祝你如愿以偿！

Answers

a. 她七岁开始喜欢跑步。　**b.** 她每天吃大量的水果、蔬菜和少量的肉食。　**c.** 她的脚受伤了。
d. 大学生运动会　**e.** 第一名

 Speaking and Writing

For part a of this activity, students might find it helpful to refer to the vocabulary in Activity 2. Walk around the classroom and listen to their conversations and provide support as necessary.

Sample answers for part a

i. 医生：你哪里不舒服？
不舒服的人：我头疼喉咙疼

ii. 医生：不舒服是什么时候开始的？
不舒服的人：今天上午

iii. 医生：到现在多长时间了？
不舒服的人：四个小时

For part b, remind students that they are writing a note to a teacher, so the style and tone need to be formal and polite.

 Students who need extra support can refer to the reading passage (Activity 3) for ideas.

Sample answer for part b

王老师您好，

对不起，我要请假一天。我头疼发烧。医生叫我在家休息一天。请您准假。

张小明敬上

Homework suggestion

Ask students to record a phone message to apologise for absence from class because of an illness or injury.

Ask students to imagine they are a doctor and record some health advice for teenagers on various common ailments.

3.6 在医院 At the hospital

Icebreaker activity

To consolidate students' knowledge of the key vocabulary associated with physical health, choose one or two ailments, for example, a headache or an allergy, and lead a class discussion. Ask:

你常常头痛吗？　　　　　你什么时候头痛？

头痛的时候你怎么办？　　你对什么过敏？

你过敏的症状是什么？　　过敏的时候你怎么办？

 **Writing**

Introduce students to the concept of simplifying expressions. Use the following examples: 台湾大学＝台大, 北京大学 ＝ 北大, 流行感冒＝流感

Ask students to give some examples of their own before tackling the ones in the Student Book activity.

Answers

a. 医药＋商店＝药店   **b.** 西＋医学＝西医

c. 中＋医学＝中医   **d.** 稻草(草)＋药＝草药

e. 生病＋床＝病床   **f.** 医疗＋院子＝医院

 Ask students to make up sentences using the combined new words.

 2 📖 Reading

Go through the questions with students and ensure they can identify the key words that will help them work out the answers: a. 哪国人, b. 什么烦恼, c. 怎样帮助了汤姆.

Answers

a. 英国人 **b.** 对花粉过敏 **c.** 传统中医治疗＋中医草药汤药

To reinforce their learning, ask students to write a different thank-you note to a doctor referring to an ailment/illness they have been suffering for a long time and how the doctor's treatment has changed their life.

Ask students to copy the original thank-you note in the Student Book but replace the following three points with their own suggestions: the sender's nationality, their illness, what treatment they were given.

Language and culture

Explain that 大夫 is the name that has been given to physicians since ancient times. Ask students if they recognise 夫 (husband, man, government official), and if they can work out what 大 means in this context (superior/respected/senior rather than big!).

3 🔊 Listening

Before they listen to the recording, ask students to go through the questions and identify the key words:
a. 怎么了 – they should listen for an ailment or illness;
b/c/d. 为什么… – they should listen for a reason.

Remind students that it is often more complicated to listen out for reasons. It is easier if the reason follows the word 因为. However, speakers may not always say 因为 out loud, in which case students need to work out the reason from the context of the dialogue.

a. 朋友：小文，你今天感觉怎么样? 好像没有发烧了。
小文：好多了。我刚刚量了体温，烧退了。今天咳嗽也没有昨天严重。

b. 朋友：马克，你饿不饿? 饿了就吃一块巧克力吧。
马克：饿，但是我不能吃巧克力。医生说我要少吃甜食，因为他说我的体重已超重。

c. 朋友：米娜，你怎么啦? 你看上去不舒服!
米娜：我牙疼得厉害，吃东西都吃不好。我得去看牙医。

d. 朋友：心美，你的感冒好像很严重，我带你去医院吧!
心美：可是我不想去，我害怕医生给我打针。你们帮我买一盒感冒药吧。

Answers

a. ii **b.** iii **c.** i **d.** i

4 📖 DP Reading

Part a: In an IB DP exam, students may be asked to give reasons for the false statements. If time allows, you may ask them to do so here.

Part b: As students act out the dialogue between doctor and patient, walk around the classroom listening and providing support as necessary.

Answers for part a

i. 错 (海伦发烧，不是牙疼。)   **ii.** 对
iii. 错 (医生只开了药，没打针。)   **iv.** 对
v. 对   **vi.** 错 (海伦去药房取了药就可以回家了。)

 Ask students to change the symptoms and the suggested treatment (they can just make one up).

Further differentiation

 Show students the first 4 minutes of "Medical office" from CNTV's *Growing up with Chinese*. Give students the following questions before they watch the video so that they know what to look out for, and ensure that they are familiar with all the vocabulary they will need.

1. 小明为什么脚腕很疼？
2. 小明认为他的脚怎么了？
3. 医生建议先做什么？
4. 医生的诊断是什么？
5. 医生给小明的处方是什么？

 Students can give answers verbally to their partners.

 Students can write out their answers.

Answers

1. 他打篮球投篮的时候不小心摔了一跤。
2. 他认为他的脚骨折了。
3. 医生要小明先去照个片子。
4. 小明没有骨折，只是严重扭伤。
5. 医生要小明卧床休息两周，按时服药上药。

Homework suggestion

Tell students to imagine they are on a school trip abroad but they've hurt themselves or fallen ill. They should write an email to their parents telling them what happened, how they are feeling, and whether or not they received medical help (and if so, what treatment they were given).

3.7 保持健康 Keeping fit

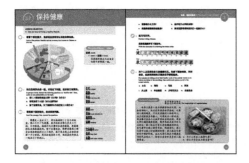

Icebreaker activity

Ask students for their views on healthy eating. List on the board their suggestions of healthy and unhealthy foods.

Lesson activities

 **Speaking**

After identifying all the food and drink items on the diagram, do a class poll to find out which food group in the picture students think is the most "healthy" food group.

Answers

香蕉，草莓，番茄，胡萝卜，白菜，吐司，白饭，面条，饼干，鲜奶，牛奶，乳酪，饮料，可乐，蛋糕，黄油，鱼，香肠，火腿肉，蛋

 **Speaking**

Ask the class if they have ever followed a special diet for a health reason. What was the diet like? Was it hard? Did they succeed? Then split students into groups for the activity. Walk around the classroom and listen to their conversations, providing support as necessary.

Sample answers

a. 我认为我的饮食很全面也很健康，因为我什么都吃，但是都不吃得过多。

b. 我尝试过节食，尤其是在圣诞节以后，因为我吃了太多巧克力变胖了。

c. 除了注意饮食，为了健康，我们还应该常常运动。

3 📖 **Reading**

The reading activity is about an actress's diet and fitness plan. Go through the questions with the students before tackling the reading passage. Help them identify the key words in each question to help them look for the answers in the passage: **a.** 什么工作, **b.** 不吃什么食物, **c.** 做哪些运动健身, **d.** 周末……和朋友做什么？

Answers

a. 张静是一名女演员。

b. 她不吃油炸的快餐速食。

c. 张静每周三去健身房跑步，每周五晚上去游泳。周末去露营和爬山。

d. 露营和爬山

Celebrity fitness regimes

Before doing this activity, research the diet and fitness regime of a few celebrities or sportspeople and create a factsheet for each person.

Tell students they are attending a press conference where the celebrities will share their diet and fitness regime and their success story. Choose 3–5 students to play the celebrities. They are given a factsheet each. They need to improvise their answers and can be as imaginative as they like. The rest of the students pretend to be journalists and ask questions on how to keep fit. You could provide 2 microphones to make the situation look authentic. After the press conference, you could ask students to write a short report about the celebrities' diet and fitness regimes.

  Writing

The strokes animation on the MGDB online dictionary is useful for showing students the sequences of writing individual characters. Apart from practising the stroke order, you may want to also ask students the radical of each character: 健 (人 / 亻); 康(广).

 **Listening**

Remind students to go through the answer options first, and write down the meanings either in pinyin or English. They can then use these as prompts when listening to the recording.

a. 我是小文。我现在每天晚上都会吃好几块蛋糕，所以长胖了。为了健康，我打算节食，以后少吃甜食，特别是巧克力。

b. 我是海伦。我的身体一直都很好。为了保持健康，我想以后多去健身房。

c. 我是马克。我最近总是眼睛疼，医生说这是因为我每天都上网的原因，所以我打算以后少上网，少玩游戏。

d. 我是阿里。最近天气很热，晚上我总是睡不好觉，所以白天觉得很累，今天我想早一点睡觉。

Answers

a. iii **b.** iv **c.** i **d.** ii

Cultural spotlight

Go through unfamiliar vocabulary with students. Then show students pictures of different kinds of Buddhist "mock" or "imitation" meat dishes. Explain that many such dishes are soy (tofu) or gluten based. Today, there are restaurants specialising in mock meat dishes across Asia, popular with both vegetarians and meat-lovers.

Assessment suggestion

In small groups, students prepare and deliver to the class a brief presentation on their New Year resolutions focusing on a new diet and fitness regime.

Homework suggestion

Ask students to research and compare a typical Chinese diet with a typical western diet. What are the similarities and differences? Which is "healthier" in their opinion?

3.8 健康的身体, 健康的心理 Healthy body, healthy mind

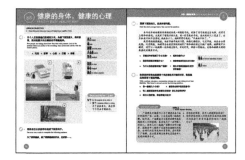

Icebreaker activity

Put students in pairs and give them each the worksheet "A questionnaire about stress" from the CD-ROM. After completing it themselves, they interview their partners and write down their answers. The class then votes for the most creative answer to the last question on the stress card, "你认为做什么事最减压？"

Lesson activities

  Listening

You could begin by asking students if they do any of the activities illustrated to relax. Ask them to jot down the pinyin for each – this will help them listen out for the activities in the recording.

Transcript

a. 我是马克。我从小跟爷爷一起钓鱼。现在如果我不开心，我就会去湖边钓鱼。

b. 我是志军。每次我觉得压力大的时候，我会听一些自己喜欢的音乐来放松自己，让自己不要太紧张。

c. 我是心美，在森林边长大，热爱大自然。每当我学习太紧张，觉得有压力了，我就会在周末去森林里走一走，看着那些又高又大绿绿的树我就会轻松很多。

d. 我是日晴。我每天都去健身房跑步，每次有麻烦事，我只要在跑步机上跑5公里我就没有压力了。

e. 我是米娜。我觉得海是很神奇的。看海是我减压的最好方式，每一次在海边看着蓝蓝的大海，听着海的声音，我就不紧张了。

Answers

a. iv **b.** i **c.** v **d.** ii **e.** iii

 **2** **Writing**

Show students how to gradually build on the sentence patterns from the grammar focus feature, as shown below:

为了……

为了……应该……

为了……除了……还应该……

Sample answers

为了保持健康，我需要健康的饮食。

为了保持健康，你应该天天跑步。

为了保持健康，除了需要健康的饮食，你还应该天天跑步。

 **3** **Reading**

To begin, ask students to compare old and young people in terms of diet, hobbies, and sports. As a whole-class activity, create a chart on the board like the one below and invite students to fill it in with ideas.

	老人	年轻人
饮食		
嗜好		
运动		

Now move on to the Student Book activity. Ask students to read the questions first and highlight the key words in each one: a. 收到了什么礼物; b. 说什么; c. 为什么; d. 做什么; e. 哪些好的生活习惯; f. 健康生活方式有哪些. Understanding what the questions are asking for will help students look for the relevant answers.

Answers

a. 一部智能手机。 **b.** 打电话，上网和玩游戏。
c. 不要玩手机了。 **d.** 早睡早起，健身
(走路和跳舞)。 **e.** 跳广场舞可以健身，还可以一边跳舞一边和朋友聊天，有说有笑，保持心情愉快。
f. 早睡早起，规律运动 (走路和跳舞)。

 MYP **Language and culture**

Show the class a video of people doing tai chi. Explain that it is a form of traditional Chinese martial arts with a focus on relaxation. Unlike other forms of martial arts using physical force, tai chi emphasises breathing and gentleness. It's a combination of Chinese philosophy and keeping fit. Some research shows that tai chi can reduce anxiety and depression. With its slow movements, it has become a popular way to keep fit and healthy.

4 **Speaking**

Before the activity, you could hold a class discussion on lifestyles in terms of diet, exercise, and sleeping habits. Ask a few students if they think they are living a healthy lifestyle; they should give a reason for their answer.

Check that students know: 健康的, 不健康的, 饮食, 运动, 睡眠. Write the reasons given by a few students on the board as examples others can use in the role-play.

During the activity, walk around the classroom and listen to the students' conversations. Provide support to individual pairs as necessary.

Sample answers

网友1：有了智能手机，和朋友联络很方便，都舍不得睡觉了！你呢？一天睡几小时？

网友2：我一天大概睡7小时，睡前一小时会上网看脸书，联络朋友。

网友1：你认为睡觉前玩手机或看社交网站好吗？

网友2：睡前玩手机或看社交网站没问题，但记得光线要充足，也不要看太久，以免影响睡意。

网友1：压力大的时候，你怎样减少压力？

网友2：我会找朋友聊天，吐苦水；或者玩喜欢的游戏舒压。

Cultural spotlight

 Find and show students a video of 广场舞. If there is space in the classroom, ask students to join in!

Homework suggestion

Students write an email to their grandparents either suggesting a healthy diet and fitness programme to them, or telling them about their research on tai chi and its health benefits for them.

3.9 运动 Sports

Icebreaker activity

Pin an image of a famous sportsperson on the board, but cover it up. Ask the class questions to which the answers are sports-related. For each correct answer, uncover a little more of the image. The first student to identify the person wins.

Lesson activities

 Listening

You could begin by asking the class what exercise they do to keep fit. Do they do any of the sports shown?

For the activity, remind students to write out the pinyin in each of the activities so that it will be easier to listen out for them in the recording.

Transcript

a. 爷爷和奶奶最近参加了一个保龄球俱乐部。他们每个星期四晚上都会去保龄球馆比赛，玩得特别开心。

b. 爸爸虽然工作忙，但是他经常健身，一个星期要去两次健身房。

c. 妈妈不太喜欢运动，但是每天吃完晚饭，妈妈都会去公园或城市广场散步。她常常说饭后百步走，活到九十九。

d. 哥哥从小打桌球就打得很好，我们家没有人在桌球上赢过他。现在哥哥把桌球当成运动，每天都会练习。

e. 姐姐每个星期五晚上都去运动中心。她在那里学跳桑巴舞。她说跟着音乐跳舞很好，让她很快乐，让她放松。

Answers

a. v **b.** ii **c.** i **d.** iii **e.** iv

2 Speaking

There are a number of possible answers in this odd-one-out activity. The important thing is that students should be able to give a reason for their answer.

Sample answers

钓鱼：其他的活动都在陆地上，但是钓鱼要到河边或海边。

放风筝：其他的活动都与陆地有关，但是风筝是飞到天空去。

乒乓球：这是唯一用到球的活动。

兵兵球：这是室内运动，其他三项则是户外运动。

3 Reading

Remind students to look for the key words in the questions to help them look for the relevant answers before reading the passage:

a. 哪些；**b.** 除了……还需要；**c.** 如果不想……可以。

Answers

a. 体育活动有：跑步、沙滩排球、爬山、森林徒步、乒乓球、网球

b. 还有语言课和文化课

c. 大家可以坐在一起聊天

To reinforce their grasp of this topic, students could work in groups of 3 or 4 to design a summer camp programme for a group of Chinese students who are coming over for a cultural exchange. The programme should include a mixture of: academic studies, sport, leisure activities, and cultural visits.

Each group presents their programme and the groups vote for the best one.

  Writing and Speaking

 For this activity, you may want to show students the website of the Weifang World Kite Museum (潍坊世界风筝博物馆) for inspiration.

Part a is a poster-designing activity. To increase students' vocabulary and help make their writing more interesting, consider teaching them the following.

Types of kites:

- 硬翅风筝 (hard-winged kite)
- 软翅风筝 (soft-winged kites)
- 立体风筝 (solid tube-shaped kites)

Descriptive phrases as reasons for/benefits of kite-flying:

- 沐浴在和煦的阳光和春风中 (soaking up the sunshine and spring breeze)
- 怡情养性 (restoring and improving your wellbeing)
- 强身健体 (toning our bodies)
- 老少皆宜 (suitable for all ages)

 For some students it is fine to keep the descriptions of the kites or "marketing talk" to a minimum. The important thing is to ensure they have covered the four questions on their poster.

For part b, walk around the classroom and listen to students' conversations. Provide support as necessary.

Sample answers for part a

风筝节海报：放风筝 – 沐浴在和煦的阳光和春风中，可以怡情养性，而且对于强身健体、防病治病都有很大帮助。老少皆宜，欢迎大家一起来！我们提供硬翅，软翅，立体等各种类风筝，还有特技风筝喔。

风筝节时间：6月1日至6月7日

地点：雷丁运动公园

Sample answers for part b

组织者：我们举办风筝节，提供各种类风筝，欢迎带家人一起参加。

参加者：听说放风筝有很多好处，是吗？

组织者：是的，放风筝可以舒展筋骨，促进人体的新陈代谢，改善血液循环。

参加者：哇，那我一定带家人一起去。

Homework suggestion

Students write an email to a friend about their experience of attending a kite festival.

 Ask students to research into the kite tradition and write a short report on it.

3.10 复习 Progress check

Lesson activities

1  **Reading**

This is a straightforward reading activity. Remind students to read the questions and answer options before they tackle the advert; it will help them look for answers more efficiently.

Answers

a. i **b.** i **c.** ii

After students have completed the reading activity, discuss what is meant by "tea culture" in the West and in China, and how they differ. For example: What is high tea and how is it different from dim sum?

 **Listening**

Remind students to look at the pictures first and write pinyin prompts for each one; this will help them find the relevant answers when listening to the recording.

Transcript

a. 我是小文。这几天天气凉了，我感冒了，经常咳嗽。

b. 我是丽青。我刚刚从香港旅游回来，那里的天气还很热，我的皮肤晒黑了很多。

c. 我是马克。昨天晚上我吃了一些海鲜，今天我的肚子很疼，很不舒服，不知道是不是因为吃了不新鲜的海鲜。

d. 我是汤姆。昨天我和爸爸在河边钓鱼时下雨了。我们没有带雨衣，所以淋雨了，我觉得我好像发烧了。

e. 我是海伦。这几个星期我不能参加长跑训练了，因为我的脚受伤了。

Answers

a. iv **b.** i **c.** ii **d.** v **e.** iii

The transcript can be used to provide additional reading practice for students. Split up the sentences in the dialogues and write them on cards. Ask students to match each condition or ailment with a cause.

Students can make up reasons of their own about each of the ailments and write sentences about them.

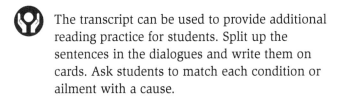 **Reading**

If students need extra speaking practice, get them to role-play the conversation in pairs and jointly find the answers to the reading comprehension. Remind them to look for key words in the questions before going through the dialogue.

Answers

a. 餐馆环境好，服务周到，上菜快，菜味道好，而且看上去很漂亮。 **b.** 逛商场。 **c.** 他们一共吃了一百八十元；给了服务员二十元小费。

 **Writing**

You may like to analyse the text first with students to help them to find the correct answers:

a. The first sentence is a combination of 2 self-contained units: 吃完饭 and 散步是一个非常好的活动。 The answer should therefore be a linking word.

b. 广场 and 河边 follow the answer for b, which indicates that b should be a place as well.

c. The answer for c sits between the subject and the verb; it could only be an adverb such as a frequency adverb.

d. The answer for d is part of a phrase indicating simultaneous tasks (一边走一边……), so it should also be a verb.

e. Use the sentence 聊一些有趣的事情 to work out what the answer for e might be (that is, it should also be a verb).

f. The answer for f comes right after 觉得, so it should be an adjective.

Answers

a. 以后 **b.** 公园 **c.** 常常 **d.** 聊天 **e.** 说一说

f. 快乐

Writing

Before the activity, you could explain that Sichuan dishes are generally very spicy; Cantonese dishes tend to be sweet and sour with some foreign influence as it is a coastal province; Hanzhou dishes tend to be bland with a sweet taste.

Write out the names of some popular dishes on the board for students who are not familiar with their names.

Remind students they are writing to their parents so the style and tone of the email should be warm and relaxed.

Sample answer

爸爸妈妈您们好,

今天一个朋友的家人带我去了一家杭州菜馆吃饭。餐馆很漂亮。我们点了龙井虾仁、金牌扣肉和青菜小笼汤包。我很喜欢龙井虾仁,非常鲜美嫩滑。吃完饭,我们还去逛了街。今天过得很开心!

儿子马克敬上

6 Speaking

Remind students to include vocabulary they have learned across the whole unit when answering these questions. Walk around the classroom listening to conversations and providing support as necessary.

Answers

a. 我认为健康生活应该是:上学,用功读书,课余运动,再加上均衡的饮食。

b. 我的生活方式是健康的生活方式,只是偶尔有赖床的坏习惯。

c. 手机可联络朋友,上网查资料,还可以玩游戏,让我很开心!但是不停的玩手机不仅伤害眼睛视力,对别人也很不礼貌。若边走路边玩手机就更危险了,甚至危害生命。

Further differentiation

Students write about whether they eat out or dine at home more often.

 Students use the simple sentence pattern: 我经常……因为……。

 Students can add an extra sentence or two to say whether or not they think their diet is healthy.

Assessment suggestion

Ask students to write an article for the school magazine promoting a healthy lifestyle for teenagers. They should include information on:

- what constitutes a healthy diet
- ways to stay fit physically
- ways to keep stress at bay.

假期
HOLIDAYS

UNIT OBJECTIVES

- Plan for school holidays.
- Learn some facts about Spring Festival and discuss how it is celebrated.
- Discuss how people celebrate Christmas.
- Plan and prepare for a study tour.

- Discuss holiday activities and experiences.
- Discuss experiences of booking and staying in a hotel.
- Discuss ways of dealing with problems during a holiday.

4.1 预习 Unit introduction

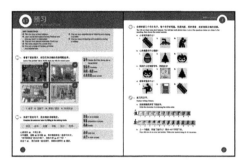

Prior learning

Students should be familiar with vocabulary relating to holidays from Units 1–3.

> **Icebreaker activity**
>
> You could begin with a holiday board race game. (For guidance, please refer to "Language-learning games and activities" on the CD-ROM.)

Lesson activities

 **1** **Reading**

You could ask students to describe each picture by responding to questions as a way to prepare them for picture-based exam questions.

 Students answer when, where, who questions.

 Students answer what, how, and why questions.

> **Answers**
>
> **a.** iii **b.** iv **c.** i **d.** ii

 **2** **Reading**

Here students fill in the missing words without the aid of pictures. Make sure they understand the meaning of each answer option first.

> **Answers**
>
> **a.** 放假 **b.** 计划 **c.** 游学 **d.** 准备 **e.** 假期
>
> **f.** 预订

 You could use the sentences in the Student Book to ask students questions to check their reading comprehension, for example:

Q: 心美什么时候放假？(A: 明天)

Q: 今年暑假汤姆去中国做什么？(A: 游学学中文)

Q: 你明天去中国要准备什么东西？(A: 行李)

Q: 妈妈叫我帮忙做什么事？(A: 预定酒店)

 **3** **Listening**

Advise students to begin by looking at the pictures and note down either the Chinese or pinyin for each one so that it is easier to match them when listening to the recording.

Before students listen to the recording for the second time, analyse each question in turn, to ensure students truly understand what they should be listening out for.

> **Transcript**
>
> **a.** 女: 在学校，你听到小明说：
> 小明：我明天放假。我明天放假。
> 女: 他明天做什么？
>
> **b.** 男: 在教室，你听到心美说：
> 心美：我最喜欢圣诞节假期。我最喜欢圣诞节假期。
> 男: 她最喜欢什么假期？
>
> **c.** 男: 在家里，你听到妈妈说：
> 妈妈：我们春节到爷爷奶奶家去。我们春节到爷爷奶奶家去。
> 男: 她什么时候到爷爷、奶奶家去？
>
> **d.** 女: 在家里，你听到哥哥说：
> 哥哥：我有很多休闲活动。我有很多休闲活动。
> 女: 哥哥有很多什么？

Answers

a. i (放假) **b.** ii (圣诞节假期)

c. ii (春节) **d.** iii (休闲活动)

4 Writing

For part a, the strokes animation on the MGDB online dictionary is useful for showing students the sequences of writing individual characters.

For part b, remind students to use vocabulary learned not just from this lesson but from previous units to help them construct their sentences.

Sample writing for part b

去年暑假我们全家去了海南岛的三亚度假，我们每天在海里游泳还吃了很多美食。

If time allows, students can share their holiday experiences with the class.

 Encourage students to write about something that happened on their last holiday, either positive or negative, and how it made them feel.

Further differentiation

 Compose a short passage about holidays, leaving gaps for students to fill in or giving alternatives to choose from.

Students interview a family member or a friend about holiday preferences and write a report.

4.2 学校假期 School holidays

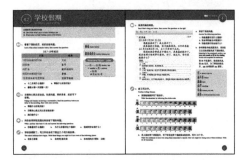

Icebreaker activity

Ask the class to say what they do during the holidays, both at home and if they go away. Introduce the Chinese for any activities they do not know.

Lesson activities

1  Reading

To practise writing dates, ask students to write friends' and relatives' birthdays. Remind them that the month comes before the day in Chinese.

 Check that students can state dates and also review vocabulary for festivals with them.

Answers

a. 圣诞节假期 **b.** 1月15日 **c.** 6月24日到8月10日

2  Listening

Remind students to read the questions first and help them to identify the focus of each question.

Transcript

日晴：寒假快要到了，一月十五日就放假了。心美，那时不用上学，你打算去哪儿玩？

心美：我在家里休息。

日晴：在家里多没意思。你忘了吗？汤姆生日快要到了，三天以后就是。心美，我们一起去他家帮他庆祝生日吧！

心美：好啊，那到时候一起去！

Answers

a. 1月15日 **b.** 汤姆的家 **c.** 帮汤姆庆祝生日

3  Speaking

Walk around the classroom listening to students' conversations and providing support as necessary.

Sample answers

a 我最喜欢寒假。

b. 因为寒假我可以去滑雪。

c. 假期的时候，我会看书，看电影和玩网络游戏。

Students could interview one another in pairs, noting their answers on the "Holiday decisions" worksheet (on the CD-ROM). You could then ask the class to vote for their favourite holiday, ask individual students which is their favourite and why, or choose one or two holiday ideas to discuss as a group.

Writing

Encourage students to write answers independently to ensure a variety of answers, particularly for part c.

> **Sample answers**
>
> **a.** 放假的时候我会在自己家里写作业 / 运动 / 听音乐。
>
> **b.** 放假的时候我会在朋友家聊天 / 玩游戏 / 庆祝他的生日。
>
> **c.** 放假的时候我会在公园散步 / 在图书馆看书 / 在法国滑雪。

  Reading

For part a, ask students for the focus of each question, so they know what to look out for as they read.

For part b, remind students to read the blog for ideas, before coming up with the missing words.

> **Answers**
>
> **a.** **i.** 寒假 **ii.** 妈妈 **iii.** 拍照片
>
> **b.** Sample answers:
> **i.** 圣诞节假期 **ii.** 下周末 **iii.** 家人 **iv.** 香港

  Writing

For part a, the strokes animation on the MGDB online dictionary is useful for showing students the sequences of writing individual characters. Ask students to identify the radical of each character.

For part b, ensure students are familiar with the following sentence patterns before the writing activity:

……的时候，我想要……

> **Sample answers for part b**
>
> 寒假的时候，我想去阿尔卑斯山滑雪。
>
> 暑假的时候，我想去中国坐火车旅行。

> **Language and culture**
>
> Remind students of the basic Chinese word order when constructing sentences:
> Time ⇒ Place ⇒ Action
>
> Examples:
> 上星期六 (Time) 我们在伦敦 (Place) 买东西 (Action)。
> 昨天 (Time) 我去奶奶家 (Place) 吃饺子 (Action)。

Assessment suggestion

Give students a set of questions about holidays for them to answer and then compose a short essay.

Sample questions:

你上一个长假期是什么时候?

你去了哪儿?

你跟谁一起去的?

你怎么去的呢?

你在那儿做了些什么?

假期过得开心吗? 为什么?

Homework suggestion

Students write a blog post about a forthcoming holiday, including holiday dates, destination, companions and proposed activities.

4.3 春节 Spring Festival

 MYP **Icebreaker activity**

Divide the class into two teams. Each team has to write down as many customs/traditions related to Chinese New Year as they can. (The video *Chinese New Year – Holidays* on the History Channel can be used for information.) For each relevant word in Chinese, the team gains 2 points; if it is in English, 1 point. The team with most points wins.

Lesson activities

  Listening

Before listening to the recording, ask students:

你和你的家人庆祝春节吗?

你们怎么庆祝?

Then, ask them for the key point in each question they should listen out for in the recording.

Transcript

小华：丽青，中国新年快到了。哪一天是春节？

丽青：小华，你不知道吗？今年春节是二月三日。

小华：知道了。谢谢！我最喜欢过春节，因为春节的假期很长。

丽青：你就只想着放假！对了，你春节到哪儿去？

小华：我会去爷爷、奶奶家拜年。

丽青：我也是。爷爷、奶奶每年都会发红包给我。

小华：红包里的钱多吗？

丽青：我才不告诉你呢！

Answers

a. 二月三日　**b.** 小华　**c.** 爷爷奶奶家　**d.** 红包

---

2 📖 Reading

Remind students to read the questions first and note down the key words in each question:

1. 节日　**2.** 说什么话　**3.** 食物

These will help them find the answers in the text.

Answers

1. 春节　**2.** 新年好，新年快乐　**3.** 饺子、汤圆

---

3  Writing and Speaking

In addition to revisiting what students have learned in the lesson about Spring Festival, it may be worth showing them pictures or videos from the internet about Chinese New Year celebrations to help them prepare their answers for both parts of the activity.

---

a. Sample writing

今年的春节在一月二十八日，我想请几个朋友来我家一起庆祝。我打算做猪肉饺子和蔬菜饺子，还要蒸年糕给大家吃。我要教朋友的小孩说说新年的中文，"恭喜"和"新年快乐"，还要给他们一人一个红包。

b. Sample answers for speaking
i. 我会吃火锅和年糕。
ii. 我会说恭喜发财。
iii. 我会请朋友来我家。
iv. 我会跟朋友一起吃饭庆祝春节。

Language and culture

Students may wonder why the date of the Chinese New Year changes every year. You can take this opportunity to explain the difference between 阳历 (solar calendar, of which the Gregorian calendar is an example) and 农历 (lunar calendar). You can also introduce 十二生肖 (Chinese Zodiac) and teach students the signs in order: 鼠、牛、虎、兔、龙、蛇、马、羊、猴、鸡、狗、猪。

Cultural spotlight

This Cultural spotlight focuses on the colour red in Chinese culture. Go through any challenging vocabulary (长辈, 晚辈, 压岁钱, 好事成双).

MYP Ask students to carry out a research project into the tradition of giving red envelopes at Spring Festival and write a short report.

Give students questions to answer about the tradition of red envelopes. These can form the basis of their report.

Assessment suggestion

In groups, students prepare and deliver a presentation to the class on either:

- a Spring Festival tradition of their choice (other than red envelopes) or

- symbols in Chinese culture and their meanings – for instance, why 8 symbolises prosperity; why a fish represents abundance.

Homework suggestions

1. Students research the recipe and history of New Year cake and answer the following questions:
- What is the cake made of?
- What is its purpose, according to legend?
- What is the name of the cake in Chinese? Why is this appropriate for the Spring Festival?

2. **MYP** Students cook egg fried rice at home following the recipe below. They can photograph their finished product and write a short paragraph to say if they enjoyed cooking and eating it!

如何做蛋炒饭：

1. 先把炒锅烧热，再把油放入锅里加热到较高的温度。

2. 把两个蛋和葱花混合打散放入热油中快炒。

3. 在蛋完全凝结以前，把冷饭放进蛋里快炒。

4. 把蛋炒饭盛进盘里，趁热吃。

4.4 圣诞节 Christmas

Lesson activities

1  Listening

Ask students to identify the key words in the questions:
a. 什么时候? b. 在哪儿? c. 怎么过?

Transcript

威廉: 圣诞节下个星期就到了。小文, 圣诞节假期去哪儿玩?

小文: 我会去中国旅行。威廉, 你呢?

威廉: 我会回美国过圣诞节。

小文: 美国人是怎么过圣诞节的?

威廉: 我们会有家庭聚会, 我们会互相送圣诞礼物, 也会吃圣诞大餐。在中国, 人们会庆祝圣诞节吗?

小文: 在中国, 有些人也会庆祝圣诞节。对了, 你会送圣诞礼物给我吗?

威廉: 我不告诉你, 下星期你就知道了。

Answers

a. 下个星期　**b.** 美国　**c.** 他家会有家庭聚会, 互相送圣诞礼物, 也会吃圣诞大餐。

2 Reading

Ask students to identify the key words in the questions before reading the passage.

 This reading passage might look alarmingly long. Ask students to break it down by underlining the most frequent word in the text, numbers, etc. then read through it paragraph by paragraph.

Answers

a. 十二月二十五日

b. 平安夜

c. 爸爸妈妈会假扮圣诞老人送孩子礼物。

d. 圣诞快乐

e. 圣诞大餐, 例如火鸡和土豆

 Students can try rewriting the reading passage by replacing certain words, for example:

In the text: 圣诞节的前一天晚上是平安夜, 有些人会去教堂唱诗。

can be replaced by: 圣诞节的前一天晚上是平安夜, 有些人会去看朋友。

In the text: 人们也会准备不同的食物, 例如火鸡和土豆

can be replaced by: 人们也会准备不同的食物, 例如烤鹅和香肠。

Students can also interview one another in pairs about their families' Christmas traditions using the "Christmas traditions" worksheet from the CD-ROM.

3 Writing

Remind students they are writing to a friend, so the style and tone of writing should be informal.

 You could change the writing activity into gap filling to make the activity easier.

 Encourage students to include reasons in their writing and write more complex sentences.

Sample answer

安娜你好,

我和家人在法国过圣诞节假期。我们白天滑雪, 晚上全家享受圣诞大餐, 非常开心! 我买了一些蛋糕给你。祝你佳节愉快!

4 Speaking

Walk around the classroom and listen to students' conversations. Provide support as necessary.

 You could prepare lists of alternative reasons, gift and food ideas for students to choose from to write in their sentences.

Encourage students to express their feelings and opinions.

Sample answers

a. 我喜欢过圣诞节，因为全家人都聚在一起。

b. 圣诞节我会送巧克力或是自己做的蛋糕给朋友。

c. 圣诞节大餐我通常吃烤鹅肉、土豆和一些青菜。

5 Writing

For part a, the strokes animation on the MGDB online dictionary is useful for showing students the sequences of writing individual characters.

For part b, remind students they can use vocabulary learned in other lessons as well as this one to help construct their answers.

 (For part b) Encourage students to give reasons for their answers if they are able to.

Sample answers for part b

圣诞节的时候，我喜欢：

街上美丽的圣诞节灯饰 / 全家人团聚 / 吃圣诞节大餐 / 跟朋友见面 / 收到自己喜欢的礼物

圣诞节的时候，我不喜欢：

街上太多人和车 / 买很多圣诞节礼物 / 花很多时间做菜 / 电视上的垃圾节目 / 收到不喜欢的礼物

Homework suggestion

Ask students to compare Christmas and Chinese New Year traditions in Chinese (80–120 words). They should cover food, family activities and presents.

4.5 假期游学 Overseas study tours

Icebreaker activity

Ask students if they have been on a school trip. Ask them to share their experiences.

Lesson activities

1  Reading

Before the activity, revise the main pen strokes by going through the strokes of a number of easy characters together.

 If necessary, students can use a dictionary to work out the number of strokes in each case.

Answers

飞机 (9)，机场 (12)，行李 (13)，夏令营 (26)，课外活动 (30)

2  Reading

Ask students for the key words in each question to help them know what to look for in the text.

Answers

a. 机场出发 b. 7月12日 c. 看中文电影，唱中文歌

d. 因为这是短途旅游

3 Listening

As usual, students should note the key words in each question to guide their listening. Note: the first two questions are true-or-false-type questions and the third question is a gap-filling one.

Transcript

马克：小华！我参加了台湾夏令营，你要一起去吗？

小华：好，我们一起去吧，因为我喜欢去以前没去过的地方。

马克：我也是。我也喜欢去外地旅游，只在本地游玩太无聊了。

小华：那你准备去台湾的哪几个著名景点呢？

马克：我听说日月潭非常好玩，我们可以坐船去那里游览。

小华：真好！对了，马克，我们在台湾能住在同一个房间吗？

马克：我不知道。我想和你住同一个房间呢。

小华：我们一起发电子邮件问问老师吧。电子邮件的地址就写在小册子上。

马克：好的！

Answers

a. i **b.** i **c.** ii

   Speaking and Writing

For part a, listen to students' conversations and provide support as necessary. Remind students to jot down their answers as a basis for their diary entries.

For part b, remind students that they're writing in their diary so they can be informal and honest, and should express personal feelings.

 If students find writing a diary entry hard, print out the sample answer, cut up the sentences and mix them up, then ask students to put the sentences back in order.

Sample conversation for part a

i.   夏令营在上海举行。

ii. 从伦敦出发

iii. 要去十二天

iv. 早上的课堂活动要学习中文和中国文化。

v.   下午和周末的时候做课外参观旅行。

vi. 我是英国人，去上海需要有中国签证。

Sample diary entry for part b

七月十五日，学校要带我们从伦敦的希思罗机场出发去上海游学十天。我们要学习汉语和中国文化，例如写书法，跳中国舞蹈。周末的时候我们还要去周庄看看江南水乡的风景。我觉得特别兴奋，希望七月快快到来。

  Writing

For part a, ask students to identify the radicals of the characters. Tell them what the radicals mean (签 = 竹; 证 = 言).

For part b, prepare a list showing nationalities that require a visa to enter China. Refer students to the list if they're not sure whether or not they need a visa.

Sample answer for part b

我去中国不用办签证因为我有中国护照。

 Homework suggestion

In groups, students carry out research on summer camps in a Chinese-speaking area, such as China, Taiwan, Singapore or Hong Kong. They then produce a presentation in Chinese on one of them, covering the date and venue; the theme (if relevant); the programme (including any special features); the cost.

Assessment suggestion

Students deliver their summer camp presentations to the class next lesson and hold a vote on which summer camp is the most appealing.

4.6 假期计划与准备 Getting ready for a holiday

Icebreaker activity

Students play the "Desert Island" game. (See the "Language-learning games and activities" document on the CD-ROM.)

Sentence patterns to use:

a.   我要去 YYY (a place)度假

b.   我要带 XXX (an object)去度假

c.   a + b = 我要带 XXX 去 YYY 度假

Lesson activities

  Reading

This activity introduces some key vocabulary to do with holiday activities and destinations. In (a) to (d), each phrase begins with a verb, so students have to find the appropriate noun to complete the action. Point out that (e) to (h) are types of holiday destinations.

You may wish to set up verb-noun-matching games on the interactive whiteboard, if available, to consolidate students' understanding of common verb-noun combinations.

Answers

a. 酒店　**b.** 护照　**c.** 旅行社　**d.** 来回票　**e.** 森林

f. 沙滩　**g.** 郊区　**h.** 海边

 ### Listening

Help students to analyse questions in advance. For example, in question b (酒店在哪儿？) they should note two important elements to listen out for: 酒店 and 在哪儿.

Transcript

志军：马克，听说你暑假的时候要到台湾去？

马克：是的，我和小华一起参加了台湾夏令营。

志军：什么时候出发？

马克：我们七月九日出发。

志军：东西都准备好了吗？

马克：行李和护照都准备好了。

志军：很好。别忘了带！对了，机票买了吗？

马克：旅行社给我们准备了来回机票，我们不用自己买，只要去旅行社拿机票，然后带机票到机场就行了。

志军：真好！你们会去台湾哪儿？

马克：我们会去台湾的日月潭。我们的酒店在郊区，在山和森林的旁边。

志军：那儿有沙滩吗？

马克：因为酒店在山区，不在海边，所以那儿没有沙滩。等我们从台湾回来以后，我们再一起去沙滩吧！

志军：好！

Answers

a. ii and iii　**b.** ii

You may also want to analyse the transcript with students to ensure understanding of all the vocabulary.

 ### 3 Writing

 Show students the video of Expedia's "Taipei Vacation Travel Guide". In pairs, they then work out a packing list for Mark's trip, before writing the items down and feeding back to the class. Remind students of the vocabulary relevant to climate and environment in Taiwan.

Sample answers

短裤，运动鞋，背包

 Students write about Taipei based on the video.

4 Speaking

Sample answers

a. 暑假我要去北京。　**b.** 我计划去北京看朋友。

c. 我要住希尔顿饭店。　**d.** 我要准备礼物和人民币。

For additional practice, students can use worksheets "Holiday plans 1" and "Holiday plans 2" (on the CD-ROM) to discuss and plan a holiday.

5 Writing

For part a, the strokes animation on the MGDB online dictionary is useful to show students the sequences of writing individual characters. Ask students what the 氵 radical means (水).

For part b, practise sentence constructions covered in this lesson. They can model their sentences on Activity 4 above.

Sample answer for part b

我喜欢去沙滩玩水，我会带墨镜和防晒霜，这样才不会被太阳晒伤。我还要带大浴巾，游泳以后可以用。

 Encourage students to practise writing complex Chinese characters.

Language and culture

Some Chinese idioms related to travelling/holidays:

游山玩水：wandering about to enjoy the beauties of nature

入乡随俗：when in Rome

名胜古迹：places of historic interest and scenic beauty

Further differentiation

 Ask students to write a checklist for their holiday preparations.

 Students write a proposal for the next school trip abroad, including a comparison between two possible destinations. They may like to use sentence constructions such as 比……更……

 Ask students to research into environmental concerns resulting from travel and holidays and write a brief report.

Assessment suggestion

Find a few holiday advertisements in Chinese on the internet and ask students questions about dates, destinations, itinerary, etc.

Homework suggestion

Give students the following scenario:

You attended a planning meeting for a school trip. A Chinese friend was too ill to attend and has asked you to update him. Write him an email giving the possible dates and destination and letting him know what to do in preparation and what essential items he will need to take.

4.7 假期休闲活动 Holiday activities

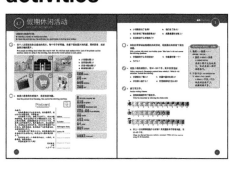

Icebreaker activity

In pairs, students take turns to ask each other the questions on the "Holiday questionnaire" worksheet (on the CD-ROM). This helps them discuss past holiday experiences using the sentence pattern (过) and a future holiday using the sentence pattern (想 / 会).

Lesson activities

1 Listening

Tell students to note down the characters or pinyin for each picture and the name in each question before listening to the recording so they know what to listen for.

Transcript

a. 女：在家里，你听到小明说：
小明：我想去公园玩。我想去公园玩。
女：小明想去哪儿？

b. 女：在学校，你听到志军说：
志军：我想去电影院看电影。我想去电影院看电影。
女：志军想去哪儿？

c. 女：在学校，你听到杰西卡说：
杰西卡：我想去参观博物馆。我想去参观博物馆。
女：杰西卡想去哪儿？

d. 女：在街上，你听到阿里说：
阿里：我想去参观动物园。我想去参观动物园。
女：阿里想去哪儿？

Answers

a. i **b.** iv **c.** ii **d.** iii

2 Reading

Ask students to read the questions first and say what the key words are in each one.

Answers

a. 约翰 **b.** 五天

c. 公园、动物园、博物馆和美术馆

d. 威廉最喜欢去百货商店买东西

e. 十点才关门。

In pairs, students can interview one another about a holiday they have been on, discussing food, accommodation, transport, people they met and what happened. They can review the past tenses "过" and "了".

Speaking

Walk around the class and listen to the students' conversations, providing support as necessary.

> **Sample answers**
>
> **a.** 假期的时候我的休闲活动是看小说、滑雪、冲浪和旅行。
>
> **b.** 我最喜欢去不同的国家旅行。
>
> **c.** 因为我可以认识不同的文化，吃到不同的美食。

 Ask students to compare their least favourite holiday activities if time allows.

Writing

Remind students they are responding to a friend, so the style should be informal and friendly. Encourage them to use vocabulary from other lessons as well.

> **Sample answer**
>
> 小明你好，
>
> 我很喜欢你的明信片。暑假的时候我去了北京，我很喜欢那儿。我在北京的四合院住了一个月，我学做了很多的中国菜。我交了很多北京朋友，他们都很友善。北京烤鸭特别好吃，我很喜欢北京，明年暑假我还要再去。
>
> 杰西卡
> 八月十八日

 Give students the a copy of the above sample answer with some words missing and ask them to fill in the gaps, or break up the sentences in the sample answer and ask students to put the sentences in the right order.

 Students use the information from the interview (after Activity 2) to write two postcards: the first complaining about food, accommodation, transport, people and unfortunate events and the other making positive comments.

 Writing

For part a, ask students to identify the meaning of the radical of each character.

For part b, remind students they are writing about the past, so should include the character 了 in their writing.

> **Sample answer**
>
> 暑假的时候我去了重庆的中国三峡博物馆，我看了里面的展览之后，了解了更多的中国的历史文化。

Homework suggestion

Students write a short story about a family holiday where everyone wanted to do something different and how the problem was resolved – if it was.

4.8 预订酒店 Making a hotel reservation

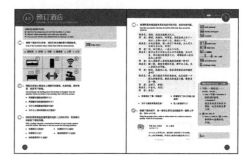

Icebreaker activity

Before the lesson, write out and cut up one or more hotel reservation conversations between a holidaymaker and a receptionist. Mix up the pieces and give one to each student. Students work out the correct order and read aloud the conversation.

Lesson activities

Reading

Point out that there are sometimes clues in the Chinese characters which can help students to remember or understand them. For example, the "water" radical can be found in 游泳, and 书桌 is a literal combination of "books" and "table".

> **Answers**
>
> **a.** vi **b.** i **c.** iv **d.** v **e.** iii **f.** ii

2 Listening

Prompt students to identify the key words in each question before they listen to the recording.

Transcript

阿里：心美，我们一家人要去中国上海旅行了！

心美：我去过上海，上海很好玩。你们住哪一间酒店？

阿里：还不知道，我喜欢酒店房间里有空调和冰箱，晚上睡觉睡得好，还可以喝冰汽水。

心美：我去上海住的酒店有健身房，那个健身房很大，我喜欢在那儿做运动。

阿里：对！我也喜欢住的酒店有健身房。

心美：你喜欢游泳吗？

阿里：喜欢，我住的酒店也要有游泳池。

心美：你会带手提电脑吗？

阿里：带的，我住的酒店房间里不但要能上网，而且里边一定要有书桌。我可以在书桌上写明信片给你。

心美：你快去订酒店吧！假期人会很多，好的酒店很难订。

阿里：嗯！

Answers

a. 阿里喜欢酒店房间里有空调和冰箱。

 Ask students to suggest a reason, for example: 因为有空调他晚上睡觉睡得好，有冰箱他还可以喝冰汽水。

b. 阿里喜欢住的酒店里有健身房。

 Ask students the following question: 你喜欢酒店里有健身房吗？为什么？

Sample answers:

我喜欢酒店里有健身房，因为我可以在度假的时候也做运动。

我不喜欢酒店里有健身房，因为度假的时候我不喜欢运动。

c. 他可以在书桌上写明信片。

d. 因为假期人很多，好的酒店很难订。

 Review with students the vocabulary for types of hotel room and hotel facilities.

3 Speaking

Ask students if the questions are about past or future activities? (Answer: future activities because of the word 要.)

Ask students what facilities they consider essential when staying at a hotel on holiday and why.

Sample answers

a. 我要预订三个房间。

b. 我要两间双人房，一间单人房。

c. 我要预订五天，十月三日到八日。

d. 酒店里要有游泳池和健身房，因为我喜欢运动。

e. 房间里要有空调和电视。

4 Reading

Ask students for the key words in the questions before they start to read the conversation.

Answers

a. 阿里预订了假期大饭店。

b. 四个晚上

c. 因为七月三日到七月七日不是假期，旅客不多。

d. 双人房有空调和书桌，可以上网还包括早饭。

5  Writing

Remind students they are writing a hotel review, so they need to be concise and descriptive.

Sample writing

上个月六号到十号，我去了布莱顿。我在快乐大饭店住了四个晚上，房间很漂亮还可以免费上网。你如果要来布莱顿，一定要住在快乐大酒店。

Further differentiation

Find some more hotel reviews and go through them with students.

 Ask students to replace the dates, the name of the hotel and the number of nights in those reviews. You could help them to write a positive or negative point about the hotel.

Encourage students to write 3 positive or negative points about the hotel in their chosen review.

Homework suggestion

Students write an advertisement for a new hotel.

Assessment suggestion

Using their homework as a basis, students present their hotels as sales reps in the next lesson. The class vote on which hotel they would most like to stay in.

4.9 假期时遇到的问题
Problems on holiday

Icebreaker activity

In small groups, students write down, in Chinese, problems they might encounter on holiday. Groups then take it in turns to read out their answers. The group with the most problems wins.

Lesson activities

1 Reading

Answers

a. iv **b.** iii **c.** i **d.** ii **e.** vi **f.** v

2 Reading

This is a long passage; go through the paragraphs one by one with the class to ensure understanding.

Answers

a. 因为那一天是假期。

b. 注意安全

c. 因为马克觉得是小偷偷走钱包的。

d. 职员说他在提款机旁边找到小华的钱包。

e. 因为他找回了他的钱包。

3 Listening

This recording is quite long; pause and repeat each section (according to the questions) if necessary to ensure students understand what they have heard.

Transcript

马克：我朋友的钱包丢失了。你能帮我报警吗？

职员：钱包是在什么时候丢失的？

马克：大概在今天下午三点吧。

职员：你知道钱包里大概有多少钱吗？

马克：我听他说，钱包里大概有一千块。

职员：钱包是不是红色的？

马克：好像是红色的。咦？为什么你会知道钱包是红色的？

职员：我们在提款机旁边找到了一个红色的钱包，可能是你朋友的。你朋友是不是姓陈？钱包里的证件好像有他名字。

马克：是的。我的朋友叫做小华。他正在急诊室里边看医生。

职员：好的。请你把地址给我，我一会儿就把钱包送到急诊室去。

马克：没问题！太好了，谢谢你！

职员：不用客气！

Answers

a. 大概在今天下午三点。 **b.** 大概有一千块。

c. 钱包是红色的。 **d.** 陈小华的。

Ask students: according to Mark, where is Xiaohua right now?

4  Speaking

Students should make use of the conversation from Activity 3 when performing their role-play. They should be able to talk about time, places, numbers and colours.

Sample answers

a. 我今天早上十一点丢了钱包。

b. 我大概在商场丢的。

c. 我的钱包里大概有两千块。

d. 我的钱包是黑色的。

5  Writing

Suggest that students use their role-play conversation from Activity 4 to write the diary entry. Remind them to adopt a personal tone and express their feelings.

Sample answer

今天中午我丢了钱包，大概是在商场丢的。我记得早上我跟妹妹一起去商场买新衣服。后来我们去一家中国餐厅要吃午饭，我就找不到钱包了。我们就马上回去商场，售货员一看到我就把我的钱包拿出来，她说我把钱包放在他们的柜台上了。找到钱包我非常开心！

Language and culture

Teach students some common expressions they may hear in Chinese when people experience a problem (or when trying to calm someone down), e.g. 真糟糕! 气死我了! 别着急!

Further differentiation

 Help students to review time expressions, locations, numbers and colours. Tell them to give different answers to the questions in Activity 4 to gain more practice.

 Give students a more complex scenario, for example: You have lost your handbag/backpack today. You are not sure about the exact time but you can give a period of time. You are not sure about the locations either and you need to backtrack through places you have been to. Describe the bag, which is multi-coloured, and list the items in it.

Assessment suggestion

Students role-play making a complaint about their hotel room/holiday with you taking the role of hotel manager/travel agent.

Homework suggestion

Ask students to write a lost property notice for something they have lost, including a description of the item, stating when and where it was lost and giving contact details.

4.10 复习 Progress check

Lesson activities

1  Writing

There is no shortcut to learning vocabulary but students might find it helpful to associate characters with pictures.

 You could write the Chinese on flashcards for students to begin by matching the pictures. They can then write the Chinese characters.

Answers

a. 红包   b. 旅馆   c. 圣诞树   d. 护照

e. 沙滩   f. 电影   g. 空调   h. 请勿拍照

i. 买东西   j. 庆祝   k. 旅行社

2 Reading

Tell students to look at the answer options at the bottom of the page first, then begin by filling in the blanks with the words they are sure of. They should then read the paragraph, trying different words and choose the one that makes most sense in each case.

 You could analyse the function of each word to help students fill in the gaps.

Answers

a. 快　b. 们　c. 没有　d. 月　e. 日　f. 把　g. 从
h. 参观　i. 虽然　j. 所以

3  Listening

Remind students to note down the Chinese or pinyin for each picture before listening to the recording.

Transcript

a. 女：在车站，你听到：
男：我们要去哪儿？
女：我们要去飞机场。

b. 女：在酒店，你听到：
男：这间酒店里有什么？
女：这间酒店里有一个电影院。

Answers

a. ii　b. i

4 Listening

Pause the recording according to the questions to give students time to think and write down the answers.

Transcript

记者：你好，你是马克，对吗？

马克：是的，你好。

记者：我是记者，想采访参加夏令营的外国学生。听说你的中文说得很好，所以我们来采访你。请问你是哪国人？

马克：我是美国人。

记者：你中文真好！请问你是怎么学中文的？

马克：我们学校有中文课，我每个星期上两节中文课。我也有几位中国朋友，我常常和他们练习说中文。

记者：为什么你会来台湾参加夏令营？

马克：因为我一直都想到台湾来看看，所以参加这次夏令营是一个很好的机会。

记者：你喜欢夏令营的生活吗？

马克：很喜欢。在夏令营里，我们就像家人一样，什么事都一起做。

记者：你们还去了台湾哪儿玩？

马克：我们一起去爬了阿里山，也去了日月潭游览。

记者：你在台湾有多久了？

马克：我来了大概一个星期吧。

记者：你最喜欢台湾的哪个地方？

马克：我最喜欢故宫博物馆，我觉得它很有趣。我在那儿参观了一整天。

记者：到了台湾以后，你有认识新朋友吗？

马克：我认识了很多台湾朋友。我回家后，打算建议我的学校邀请台湾学生到我的国家来参加夏令营。

记者：这是个好主意。谢谢你接受采访。

马克：不客气，再见！

Answers

a. 因为他的中文说得好。

b. i) 他每周上两次中文课。
　 ii) 他常常跟中国朋友练习说中文。

c. 他觉得它很有趣。

d. 他打算建议他的学校邀请台湾学生到美国来参加夏令营。

5 Speaking

Walk around listening to the students' conversations and noting which students require additional support.

Write out questions and sample answers on flashcards. Tell students to match each question with an answer. If necessary, help students to compose their own answers.

Sample answers

a. 我要去意大利旅行。

b. 我准备去一个星期。

c. 我跟两位好朋友一起去。

d. 我会带背包、照相机、护照和信用卡。

e. 我会换两百欧元。

6  Writing

Remind students they are writing to their grandfather, so the tone should be friendly but not too informal.

Sample answer

亲爱的爷爷，

好久没有写信给您，您身体好吗？

上个月我跟同学和老师一起去了巴黎，我们坐了十二个小时的飞机才到。到了巴黎我们先上了一个礼拜的法文课，然后我们去参观了很多名胜古迹。我爬上了巴黎铁塔，最喜欢莫内的花园，因为那里的风景真是美极了！

我也买了一些马卡龙给您，下周末给您带去。祝您身体健康，心情愉快！

小明 敬上
八月十日

Further differentiation

Ask students to write a paragraph about a holiday.

 Give students a few holiday-related pictures and ask them some questions. Then help them to arrange their answers into a sensible paragraph about a holiday.

 Students write about a real or imagined study tour, what they did and any problems they had.

Assessment ideas

1. **DP** Students write a report comparing city and country holidays.

2. **Listening** – Play students clips from "Finding and booking a hotel" on the **MYP** BBC *Real Chinese* website as a listening comprehension. (Click on "Videos" and choose clips from "Beidaihe" and "Boating".) Suggested questions:

Clip 1 – A couple are hiring a boat (Boating 2.05–2.15)
Q: 租船要多少钱？   A: 一个小时二十块
Clip 2 – A couple are booking a room in a hotel (Beidaihe 2:05–2:20)
Q: 一间房间多少钱？   A: 一个晚上五百元。
Clip 3 – People are talking about their favourite sporting and leisure pursuits (Beidaihe 3:25–3:42)
Q: 女士们喜欢什么运动？
A: 排球、羽毛球、乒乓球和游泳。(Tell students to listen for 2 women's comments.)
Clip 4 – People are talking about their favourite sporting and leisure pursuits (Beidaihe 3:25–3:42)
Q: 先生们喜欢什么运动？
A: 篮球、乒乓球、游泳、足球、跳绳
Clip 5 – Some tourists are hiring bicycles (Beidaihe 4:30–4:45)
Q1: 租一辆自行车多少钱？   A1: 二十块
Q2: 他一共付了多少钱？
A2: 四百四十块。 (2小时租金＋400块押金)

2. **DP** Provide a selection of posters and a few Chinese articles on tourism and the **MYP** environment. Students refer to these and to the short podcast on China's environmental problems on the *Slow Chinese* website, before writing a brief report about how the air pollution in China has affected their decision to go on a holiday there.

UNIT OBJECTIVES

- Describe your home town and the surrounding area.
- Give information about the public facilities in your home town.
- Give information about the local customs and specialties of different places.

- Describe and discuss your shopping experiences.
- Describe a range of banking-related activities.
- Describe and discuss a range of activities and events organised by your local community.

5.1 预习 Unit introduction

Prior knowledge

Students should be able to give personal information about themselves, describe their home and school environments, their diet and health, their favourite leisure activities, and their holiday plans.

Icebreaker activity

Show students the music video *我们的上海* by Shanghai Tourism Administration and Shanghai Media Group. Ask the following questions (answers and timings shown in brackets):

Q1: 上海的地标是什么？（东方明珠塔 [0:57]）

Q2: 每个到上海的人都带着什么？（梦想 [1:00]）

Q3: 上海是个繁忙、充满机会的城市。大家觉得自己将来的生活如何？（越来越好 [1:24]）

Q4: 上海是港湾还是山城？（港湾 [1:42]）

Lesson activities

  Reading

Before the activity, write the Chinese vocabulary on the board and go through the pronunciation. Ask students if they can work out any of the meanings. 电影院, 美术馆, 动物园 and 剧场 should be easy because students should recognise 电影, 美术, 动物, 剧, having learned them in previous units.

Answers

a. v **b.** vi **c.** i **d.** vii **e.** iii **f.** ii **g.** iv

Students could try to work out the meanings of the Chinese vocabulary from the radicals and pen strokes of the characters. They should recognise some, such as 山, 海, 城市, 村, from previous units.

Answers

a. ii **b.** iii **c.** iv **d.** i **e.** v

For part a, the strokes animation from the MGDB online dictionary is useful for showing students the sequences of writing individual characters.

For part b, remind students to use vocabulary learned not just from this lesson but from previous units to help them construct their sentences.

Sample answer for part b

我妈妈住在城市，因为她觉得城市方便，也因为她喜欢热闹。

Remind students to read the questions first and note any key words that will act as prompts to locate the answers (a. 住在; b. 公寓; c. 一起住; d. 喜欢; e. 旁边).

Transcript

我是小明，来自香港，现在我跟爸爸妈妈一起住在伦敦。

我们住的是高层公寓的十八楼。我们喜欢住在那里，因为公寓楼很新，很干净，而且旁边就是公园。

Answers

a. ii **b.** iii **c.** i **d.** ii **e.** iii

Make use of the listening comprehension questions to ask students about where they live. For example:

- 你住在哪里?
- 你家是公寓还是房子?
- 你跟谁住在一起?
- 你家旁边有什么?

 5 ✏ **Writing**

Before tackling the activity, analyse the questions with students and highlight the key words. Then, in the passage, they should look for: a. a city name appearing in the text after 来自; b. an activity after the place name 杭州; c. either the city centre or the suburbs; d. the question is 为什么......? so students should look out for 因为 and 所以.

Answers

a. 苏格兰的爱丁堡 **b.** 参加中文夏令营

c. 在市中心 **d.** 因为他家的公寓很大，而且在高层十楼可以看到西湖

 6 💬 **Speaking**

Write out the following questions as prompts for students' conversations.

1. 你家在哪儿? **2.** 怎么去你家?

3. 你家有什么特别的地方?

Sample answer

我家在英国南部的一个小乡村，从伦敦坐火车只要四十分钟就到了。村子里有小超市、图书馆还有三家咖啡店。我家门前是漂亮的泰晤士河，我常常在河边散步。

 Provide a "ready-made" structure for students who need more support, for example:

我叫____，我现在住在_____，我们住的是_____。
我住的地方有_____。我喜欢___因为_____。

 Show students the first 2 minutes of the video 这样的杭州你不得不爱 by Zhejiang TV Official Channel. Explain that Hangzhou is in Zhejiang province, eastern China.

 After watching the video, ask the following questions (answers and timings of clips shown in brackets):

Q1: 影片一开始 [00:45–00:50]，很多人早早起床做什么呢? (拍照)

Q2: 为什么杭州让人们不得不爱? (自然生态和人文历史 [1:22])

Q3: 杭州哪一个湖最美? (西湖 [1:50])

 Students can pick three things they liked about Hangzhou from the video and write a short paragraph about it.

5.2 我的家乡 **My home town**

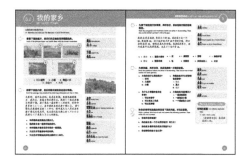

Lesson activities

 1 📖 **Reading**

This activity should not pose too much of a challenge since students should recognise the vocabulary (or characters) from previous units.

Answers

a. i **b.** iv **c.** v **d.** iii **e.** ii

 2 📖 **Reading**

 Students should read the statements first and note the key words before comparing them with what's in the passage. To make the most of this activity, ask students to give a reason for each false statement.

Answers

a. 错 (本杰明来自苏格兰的爱丁堡。)

b. 错 (爱丁堡是一座非常古老的城市。)

c. 对

d. 错 (文化艺术节是在夏天七八月的时候。)

e. 错 (文化艺术节期间的活动也在大街上在举行。)

 Students research and give a 2-minute presentation on any city. They can follow the structure of the reading passage. Record the presentations and show students later for analysis.

  **3** **Listening**

Before the activity, ask students to read the questions and note down the pinyin of the answer options. Having the pinyin beside the options makes it easier for students to know what they need to listen out for.

Transcript

我的名字是海英，来自韩国的釜山。我的家乡是一个旅游名城，离海很近。这个地方因为有美丽干净的沙滩，所以会有很多游客，特别是夏天的时候。我爱我的家乡，因为这里不仅风景很美，而且居民也十分热情好客。

Answers

a. ii **b.** ii **c.** i **d.** i **e.** i **f.** i

 4 **Listening**

Remind students to read the questions and note the key words. This will help them work out what to listen out for: a. a place; b. a time/season; c. 因为 or 所以 to find the reason; d. a place.

Transcript

a. 我叫大海，我和家人一起住在一座大城市里。这座城市有很多高高的楼、宽宽的马路和来来往往的汽车。

b. 我叫朱莉，来自澳洲的西北部。我的家乡是一座海边小镇，非常美丽，特别是夏天的时候有很多游客去那儿度假。

c. 我的名字是小婷。我的家乡在中国的东北。我最喜欢家乡的冬天，因为冬天的时候常常下雪，可以玩滑雪。

d. 我叫小宝。虽然现在我住在上海，但是我的家乡是一个在中国西南部的小山村，村子的四面都是大山，风景很美丽。

Answers

a. ii **b.** ii **c.** iii **d.** iii

5   **Writing and Speaking**

Remind students to include two-syllable verbs and stative verbs in their answers where possible.

Sample answers

a. 我现在住在英国雷丁 (Reading)。

b. 我的家乡是一个海边小镇，叫圣艾夫斯 (St Ives)。从我家我可以看到蓝蓝的大海。夏天时有很多来来往往的游客。

c. 我家乡最有名的名胜古迹就是故宫博物院。

d. 我觉得我的家乡很美，有高高的山，绿绿的田。

Language and culture

Discuss the concept of nostalgia for one's home town or birthplace. Introduce the phrase 落叶归根 (literally "fallen leaves returning to the roots"). It is used to describe people who wish to return to their home town when they are old. There are many poems and stories in Chinese literature that express this longing.

Show students the poem 回乡偶书 (Coming home) by 贺知章 (He Zhizhang) (c. AD 659–744).

Ask them what they think is meant by the lines 乡音无改鬓毛衰 /儿童相见不相识.

回乡偶书	**Coming Home**
少小离家老大回	When I was young, I left my home town. Now that I am older, I have come home.
乡音无改鬓毛衰	My accent unchanged, my hair has grown thin.
儿童相见不相识	Children saw me but did not recognise me.
笑问客从何处来	Smiling, they asked, "Hello, visitor, where do you come from?"

Extra vocabulary: 离 (lí) leave; 乡音 (xiāng yīn) home town accent; 鬓毛 (bìn máo) hair at the temples; 衰 (cuī) thin; 何处 (hé chù) where

Homework suggestion

Students write about their home town, describing 3 things they like and dislike about it, and saying if they would want to live there when they are older.

5.3 家乡的环境 Home town environment

Lesson activities

1  Reading

Remind students to study the radical and parts of each character to find clues to the meaning.

> **Answers**
>
> **a.** v **b.** iv **c.** ii **d.** iii **e.** i

This is also an opportunity to review the vocabulary for colours.

2 ✏️ Writing

Students will have been taught these terms in previous units so the activity should be a straightforward one.

 If students struggle, write the answers on the board and turn the activity into a matching one.

> **Answers**
>
> mountain: 山 sea: 海 river: 河 lake: 湖
>
> geography: 地理 scenery: 风景

3 📖 Reading

Before they fill in the blanks, you could help students to understand the meaning of each of the answer options by using it in a sentence.

> **Answers**
>
> **a.** 美丽的   **b.** 秋天   **c.** 高高兴兴地
>
> **d.** 一条   **e.** 一点儿   **f.** 因为

4 🔊 Listening

Give students a few moments to go through the questions and answer options. Explain that the answers are paraphrases (so they may not exactly match what students hear on the recording). It is therefore important to make sure students understand the meaning of each answer option first.

> **Transcript**
>
> **a.** 我叫露西。我的家乡在一座海岛上。海岛因为美丽的海景、好吃的海鲜和新鲜的空气吸引了很多游客。
>
> **b.** 我叫小文。我的家乡是一个国际大城市，这里有许许多多高高的大楼和来来往往的车辆。这里有很多商店和购物中心，是买东西的好去处。
>
> **c.** 我叫保罗。我的家乡是一座古老的小镇，镇上有许多有几百年历史的建筑。镇上没有很多汽车，所以比较安静。
>
> **d.** 我叫小月。我的家乡是一个很无聊的地方，没有名胜古迹，也没有高山大河，只有工厂，所以我以后不想住在这里。

> **Answers**
>
> **a.** iii **b.** i **c.** ii **d.** i

5 📖 Reading

Go through the questions with students and help them identify the key words in each one. They should look for: a. a city; b. directions (东西南北); c. three geographical features; d. two activities; e. sentences around the phrase 多元文化.

> **Answers**
>
> **a.** 艾玛的家乡是温哥华。
>
> **b.** 温哥华在加拿大的西海岸。
>
> **c.** 高山、森林和海洋。
>
> **d.** 滑雪和冲浪。
>
> **e.** 温哥华居住着来自世界各地的人，是一个多元文化的地方。

 6 💬 Speaking

Prompt students to use 我觉得……, 因为…… to express opinions and reasoning. Remind them again that Chinese verbs and stative verbs can be duplicated for emphasis. For example: 高高的大楼, 宽宽的马路, 许许多多的车辆, 来来往往的行人, 安安静静地喝咖啡. Ask students to make notes on what their partners say.

Sample answers

a. 我的家乡在台北。

b. 我觉得台北的环境很不错，不仅有高山还有河流。你可以去阳明山看花，还可以去淡水河看日落。

c. 台北是一个很热闹的地方，市中心除了有高高的大楼，宽宽的马路，还有许许多多的车辆和来来往往的行人。但是我喜欢去101大楼安安静静地喝咖啡。

d. 去台北最好的季节是秋天，因为秋天气温不冷不热刚刚好。

Assessment suggestion

DP Create a true-or-false reading and writing activity for students, using the listening transcript from Activity 4. Give them five statements based on the content, and ask them to say if each is true or false.

📈 Students can give reasons why the false statements are false.

Homework suggestion

Ask students to write about the home towns of their partners, based on the notes they made in Activity 6. They should write in the third person.

5.4 休闲设施 Leisure facilities in my home town

Icebreaker activity

Conduct a vote to find out the most popular leisure facility in their local town.

Lesson activities

1 ✏️ Writing

If students struggle to use the correct location suffix with an activity (e.g. 电影场 instead of 电影院), remind them of the meanings of the suffixes: 院 (an enclosed space often with an outdoor area), 场 (a court or field), 房 (room), 池 (pool), 馆 (large, indoor public space or building).

Sample answers

游泳池、健身房、网球场、溜冰场、电影院

2 🔊 Listening

Go through the questions with students and highlight the key words that will help them when looking for the answers. a. 哪天不开放? b. 除了……还可以……; c. 没有什么? d. 因为附近有……

Transcript

a. 我是马克。我住的城市中心有一座新的现代图书馆，除了星期日和星期一不开放，其余每天都从上午十点开放到傍晚八点。

b. 我是小月。我家附近有一个休闲娱乐中心，在那里既可以去健身房跑步、去游泳池游泳，还可以打羽毛球。

c. 我是本杰明。在我住的那个小镇上没有电影院，所以每次我想看电影的时候我得开车去另一个城市。

d. 我是日晴。我们居住的小城很方便，因为这里不仅有一个比较大的购物中心，还有好几家大超市。

Answers

a. i b. iii c. ii d. iii

3 📖 Reading

Remind students to read the statements first and note the key words, before finding similar words in the passage. This will help them identify any discrepancies quickly.

Students can give reasons for the false statements.

Answers

a. 对 **b.** 对

c. 错 (我家离图书馆很近，走路可以到。)

d. 错 (图书馆里有咖啡厅没有小吃店。)

e. 对

4 Writing

Before the activity, put the students in pairs and ask them to interview one another about the popularity of a number of meeting places. They can use the notes from their discussion to help them with the writing activity.

Sample answer

我住的镇上有一个溜冰场，周末的时候很多年轻人都喜欢去那儿跟朋友见面。有的人喜欢和朋友们一起享受溜冰的自由快乐，有的人喜欢在溜冰场里面的咖啡店跟朋友一起喝咖啡聊天。

5 Speaking

Walk around the room and listen to students' conversations. Provide support as necessary.

Sample answers

a. 我认为雷丁最好的游泳馆是中央游泳馆。因为那里的游泳池不仅大而且水很暖和。

b. 我一个月去一次游泳馆，都是跟好朋友一起去。

c. 除了游泳馆，青少年还喜欢去电影院看电影。

d. 这个周末我们可以先去喝咖啡，再一起去足球馆看比赛。

Assessment suggestion

MYP Students design their ideal youth centre, explaining which facilities it should have and why.

Homework suggestion

Ask students to imagine that a Chinese teenager is coming over on a cultural exchange programme. They should write an email to him/her describing some popular leisure activities, as well as what leisure facilities are available in their home town.

5.5 家乡特产与文化活动 Local specialities and cultural practices from my home town

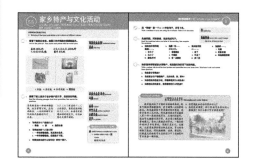

Icebreaker activity

In groups of 3–4, students write down in Chinese as many specialities, local customs and festivals as they can in 3 minutes. Accept ones from other regions as well. The group with the most items is the winner.

Lesson activities

1 Reading

This is a good opportunity to revise Chinese number characters. Do some simple sums on the board and ask students to solve them, using Chinese number characters only.

Answers

a. i **b.** ii **c.** iii **d.** iv

2 Reading

Before tackling the activity, read the passages as a class and go through any new vocabulary together.

Answers

a. iii **b.** i **c.** 皮影木偶、咖啡。

3 Writing

To help students with the task, before they start writing, ask the class for some examples of a tradition or a traditional food people are familiar with.

Sample answer

英国的传统早餐很丰富，有鸡蛋、香肠、土豆、烤豆子、西红柿。

4  Listening

Give students a few moments to go through the questions and answer options before listening to the recording. Remind them that what they hear in the recording may not always match what is written in the Student Book questions exactly, so they need to listen right to the end of each character's clip before choosing the answer.

Transcript

a. 您好。这是我昨天在您店里买的中国传统服装，打算送给朋友的，但是朋友告诉我他穿中号的衣服。这件是大号的，所以我能换一件中号的吗？

b. 服务员您好。我要来一份这里的特色菜麻婆豆腐。但是我不喜欢太辣的。我要有一点点辣的麻婆豆腐。

c. 您好。昨天我在您这儿买了一张民歌CD。可是回去发现这张CD是坏的。

d. 明天上午博物馆有传统舞表演。我们一起去看吧!

Answers

a. i b. iii c. iii d. iii

5  Speaking

You could provide pictures of local specialities or souvenirs to help students with their discussions. Walk around the classroom and listen to students' conversations, providing support as necessary.

Sample answers

a. 我的家乡在新加坡。

b. 新加坡有很多特产，比如榴莲、巧克力和白咖啡。

c. 如果你来我的家乡玩，我推荐你买手工艺品的纪念品。

d. 如果你来我的家乡玩，我推荐你吃娘惹菜 (niáng rě cài, Nyonya dishes)，又酸又辣，真好吃。

 In small groups, students could research a country, focusing on its climate, tourist attractions, foods or local traditions and create a presentation to show the rest of the class.

Cultural spotlight

 For more information on how the Dai people celebrate their new year (including some excellent footage of the water festival), show students a short video entitled *航拍中国 "西双版纳 – 泼水节"* produced by Youku / DJI Studio.

Assessment suggestion

Ask students to research and write about cultural events in their home town or local area. They should aim to answer the following questions:

- 家乡有哪些有意思的风俗习惯？

- 家乡每年重要的文化活动有哪些？

- 家乡最近举办过的重要的文化活动是什么？

- 将来会举办什么重要的活动？

Homework suggestions

1. Students can design a poster illustrating 10 countries and their specialties (be it a type of food, a product or a cultural tradition).

2. Students can research into a tradition of a specific country and write a report about it. They can follow the structure of the passage in the Cultural spotlight feature. The report should contain the following points:

   - 国家名称

   - 风俗习惯/文化活动名称

   - 什么时候举办

   - 特别意义

   - 当地居民的看法

5.6 购物 Shopping

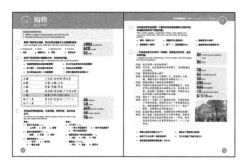

Lesson activities

  1 **Reading**

Remind students to look at the individual characters to help them work out the meanings of the Chinese terms, for example, they should recognise 书 (book) and work out that 书店 means "book shop"; they should remember 场 (court, field, or outside space), so 市场 is "market". Go through the pronunciation of each term with the class.

> **Answers**
>
> **a.** ii **b.** iii **c.** iv **d.** i

You could ask students to name some things they can buy in each of the above shopping places.

  2 **Reading**

> **Answers**
>
> **a.** 二楼　　　　　　**d.** 地下一层
>
> **b.** 三楼　　　　　　**e.** 地下一层
>
> **c.** 五楼或地下一层　**f.** 地下二层

After the reading activity, pairs of students could take turns being the customer (asking the questions) and the member of customer service staff (answering the questions).

  3 **Listening**

Give students a few moments to go through the questions and remind them to familiarise themselves with the different answer options before listening to the recordings. They may find it helpful to note down the pinyin for the answer options.

Transcript

Recording 1

我是杰西卡，现在在北京旅游。后天我就要回英国了，今天我在百货商场买纪念品。因为妈妈很注意健康，所以我给妈妈买了一些绿茶。爸爸对艺术很感兴趣，所以我给爸爸买了一幅中国传统的山水画。我还给每个人买了一双精美的中国筷子和一件T恤衫。

Recording 2

顾客: 服务员您好。请问这条裤子有没有小号的?

服务员: 您等一下，我帮您看看。我们店里还有小号的。

顾客: 太好了! 这个周末您们店里打折吗?

服务员: 是的，这个周末我们店里的每一件商品都半价。

顾客: 那这条黑裤子您帮我拿一条小号的。谢谢!

服务员: 一共两百二十元。您用现金还是银行卡?

顾客: 用卡吧。

服务员: 收据给您放在购物袋里了。谢谢!

> **Answers**
>
> | | | | |
> |---|---|---|---|
> | Recording 1 | **a.** iii | **b.** i | **c.** iii |
> | Recording 2 | **d.** i | **e.** iii | **f.** iii |

 4 **Speaking**

Put students in pairs. You could give each pair some pictures showing different items of clothing and their prices to support their conversation. Students can take turns at being the customer and the shop assistant, choosing a different picture each time.

 Encourage students to provide more detail in their questions and answers.

> **Sample answers**
>
> **a.** 我要买一条裙子来配这件上衣。
>
> **b.** 我喜欢绿色的。
>
> **c.** 噢! 我有时候穿小号，有时候穿中号。
>
> **d.** 两个号都试试吧。
>
> **e.** 除了上衣以外，我还需要买长裤。
>
> **f.** 我要用信用卡付款。

 5 **Reading**

Ask students to go through the questions and highlight the key words in each one before reading the dialogue

(a. 几次; b. 哪些地方购物; c. 买了什么 / 给谁买;
d. 为什么买巧克力; e. 最后推荐/为什么).

Answers

a. 四次了

b. 有名的百货公司，牛津街

c. 她给弟弟买了一个很时尚的蓝色书包，她给自己
买了一件深绿色的毛衣。

d. 她打算送巧克力给朋友们。

e. 伦敦各区的二手市场，因为在市场的小店里常常
能找到很独特的纪念品。

Homework suggestion

Ask students to write 80 to 100 characters about their
favourite local shopping place. They should answer
the following questions:

- 那个地方是个购物中心、购物街还是有意思的
  市场?

- 你在那里买过最特别的一件东西是什么?

- 你最希望去世界哪个城市买东西? 想买什么? 为
  什么?

Sample writing

我住在牛津北部，附近有一个购物中心叫做比斯特购
物村。我很喜欢去那里逛街，但是我买得不多，因为
那些名牌商品很贵。有一次我买到一顶可爱的毛帽
子。我最希望去法国的巴黎，买一些独特和比较便宜
的衣服。

5.7 在银行 At the bank

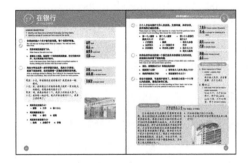

Lesson activities

1 🔊 ✏️ Listening and Writing

For part a, students can write their answers either using
pinyin or Chinese characters.

For part b, let students count the strokes themselves
first. If they are struggling, you can write out each
character on the board, counting each stroke aloud with
the rest of the class.

Transcripts

a. 银行，银行   **d.** 信用卡，信用卡

b. 现金，现金   **e.** 取款机，取款机

c. 钱，钱   **f.** 支票，支票

Answers

a. 银行   现金   钱   信用卡   取款机   支票

b. 钱 (10)   支票(15)   现金(16)   银行 (17)
    信用卡 (19)   取款机(26)

 Students can make a sentence with each term.

2 📖 Reading

Before they do the activity, you could put students
in pairs and ask them to read the dialogue aloud with
their partners. Provide additional support as necessary.
Then go through the questions as a class, highlighting
key words to help students understand what to look for.

Answers

a. iii   **b.** ii   **c.** iii

3 🔊 Listening

Remind students to read the questions and answer
options before listening to the recording. They may find
it helpful to jot down the pinyin of the answer options
to help them identify the correct answers.

Transcript

a. 我需要换美元，请给我兑换五百美元，换成人民
币。这个是我的护照。谢谢。

b. 我在北京大学做交换生。 我需要办一张银行卡。

c. 您好。我需要给我在美国上学的女儿汇款，请问
汇2000美元需要多少人民币?

Answers

a. ii   **b.** ii   **c.** ii

Language and culture

Students are already aware that measure words are applied when talking about a certain amount of a certain object. Point out that each currency has its own measure word. Refer them to examples in the Grammar focus.

 **4** **Speaking**

Check that students are pronouncing 您 correctly (nín).

 You could print out the transcript from Activity 3 for students to read as a guide.

Sample answers

a. 我要换钱。   **b.** 我要用英镑换人民币。

c. 我有两百英镑。   **d.** 我带了护照。

e. 我还想开个银行账户。

5 **Writing**

Remind students they are writing a text message, so they should be concise but retain a sense of urgency.

Sample writing

妈，请帮个忙！昨天我坐火车时钱包不见了。我还有两个星期的旅游，钱不够了，可以汇款到我的银行账户吗？谢啦！

Cultural spotlight

The passage about HSBC contains a number of terms and phrases students may find unfamiliar and challenging. Go through these as a class: 汇集财富 (an influx of wealth), 创始 (founding), 频繁 (frequent), 业务网络 (business network).

Banking role-play

1. Photocopy the four "At the bank" worksheets (on the CD-ROM) so there is enough to be shared by the class. Cut out all components beforehand.

2. Put students into pairs: one playing the customer, the other the bank clerk. The customer needs the following resources:

   • customer role-play form

   • one form of ID (passport or driving licence)

   • a bill, some currencies, or a cheque

The clerk gets the clerk role-play form and some banknotes. Also give each pair the vocabulary worksheet.

3. The customer needs to carry out a transaction using the resources they have (e.g. if they have a cheque, then their task is to cash it; if they have a bill, they need to pay it in; if they have cash, exchange them for a different currency). They can also choose to open a bank account.

4. The clerk needs to respond to the customer's request accordingly (e.g. give the right change, ask for ID where necessary).

5. Both customer and clerk note down their transactions on the role-play slip.

6. Once they have completed their role-play, students can swap resources with each other and perform different tasks, or swap roles with each other.

MYP Assessment suggestion

Students give an oral presentation comparing what they can do in a bank physically and what they do with online banking.

Students should give their opinion about which method of banking they prefer.

Homework suggestions

1. **MYP** Ask students to produce a poster for a bank to attract new students to open an account with them.

2. Students write 50–70 characters about a visit to the bank when something went wrong. They can make up their own story if necessary.

5.8 居住的小区 My community

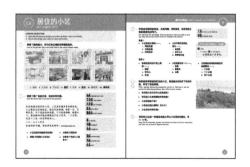

Icebreaker activity

Ask students what facilities they consider important in a town. Write them on the board and ask students to vote for those they consider the most important.

Lesson activities

1  Reading

Remind students to study individual characters (including the location suffixes) in a word, as they can offer clues to the meaning. For example, 停车场 means "car park", given that 停 means "stop", 车 means "car", 场 means "court" or "field". 站 means "stand", "station", or "terminal", so a term ending in 站 refers to a stop or station of some sort. 局 is a location suffix used to describe buildings that offer public services.

Answers

a. v **b.** iv **c.** vi **d.** vii **e.** ii **f.** viii **g.** i **h.** iii

2 Reading

This activity contains "which", "how far", "how many", and "how much" questions. Ask students to identify which is which.

Answers

a. 健身房和游泳池 **c.** 三百米

b. 两间卧室 **d.** 六千人民币

3 Listening

Before the activity, ask students to read the questions first, then note down the pinyin of the answer options. This makes it easier for students to know what they need to listen out for.

Transcript

Recording 1

我是小云。我来自香港。我和家人住在三室一厅的公寓里。我们的小区在城市的郊区，小区里除了有游泳池，还有儿童游乐园。我不喜欢住这里，因为离我的学校太远了。

Recording 2

我是珍妮。现在我和父母住在上海的市中心。我们很幸运租到了一栋独立的老房子。我们喜欢住在这里，因为小区的环境很好，外滩公园就在我家的附近，夏天晚上吃完饭，我们和父母会去江边散步。而且这里离我的学校一点儿都不远，坐地铁十分钟就到。

Answers

Recording 1　　a. ii　　b. iii
Recording 2　　c. ii　　d. iii　　e. i

4 Speaking and Writing

Remind students to make notes during the speaking part of the activity, so they have something to refer to when they are writing out their answers.

Sample answers

a. 我们的小区在市中心。

b. 我们小区里的体育设施不多，只有一个运动场。

c. 小区的树不多，但是汽车很多。

d. 小区的交通不是很方便，公车一小时才一班，我爸爸妈妈常常要开车带我出去。

e. 小区有很多停车场，而且很便宜。

5 Writing

You could ask students the following questions to guide and expand their writing:

- 你的小区在哪里？
- 小区的优点是什么？
- 小区的缺点是什么？
- 你有什么建议可以改进这些缺点？

Sample writing

我住在郊外的一个小区。小区又美丽又安静，但是交通不方便，而且年轻人的活动太少。我建议公车能够多开班次，小区活动中心多举办一些年轻人喜欢的活动。

Assessment suggestion

DP Ask students to complete the worksheet "Reading comprehension" (on the CD-ROM). True-and-false activities are typical IB questions, so this will be a good practice for students.

They should give reasons for the false statements.

Homework suggestion

Students should write an email of 80–100 characters to their local councillor (议员), suggesting one thing the council (区议会) should do to improve the local community.

Remind students they are writing a formal email, so they need to make it sound respectful and sincere.

5.9 社区活动 Community life

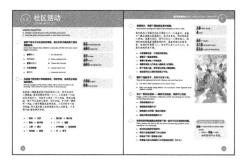

Lesson activities

1  Reading

Remind students to study individual characters in each term, as they can offer clues to the meaning.

Answers

a. iii **b.** ii **c.** iv **d.** v **e.** i

2 Listening

Students may find it helpful to note down the pinyin of each answer option before doing the activity.

Transcript

我和家人都很喜欢我们现在住的小区，因为这里的人都很友好，看到你都会和你打招呼。小区里有一个很大的社区活动中心。活动中心里有一个小的图书馆，那里比较安静，除了可以在那儿看书，还可以上网。中心的一楼还有一间乒乓球室，小孩子都喜欢去那里玩。小区活动中心因为有空调，所以夏天晚上去那里聊天的人比较多。小区每个月都会举行活动。

Answers

a. ii **b.** i **c.** ii **d.** ii **e.** i **f.** i **g.** ii **h.** i

3 Reading

Remind students to read the statements first, so they know what to look for, before reading the passage.

Answers

a. 对	**d.** 错
b. 对	**e.** 错
c. 错	**f.** 对

  Students can also give reasons for the false statements.

4  Writing

Remind students of the basic word order when writing in Chinese: time → place → action (e.g. subject → verb → object).

If students struggle with word order, provide extra practice by giving them some jumbled-up sentences in Chinese and asking them to put them back in order.

Answers

a. 去年我没有参加任何慈善活动。

b. 每年春节的时候，我们小区中心都会组织很多不同的活动。

5 Writing

MYP Remind students that the purpose of a poster is to provide important information in a clear and concise way.

Sample writing

植树日

一人一棵树，树下好乘凉，
一人一棵树，大家好朋友。

时间：三月十二日，早上十时整
集合地点：小区中心门口
注意事项：请穿轻便的衣服鞋子

Students can provide some extra marketing copy by writing a fuller description of the event using the details in the poster. They can provide additional information such as what activities will take place on the day.

6 Speaking

Conduct a class discussion about students' experiences of and views on participating in local community activities, before putting students into pairs for the activity.

 Ask students to expand on their answers, using grammar structures like 除了...... 还可以/有......, 因为 ...... 所以 ....

Sample answers

a. 我们社区经常有活动。

b. 我们小区最近组织了捡垃圾活动。

c. 我参加了，觉得很有意思。

d. 我希望以后有更多机会让年轻人参加有意思的社区活动，例如拜访老人家。因为这些活动可以让我们觉得自己是社区的一分子，对社区有更多的了解。

Further differentiation

Ask students to read the passage in Activity 3 again.

 Students should identify all the action verbs and adjectival stative verbs.

 Students should rewrite the passage by replacing the existing community activities with their own, as well as using their own adjectival stative verbs where relevant.

Homework suggestion

Tell students to imagine that they attended the tree-planting day (from Activity 5). They now need to write an email of 80–100 characters to a friend, describing what happened on the day (what they did, whether or not they enjoyed it, and why).

5.10 复习 Progress check

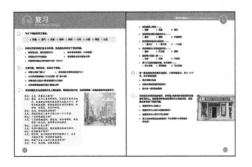

Lesson activities

1  Reading

For additional practice ask students to make a sentence with each term.

Answers

a. environment b. air c. scenery d. forest

e. woods f. big river g. small lake h. seaside

i. hillside

2 Speaking

Walk around the classroom and listening to students' conversations. Provide additional support as necessary.

If some students struggle to remember key vocabulary, direct them to the relevant flashcard sets on Quizlet for further practice.

Sample answers

a. 我住在伦敦市区。

b. 我的家乡没有森林或湖，但是离泰晤士河不远。

c. 我的家乡不在海边。

d. 我觉得家乡的风景不错。我家在35层高楼，可以看到漂亮的伦敦城市风景。

e. 我觉得家乡的环境很不错，交通方便，小区还有运动中心和一大片草地。

3 Listening

Remind students to read the questions first, noting key words to help them listen for the answers. They don't have to answer in full sentences – their answers just need to contain the underlined information in the answers given below.

Transcript

a. 我是米娜。这个星期我们家来了一个美国朋友。今天我带朋友参观了家乡的美术馆，看了很多有意思的画。朋友觉得这个美术馆太漂亮了！

b. 我是杰克。我的家乡在海边，家乡最有名的就是这里美丽的沙滩和新鲜的海鲜。每年的夏天都会有很多人来我的家乡度假。

c. 我是小文。现在在在百货商场买礼物，我给妈妈买了杭州有名的绿茶，给爸爸买了一张民歌CD，一共花了两百元。

d. 我是日晴。我住的小区这个星期六组织慈善日，有的人会去老人院帮助老人们，有的人会去大街上捡垃圾，让我们住的城市更干净。

e. 我是本杰明。我住的小镇上没有电影院，也没有娱乐中心，我觉得很无聊，很没有意思。

Answers

a. 米娜今天去了美术馆。

b. 杰克的家乡最有名的是(美丽的)<u>沙滩</u>和(新鲜的)<u>海鲜</u>。

c. 小文给妈妈买了<u>绿茶</u>，给爸爸买了一张<u>民歌CD</u>，一共花了<u>两百元</u>。

d. 他们要组织<u>慈善日</u>。

e. 本杰明觉得他住的小镇很<u>无聊</u>也很<u>没有意思</u>。

---

4 📖 Reading

In addition to the activity, you can also use this as an opportunity to test students' understanding of action verbs and adjectival stative verbs by asking them to highlight them, and replace any adjectival stative verb with their own where relevant.

Answers

a. iii **b.** ii **c.** ii **d.** i **e.** i **f.** ii

---

5 ✏️ Writing

This activity (especially parts b and c) requires students to recall vocabulary learned in previous units (for example, on food and drink). Because of the word limit (60–80 characters), students should just write about one thing in each category.

 If it is difficult to write about these aspects of their own home town, help students choose a well-known city or village that they can easily write about.

Sample writing

珍妮：

让我介绍一下我的家乡: 坎特比亚 (Canterbury)。那是一个古老的小城，人口不多。城里最有名的建筑物是坎特比亚大教堂。 这儿有很多海鲜餐厅，每年九月底的时候还有美食节，你可以吃到各式各样的美食。

小梅

---

6 🔵 Speaking

To make it easier to assess students' progress, you could provide a simplified map of a city centre (showing just a few facilities, including the tourist information centre).

Sample answers

a. 旅游咨询中心在火车站旁边。

b. 旅游咨询中心有厕所、免费地图，可以上网，服务人员可以帮你订旅馆和车票。

c. 旅游咨询中心也可以换钱。

d. 那儿有一家买纪念品的小商店，可以买到导游书和一些当地的手工艺品。

Further differentiation

Show students the following passage:

小时候，我们家住在农村，那里有山有水，空气新鲜，风景很美也很安静，可是有时候太安静了，生活很无聊。后来爸爸在上海找到了新工作，我们也搬到了大城市。我喜欢城市，因为城市很热闹，可以做很多有意思的事。但是住在城里也有缺点，空气污染，噪音也大。

 Students find three things the writer says about the countryside, and three things about the city.

 Students rewrite the paragraph, adding two additional things about both life in the countryside and city living.

Assessment suggestion

 Each student should give a 3-minute presentation about their home town or a well-known city, talking about the amenities or interesting local customs. Afterwards, the other students – and you – can ask questions. You can record the presentations and show them to students afterwards for analysis. You can also compare these presentations with the ones students gave back in Lesson 5.2, Activity 2 (extension), to check the progress they have made.

自然和人造环境
NATURAL AND MANMADE ENVIRONMENT

UNIT OBJECTIVES

- Describe and discuss the weather and climate in different places.
- Discuss what to wear in different weather conditions.
- Share information about your location and give directions.

- Share your views on a range of environmental and conservation issues.
- Discuss your experiences of being around animals.

6.1 预习 Unit introduction

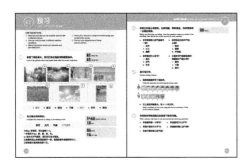

Prior knowledge

This unit recalls and builds on students' ability to use vocabulary relating to their local community and its amenities, so do make sure students are familiar with the essential vocabulary they have learned in Unit 5.

Icebreaker activity

Show students the CGTN video *China's most beautiful summer scenery in three minutes*. Pause it at these times and ask students what they can see: 00:24 (云), 00:32 (树和山), 00:36 (花), 00:46 (河), 1:10 (羊), 2:00 (森林). Alternatively, pause at various points and ask students to describe the weather or what colours they see.

Lesson activities

1 **Reading**

Before the activity, point out to students that pictures a, b, f are to do with weather conditions while pictures c, d, e, g are to do with seasons. This will make it easier to match the right words to the pictures.

Answers

a. iv   **b.** v   **c.** vi   **d.** ii   **e.** vii   **f.** i   **g.** iii

2 **Reading**

Remind students to read each line of text once for context before trying to work out the missing words.

Answers

a. 天气   **b.** 季节   **c.** 天气预报   **d.** 气候

Help students to distinguish between 天气 and 气候: 天气 contains the character 天 (day), so 天气 is all about *daily* conditions (weather). 气候 contains the character 候, which is found in the phrase "……的时候" (which refers to a period of time), therefore 气候 is about the condition over a *period of time* (climate).

3 **Listening**

Give students time to read the questions and answer options before listening to the recording. Remind them to jot down the pinyin of the answer options if it helps them to listen for them in the recording.

Transcript

小明：志军，你到了北京也有一个星期了，还好吗?

志军：还不错。北京的气候很不一样，冬天特别冷，特别干燥，这几天我都不想出去。听天气预报说明天天气很好，有太阳，明天我会去公园玩。

小明：你不喜欢北京的冬天吗? 听说会下雪，很好看。

志军：一点儿也不喜欢! 我还是喜欢春天，天气比较暖和、舒服。对了，小明，英国那边的天气怎么样?

小明：不太好。这几天都是阴天，听天气预报说明天会下雨。

Answers

a. i   **b.** i   **c.** i   **d.** ii

4 **Writing**

For part a, the strokes animation from the MGDB online dictionary is useful for showing students the sequences of writing individual characters.

For part b, encourage students to use conjunctions to make longer sentences.

Sample writing for part b

我很喜欢春天这个季节，因为那时候我可以看到很多漂亮的花。

哥哥最喜欢的季节是夏天，因为那时候他可以常常去海边游泳。

妈妈最喜欢的季节是秋天，因为她觉得秋天的气候特别舒服。

弟弟最喜欢的季节是冬天，因为那时候他可以去滑雪。

---

 5 **Speaking**

Encourage students to give reasons for their answers.

Sample answers

a. 我最喜欢冬天，因为冬天的时候我可以出去滑雪。

b. 我最喜欢晴天，因为阳光让我心情愉快。

c. 我最不喜欢雨天，因为潮湿的天气让我心情不好。

d. 我最喜欢美国亚利桑那州 (Arizona) 的气候，因为那儿有全世界最多的阳光。

e. 我最不喜欢英国冬天的气候，又湿又冷，最没有意思。

Further differentiation

 Students list activities and food or drink items associated with particular seasons.

 Students write full sentences describing what they like to do and eat in different seasons.

6.2 天气与气候 Weather and climate

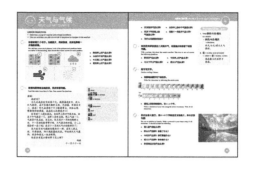

Lesson activities

  1 **Listening**

Before the activity, discuss with students what each picture represents: a. 冷, b. 热, c. 下雨, d. 凉快, e. 有太阳.

Transcript

a. 昨天早上天气怎么样？

昨天早上天气很冷。

b. 今天中午天气怎么样？

今天中午天气很热。

c. 今天晚上天气怎么样？

今天晚上天气很凉快。

d. 明天早上天气怎么样？

明天早上会有太阳。

Answers

a. i **b.** ii **c.** iv **d.** v

This activity revisits expressions of time: ask students what 昨天, 今天, 明天, 早上, 中午, 晚上 mean.

 2 **Reading**

Give students time to go through the questions and note the key words before they read the passage.

 Encourage students to give supporting statements in their answers, preferably in their own words.

Answers

a. 东京天气很好，几乎每天都有太阳。

b. 东京早上和中午很凉快。

c. 东京下午气温会升高，没有风的时候会比较热。晚上气温下降的时候会有点冷。

d. 伦敦十一月的天气很潮湿，常常下雨，最冷的时候还会结冰。

e. 玛莉喜欢东京，因为那儿的气候温和，跟伦敦不一样，而且人很好，风景很美。

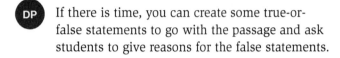 **DP** If there is time, you can create some true-or-false statements to go with the passage and ask students to give reasons for the false statements.

3 ⬤ Speaking

Remind students to use appropriate language when talking about the past and future – for example, use 了 after a verb when talking about a past action, and 会 when talking about something about to happen.

Sample answers

a. 昨天的天气很潮湿，下了一天雨。

b. 今天早上是晴天，阳光很暖和。

c. 今天下午气温下降到一度，好冷。

d. 天气预报说明天可能会下雪。

4 ✏️ Writing

For part a, ask students for the meaning of the radical for each character (日 = sun and 禾 = grain).

For part b, remind students to use vocabulary from previous units, not just this lesson, to make sentences.

 You could write on the board other vocabulary associated with 暖和 (for example, seasons or things people to do keep warm) to help students develop ideas on what to write.

Sample writing for part b

春天的时候天气变得很暖和。

每次出门，我得穿很多衣服才暖和。

5 ✏️ Writing

Remind students they are writing a postcard to a friend, so the tone should be friendly and informal, but they need to be brief as postcards don't have much space!

Sample writing

家明你好，

我跟着学校在温哥华旅行，虽然现在是冬天，但不太冷。昨天下雨，我们去了博物馆参观。今天天气晴朗，我们去逛唐人街 。明天也是晴天，我们要上山滑雪，我很兴奋！这次旅行真是太棒了！国华

Further differentiation

Ask students to write about how different kinds of climate make them feel by using weather-related terms and stative verbs describing feelings.

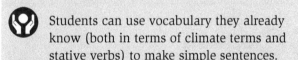 Students can use vocabulary they already know (both in terms of climate terms and stative verbs) to make simple sentences.

Give students a selection of new stative verbs for different kinds of moods and feelings, for example: 愉快 (yú kuài; happy), 开朗 (kāi lǎng; cheerful), 舒畅 (shū chàng; comfortable), 忧郁 (yōu yù; melancholy), 烦恼 (fán nǎo; worried), 苦闷 (kǔ mèn; depressed).

They can also use the language pattern: 使我 / 让我 to make sentences.

Sample sentences:

春天的气候不冷不热，让我心情愉快。

夏天的阳光暖和，使我心情开朗。

Homework suggestion

Students write a short paragraph describing their favourite city's climate in the winter and in the summer.

6.3 天气预报 Weather forecasts

Lesson activities

1  Reading

Before the activity, go through the new vocabulary: 刮风, 下雾, 下雪, 打雷, 多云. Help students to associate some of the vocabulary with pictures. For example, 云 looks a bit like a cloud overhead, while the dots in 雨 resemble water droplets. Point out that 雨 is also a radical; many terms relating to precipitation have this radical.

Answers

a. v **b.** vi **c.** i **d.** iii **e.** iv **f.** ii **g.** vii

Ask students to make sentences about the weather conditions they like best and least.

Language and culture

Point out to that some weather conditions, for example, 下雪, 下雨, 打雷, 刮风 are verb–object constructions. 雪 and 雨 tend to be paired with the verb 下 because that's how snow and rain behave (i.e. they fall or drop). 雾 can be paired with 下, though some people prefer to say 起雾, because fog rises from the ground. For weather phenomena like thunder or wind, the verb in the verb–object combination does not carry a literal meaning. Instead, it is added to conjure up an image of that experience.

2  Listening

You could revise days of the week and other time expressions with the class before this activity.

Transcript

以下是北京未来五天的天气预报：

星期一大雨，会打雷，外出时需要带雨伞和雨衣；

星期二下雾，请小心开车；

星期三是晴天，最高气温二十五度；

星期四阴天多云；

星期五下午以后会刮风，请注意安全。

Answers

a. iii **b.** v **c.** i **d.** iv **e.** ii

Word weather report

In pairs, students complete the "World weather report" activity (on the CD-ROM). Each is given a table with some missing information; the aim is to complete the table by asking their partner about the weather in a city (e.g. 伦敦星期一天气怎么样?) or what the temperature is (伦敦星期一多少度?). The other person will have to find the answer on their own table and respond. At the end, both students should have identical information.

Language and culture

When asking about the 气温 (temperature) in Chinese, the measure word 度 (degree) is used. 多少度 or 几度 (how many degrees) comes at the end of the question: 明天多少度? or 明天几度?. 摄氏二十六度大概等于华氏八十度 means "26 degrees Celsius roughly equates to 80 degrees Fahrenheit".

3  Reading

DP True-or-false questions often require students to give reasons why the statements are false.

Answers

a. 错 (是下雪，不是下雨)

b. 对 (根据天气预报)

c. 对 (根据天气预报，下星期四和星期五会刮大风。)

d. 错 (气温会下降五度，不是十五度。)

4 Speaking

You could ask students to say what they were/are doing on the day in question. This helps to test understanding of the weather forecast terms.

 Add a couple of weather forecast terms for students to use:

晴见多云   晴见多云偶阵雨
(sunny intervals)   (heavy showers)

Sample answers

a. 昨天是星期四，下雨，我一整天都在家里。

b. 今天是星期五，气温是零下3度，早上下了一场大雪。我在花园里堆雪人。

c. 明天是星期六，天气预报说会是晴天，我希望天气暖和一点，这样我就可以出去玩。

d. 天气预报说下个星期天气会很好，因为春天快来了。

5 Writing

Keep an eye out for students who struggle to write their sentences using the correct word order.

 If students need further practice with word order, create some jumbled-up sentences and ask students to rearrange the words.

Answers

a. 昨天我看不到太阳。/ 昨天一整天都没有太阳。

b. 明天天气多云又刮风。

c. 星期三气温会下降五度。

Homework suggestion

Students imagine they have just watched a weather forecast on TV. They should write a note of 50–80 characters to a family member, telling them what the weather will be. Give them these stimulus questions:

• 你是怎么知道最近的天气？

• 今天的天气会怎么样？

• 下星期一到星期三的天气会怎样？

• 要注意什么？

6.4 季节和衣服 Seasons and seasonal dress

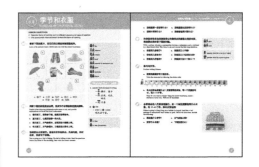

Lesson activities

1 Reading

Ask students to work out the meanings of the Chinese vocabulary by looking at the radicals or the pen strokes of the characters. Most should be able to work out that 雨伞 is "umbrella" and 雨衣 is "raincoat" since both contain the character for rain (雨); 伞 even resembles an umbrella! They should also be able to work out 手套 means "gloves" since it contains the character for hand (手).

Answers

a. ii   b. viii   c. i   d. vii   e. iii   f. vi   g. iv   h. v

It is also a good opportunity to review measure words with these items of clothing. For example:

一件大衣	一条短裤	一顶帽子	一把雨伞
一件毛衣	一双手套	一条围巾	一件雨衣

2 Reading

Encourage students to give their reasons in full sentences.

Answers

a. 合理

b. 不合理 (夏天很热，不应该穿大衣。冬天冷的时候才需要大衣。)

c. 不合理 (天气变冷应该穿大衣戴围巾，而不是穿短裤。)

d. 合理

If time allows, put students in pairs, and ask them to think up similar statements for their partners to consider.

3   Listening

Remind students to go through the questions first and note the key words in each one, so they know what to listen out for in the recording (a. 星期一应该带; b. 星期三应该带; c. 不用带; d. 买不到). Encourage students to give reasons for their answers.

 Students should write their answers using full sentences.

Transcript

爸爸：汤姆，根据天气预报，北京星期一会下雨，你应该带雨伞；星期三北京开始下雪，气温会下降，你应该带围巾。手套你不用带了，你常常丢，到了北京再买吧。

汤姆：谢谢爸爸。对了，我那旧大衣不合穿，您能买一件新的给我吗?

爸爸：你怎么不早说? 现在太晚了，百货公司早就关门了，应该买不到了。你就拿我那件大衣去北京穿吧。

Answers

a. 雨伞。(星期一会下雨。)

b. 带围巾。(星期三会下雪，气温下降。)

c. 不用带手套。(汤姆常常丢手套，爸爸要他到北京再买。)

d. 汤姆爸爸买不到新大衣。(百货公司早就关门了。)

What to wear?

Ask students to list some other things they might pack for the weather conditions described in Activity 3, for example:

下雨：雨衣、雨鞋。

下雪：帽子、雪鞋、毛衣。

4   Speaking

Remind students to use the correct measure words and also encourage them to use adjectival stative verbs when describing what they want to buy.

Sample answers

a. 我要买三条中号的裤子，都要黑色的。

b. 我要买两双手套，一双黑色的，一双红色的。

c. 我要买一条五彩缤纷的长围巾。

d. 我要买两件厚厚的毛衣和一件长大衣。毛衣要红色的，大衣要黑色的。

e. 我要买一件黄色的雨衣。

f. 我要买一双打篮球穿的运动鞋和三双短袜子。

5   Writing

Part a provides a good opportunity to explain to students the differences between 穿 and 戴.

穿 (relate to clothing)	戴 (relate to accessories)
Examples	Examples
穿大衣／穿红色的上衣／穿裙子 穿泳衣／穿雨衣／穿鞋子	戴帽子／戴围巾／戴手套 戴眼镜／戴耳环 (ěr huán; earrings)

For part b, you may want to write a few adjectival stative verbs associated with winter clothing on the board as prompts, for example: 厚厚的, 暖暖的, 羊毛做的. Remind students that for some terms (like the first two) the characters are often reduplicated for emphasis.

6   Writing

Before the writing activity, you could give students some information about Hong Kong, either on the board or in the form of a factsheet.

八月的香港

天气	很热，很潮湿，常常下雨，有时有台风。
气温	最高35°C, 最低25°C
衣物	T恤，短裤，凉鞋，雨伞，墨镜，防晒油
去哪儿玩?	看香港天际线，海洋公园，迪士尼乐园，逛百货公司

Given the word count (25–40 characters), remind students to be concise; instead of listing every garment, they can consider using an appropriate adjectival stative verb to describe the clothes they need to bring.

Sample writing

八月是香港的夏天，天气又热又湿。最好穿薄薄的衣服，带墨镜，擦防晒油。别忘带雨衣或雨伞。

Homework suggestion

  Ask students to research a country and compile some facts about it, like the Hong Kong example in Activity 6. They should then write a short message about what clothing will be needed for a visit at a specified time of year.

Assessment suggestion

Find two magazine images showing people in different types of clothing (one in summer clothes or outdoor clothing, and the other one in winter wear). Ask students to write a paragraph describing what the people in the images are wearing.

6.5 方位 Locations

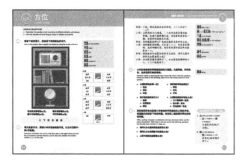

  Icebreaker activity

First, go through the six positional words from the Key terms box in the Student Book with the class. Once students are familiar with 上，下，左，右，前，后 and 对面, show them the music video *对面的女孩看过来* ("Hey girl, look this way"), by 任贤齐 (Richie Jen). (The song deals with unrequited young love in an amusing way.) Ask students to see how many positional words they can recognise in the song.

Lesson activities

  Reading

This is a straightforward activity. If students finish quickly, they can get into pairs and take turns to ask one another about the positions of the other items on the shelves.

> **Answers**
>
> **a.** 上　**b.** 下　**c.** 右　**d.** 左

 **Reading**

Ask students to look at the floor plan before they do the activity. They should note down that the facilities in questions are located on 一楼, 三楼 and 四楼. So when they look for the answers, they should look for sentences that mention these floors.

> **Answers**
>
> **a.** 礼堂　**b.** 小华的教室　**c.** 办公室

Language and culture

Point out that in Chinese 一楼 does not mean first floor – it means ground floor! 二楼 means first floor, 三楼 means second floor, etc. 地下 actually means basement (even though 地 normally means ground or floor!). This system may be confusing to Westerners, so it's important for students to grasp this early on.

Students may be interested to know that some buildings in East-Asian countries do not have 四楼, 十四楼 or 二十四楼, because 四 (sì) sounds similar to 死 (sǐ), the word for death!

  Listening

It may be helpful for students to jot down the pinyin of the answer options first, so they know what to listen for when the recording is playing.

> **Transcript**
>
> **a.** 爸爸：请问公园在学校的哪一个方向？
>
> 路人A：公园在学校的后边。
>
> **b.** 爸爸：请问博物馆在学校的哪一个方向？
>
> 路人B：博物馆在学校的前边。
>
> **c.** 爸爸：美术馆附近有什么？
>
> 路人C：美术馆附近有百货商店。
>
> **d.** 爸爸：请问从博物馆到美术馆怎么走？
>
> 路人D：顺着博物馆的方向，往前边一直走就看到了。

> **Answers**
>
> **a.** ii　**b.** i　**c.** ii　**d.** i

4 Speaking

This is a good opportunity to check students' understanding of the floor-numbering system. Listen to students' conversations and provide support as necessary.

Remind students to follow the sentence structures in Activities 2 and 3 when answering the questions.

> **Answers**
> **a.** 办公室在三楼，你要先下楼梯到二楼，实验室就在卫生间的右手边。
> **b.** 办公室在三楼，你要先上楼梯到四楼，图书馆就在两个教室的中间。
> **c.** 图书馆在四楼，你要先下楼梯到一楼，食堂就在礼堂对面。

School treasure hunt

This game may take a little while to set up, but it's an enjoyable activity. You need to hide a "treasure" somewhere in the school and work out three or four different routes (of roughly the same distance) for getting to it, depending how many teams of students you have. Write out a series of clues for each route (e.g. "下一个线索在二楼图书馆对面的教室"), and place these in various locations along the route. The teams all pick up their first clue in the classroom, this contains directions to a different location where each team will find their second clue, and from there they will find a new clue to the next location, and so on. Students can record their team's efforts using a camcorder or a phone. The first team to reach the "treasure" wins.

> **Homework suggestion**
>
> Tell students they are helping out at their school's annual open day. They need to provide written directions to the following places on a leaflet for the visitors:
> **a.** from the school reception to the library
> **b.** from the library to the sports hall
> **c.** from the sports hall to the canteen
> **d.** from the canteen to the music department
> **e.** from the music department back to the reception.
>
> Feel free to change the locations depending on what facilities you have at your school.

6.6 迷路了 Help, I'm lost!

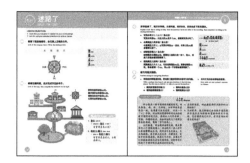

> **Icebreaker activity**
>
> Draw or display a picture of a maze or town map on the board. Students take it in turns to find the centre, guided by instructions from the other students.

Lesson activities

1 Reading

Students should recognise three of the four cardinal points as they will have seen the characters in the vocabulary from earlier units (e.g. 北京, 东京, 西餐). 南 will be the only new character here.

> **Answers**
> **a.** 东 **b.** 南 **c.** 西 **d.** 北

> **Language and culture**
>
> In western culture, north and south are viewed as the main directional reference points; intermediate directions are given as *north*east, *north*west, *south*east, *south*west (note how the words "north" and "south" come first). In Chinese culture, east and west are the main directional reference points, so the words 东 and 西 come first in the names of the intermediate directions.

2 Reading

This activity requires students to recall the Chinese names for a number of public buildings and facilities. Before the activity, go through the facilities listed on the map with the class.

> **Answers**
> **a.** 北 **b.** 西 **c.** 东 **d.** 南

In pairs, students create questions for each other that require answers involving intermediate directions, e.g. 动物园在医院的哪边？

3 Listening

Before the activity, go through these phrases so students get used to hearing (and writing) them:

近 / 远 near / far
往(东)走 to go (east)
顺着 to follow
往右拐 / 往左拐 to turn right / turn left
一直走 to go straight on
路口 junction / intersection
十字路口 crossroads

For the listening activity itself, remind students to focus on what the passers-by say (since they are the ones giving the directions), rather than what Sophie says.

Some students may find this activity challenging; you may need to provide some answer options on the board.

Transcript

a. 苏菲: 请问百货公司离这儿远吗？

路人A: 百货公司很近，它在这儿的东边。

苏菲: 百货商店怎么走？

路人A: 从这儿往东走五十米，就看到百货公司了。

b. 苏菲: 请问公园离这儿有多远？

路人B: 公园离这儿不远，在南边。

苏菲: 请问公园怎么走？

路人B: 顺着百货公司往南一直走，在路口往左拐就会看到公园了。

c. 苏菲: 请问动物园在哪儿？

路人C: 动物园在公园的西边。

苏菲: 动物园怎么走？

路人C: 顺着这儿的路口走一百米，往右拐，到那儿，你就会看到动物园了。

d. 苏菲: 请问医院离这儿远吗？

路人D: 医院离这儿有点儿远，它在动物园的北边。

苏菲: 医院怎么走？

路人D: 顺着动物园方向一直走，你会看到一个十字路口，在十字路口向北走一千米就会看到医院了。

苏菲: 麻烦你了。

Answers

a. i 近 ii 东 iii 米 **b.** i 顺着 ii 南 iii 左拐

c. i 西 ii 右拐 **d.** i 远 ii 北 iii 方向一直 iv 十字路口 v 北

4 Speaking and Writing

Students can practise asking for and giving directions themselves (both orally and in written form) using the map in Activity 2. Listen to students' conversations, providing support as necessary.

Sample answers

i. 百货商店离学校不远，在学校的南边，你从学校大门往南一直走，第一个路口往左拐就到了。

ii. 从百货商店继续往南走，经过志军的家，再继续一直往南走，你就可以看到公园了。

iii. 动物园离公园很近，在公园的东北边，走3分钟就到了。

iv. 医院离动物园有点远，从动物园出来，你往西南走，到了公园往右拐，然后往北走，经过志军的家，到了第二个路口往左拐，就可以看到医院了。

Cultural spotlight

This feature contains a lot of unfamiliar vocabulary and phrases; take time to go through these with students. Show the class additional photos of 四合院 from the internet.

Assessment suggestion

DP Find a very simple map of your local town or city. Write a set of true and false directions to and from different places. Students decide which are false and rewrite them correctly.

Homework suggestion

Students draw a map showing two famous landmarks, either in your city or in a foreign city. They then give directions from one to the other, using all the direction words they have learned in this session.

6.7 自然环境 The natural environment

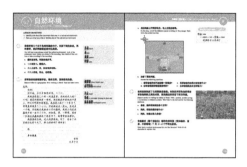

Lesson activities

1  Listening

This activity both consolidates students' knowledge of vocabulary to do with the natural environment and checks their understanding of 有 and 没有.

Transcript

a. 在森林，你听到：

男: 这儿有什么？

女: 这儿有河。河里有很多鱼。

b. 在沙漠，你听到：

女: 这儿有什么？

男: 这儿有湖。湖很大。

c. 在高原，你听到：

男: 这儿有什么？

女: 这儿有草，没有花，也看不到动物。

d. 在平原，你听到：

女: 这儿有什么？

男: 这儿有花，没有山，也没有湖。

Answers

a. 错 (河里有很多鱼。)　　b. 对

c. 错 (没有花，也看不到动物。)

d. 错 (没有山，也没有湖。)

---

2  Reading

For part a, explain that students need to identify the features that *should* appear on the map based on the contents of the letter, not those already on the existing map.

For part b, remind students to look for key words in the questions to help them work out where in the passage they can find the answers.

Answers

a. i 山　　ii 森林　　iii 湖

b. i 河南酒店 ii 有一条河 iii 志军爸爸要找濒危物种的花、草、树等等。iv 志军爸爸的朋友住在森林里。

---

3 Speaking

This activity is an opportunity for students to practise the vocabulary learned in previous lessons. Encourage them to be creative in their answers.

Sample answers

a. 森林在酒店的北边。

b. 我想看看巴西森林里的动物和花草。

c. 这是我第一次去巴西，我想参观一些名胜古迹，我想去看看有名的亚马逊河，去爬爬面包山看里约全景，也想去看看你工作的森林。

---

4 ✏ Writing

Because of the word count (35–40 characters), remind students to write concisely, giving just one reason why they like a particular natural environment.

Sample writing

我很喜欢台湾的高山，因为山底、山腰和山顶都会有不同的气候和不同的风景。

Further differentiation

DP　**MYP**　Ask students to do some internet research on an endangered species and create a presentation to share their findings with the class. Give them some guide points:

- What is the definition of an endangered species?

- Location – any place they choose.

- They should choose a category – animals, birds or plants – then a specific species.

They could find a poster or design one to support their presentation.

Students can keep their presentation brief by writing 5 sentences on their chosen animal, bird or plant, using the new vocabulary they have learned in this unit. They should write 20–30 characters for each sentence.

Homework suggestions

 Give students each a copy of the worksheet "Reading comprehension" on the CD-ROM to complete.

Students can choose an outdoor destination and write about it, following the style of the passage but using their own words.

6.8 环保意识 Think green!

Icebreaker activity

Introduce the new vocabulary for this lesson, and then organise a board race on the theme of saving energy (节省能源). Instructions for board races can be found in "Language-learning games and activities" on the CD-ROM).

Lesson activities

1 Reading

Agree with students what each photo represents in English before this activity, as the meanings of some photos may not be immediately clear (for example, photo c shows the effect acid rain has on trees, while photo e shows the effect of global warming on polar bears).

Answers

a. ii **b.** i **c.** v **d.** iv **e.** iii

2  Reading

DP This activity does not ask students to give reasons for the false statements, but you can ask them to do this – it provides a good opportunity to check their understanding.

Answers

a. 对 **b.** 对
c. 错 (人类一直在破坏自然环境。)
d. 错 (活动将会在下个月开始。)
e. 错 (可以找日晴报名。)

3 Listening

Remind students to read the questions and answer options first. They can jot down the pinyin of the answer options to help with the listening task.

Transcript

a. 同学: 请问环保小组将会举办什么活动?

日晴: 我们将会举办垃圾回收利用和环境绿化活动。

b. 同学: 为什么要回收利用垃圾?

日晴: 为了节约自然资源，我们要回收利用垃圾，这对环保很有用。

c. 同学: 绿化环境活动做什么?

日晴: 我们将会和同学们一起去植树。

d. 同学: 除了这些活动之外，环保小组以后还会举办其他活动吗?

日晴: 会的。我们打算请地理老师来演讲，教大家怎样节省能源。

Answers

a. ii **b.** iii **c.** i **d.** iii

4 Speaking

Since students will be discussing their opinions and plans, remind them to use appropriate phrases and sentence constructions, such as 我觉得......, 我打算......, 我将会......, 我以后还会.......

Tell students to make notes during this activity, as they may re-use them for Activity 5.

Sample answers

a. 环境问题是全世界所有人的问题，我在学校听过关于全球暖化、森林减少、自然资源短缺、垃圾回收问题等等。

b. 因为人类一直在破坏自然环境。

c. 我打算参加绿化环境活动。

d. 我觉得植树可以一方面在自然环境里呼吸新鲜的空气，另外一方面把希望带给我们的下一代。

5 Writing

 This is a good opportunity to show students ways of using language creatively to produce an effective poster — for example, through the use of rhyme: 垃圾分类做得好，世世代代没烦恼，(students should also recognise the reduplicated noun, 世世代代) or, through the use of short, bold statements: 美化家乡活动，让家乡更美丽。

Remind students they are designing a poster promoting an event, so they need to make sure they include 时间 (time), 地点 (location), 联系人 (contact person), 联系方法 (contact details).

> Show students the video of a news report about a recent recycling initiative introduced in Beijing. You can find the report on the internet by typing "Recycling Initiative in China (CNN)" or "Incom Recycle China CNN". Watch the video together and ask:
>
> **1.** 在这段视频中，人们用什么来回收塑料瓶子？
>
> **2.** 在哪里可以找到这些回收瓶子机？
>
> **3.** 为什么有人反对这种垃圾回收方法？

Homework suggestion

Students write a report on saving energy using the ideas generated during the board race at the start of the lesson. The following questions could be used to help them structure their report:

- 如果我们不节约自然资源，地球会有什么变化？
- 你知道你最常用的资源是什么？
- 你有什么节约自然资源的好方法？

6.9 动物园一日游 A day out at the zoo

Lesson activities

1 Reading

This activity offers a good opportunity for students to revise vocabulary to do with animal names, body parts, physical attributes, and characteristics.

> **Answers**
>
> **a.** i **b.** ii **c.** iii

Animal families

Write the Chinese names of several animals (using new vocabulary from this lesson and also from Unit 1) on small pieces of paper and put them in a container. (The number of animals depends on how many students you have in the class, but there must be 3 of each kind.) Students pick a piece of paper each and go around the room describing in Chinese the physical attributes and characteristics of their animal without giving its name. If two students think they are the same kind of animal, they join forces and look for their remaining "relatives". The first complete animal family group to get all its members together wins.

2 Reading

Remind students to identify the key words in each question to help them look for answers.

> **Answer**
>
> **a.** 老虎 **b.** 熊猫 **c.** 大象
>
> **d.** 喂猴子很危险，只有动物园的饲养员才可以喂。

Using their own words, students should write a different description for each of the animals mentioned in the diary entry.

3 Speaking

Walk around listening to students' conversations. Provide support to individual pairs as necessary. Encourage students to use the reduplicated form of adjectival stative verbs in their answers where they can.

Some students may benefit from having a list of adjectival stative verbs written up on the board.

Sample answers

a. 我两年前去过野生动物园。

b. 我看了很多动物，有狮子、老虎、斑马、猴子等等各式各样的动物。

c. 我最喜欢的是胖胖的企鹅。

d. 我喜欢看企鹅游泳，它们看起来很优雅，走路的时候，它们又滑稽又可爱。

(New word: 滑稽 huá jī; comical)

4 Writing

This activity offers an opportunity for students to revisit vocabulary relating to directions.

Answer

动物园在博物馆的南边，公园的东北面，离志军家不远。

Ask students to imagine they visited three places on the map yesterday. They should write a diary entry about their day, mentioning one interesting thing they did/saw in each place, using at least one stative verb in reduplicated form, one emotion word, and the sentence structure 又⋯⋯又⋯⋯.

Homework suggestions

1. Ask students to design and describe their ideal zoo. They should take into account the following:

   a. What is their concept of an ideal zoo? What difference will it make to the animals and the visitors?

   b. What animals will they keep in their zoo? Why?

   c. Which animals will they put together and which will they keep separate from the others? Why?

2. Ask students to draw a simple map of their ideal zoo, and write a set of rules for it. They can work out the dos and don'ts for the zoo by filling in a table:

动物园规定

可以	不可以
喂鱼	喂猴子
摸小老虎	摸大老虎

If they wish, students can also write a paragraph describing their zoo.

Assessment suggestion

This assessment follows on from the homework suggestion. Put students in groups of 3 or 4. In each group, assign at least one person as the zoo designer and one as the rule setter. Ask them to discuss the following questions and then present their ideal zoo to the class, displaying their map.

a. 动物园怎么走？   b. 动物园有什么动物？

c. 你的动物园有什么特别之处？ d. 你的动物园有什么规定？

The class can vote on their favourite zoo.

6.10 复习 Progress check

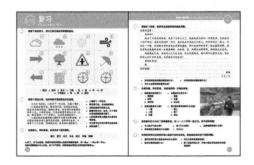

Lesson activities

1 Reading

In addition to the picture–word matching, you could check students' writing and pronunciation skills by asking them to write out the characters together with the tone each should be in.

Answers

a. iii **b.** iv **c.** i **d.** ii **e.** viii **f.** xi

g. ix **h.** xii **i.** vii **j.** x **k.** vi **l.** v

Answers

a. 夏天 **b.** 冬天 **c.** 围巾 **d.** 手套 **e.** 毛衣

f. 秋天 **g.** 短裤

2 📖 Reading

In addition to identifying the false statements in this activity, students can also give reasons for them. Remind students to watch out for possible traps in the questions. For example: According to question d, you should turn at the crossroads but the text says that you should turn left *after* passing the crossroads.

Answers

a. 错 (她穿了一件大衣。)

b. 错 (在心美家附近。)

c. 错 (他不知道图书馆怎么走。)

d. 错 (往十字路口走，之后左拐就到图书馆了。)

e. 对

f. 错 (中文图书区在英文图书区的前面。)

g. 对

3 🔊 Listening

You can either do this as a listening task or treat this as a reading task. It is possible for students to fill in the blanks based on the context of the passage, as explained here:

- Blank a is followed by 天气会变热 (the weather is turning hot) so the answer is 夏天 (summer).

- Blank b is about putting some clothes away so it is likely to be winter clothing, hence 冬天.

- Blanks c, d, and e all have measure words so students should fill in the blanks with nouns, in this case the clothing. Students can also use the measure words to help them to find the answers.

- Blank f is about some season in the last year; as we have already used summer and winter, the answer can only be 秋天 (autumn).

- Blank g is some clothing for the summer; hence the answer has to be 短裤 (shorts).

Transcript

夏天来了，天气会变热。妈妈叫我把衣柜里冬天穿的衣服都收起来，有一条围巾、一双手套和一件毛衣。这些衣服都是去年秋天买的。由于天气变热，妈妈说她会带我去百货商店买新的短裤。

4 📖 Reading

Remind students to note the key words in each question to help them look for answers (a. 酒店附近; b. 去森林看……; c. 喜欢巴西).

Sample answers

a. 酒店的附近有一条河。

b. 她要和爸爸到森林里去看一些濒危物种，例如花、草、和野生动物等等。

c. 因为巴西风景很美，每天都可以看到太阳。

5 🔊 Listening

Students can jot down the pinyin of the answer options to help them know what to listen out for.

Transcript

妈妈: 丽青，明天我要去你的学校，礼堂怎么走？

丽青: 从学校的大门进来，一直往前走就会看到教学楼。礼堂在地下。走进了教学楼以后，您会看到食堂，食堂的左边就是礼堂。

妈妈: 你的教室在哪儿？我要去教室见你的班主任。

丽青: 我的教室在三楼。从礼堂往左拐，您会看到楼梯，走到三楼以后，您会看到图书馆在两间教室的中间。我的教室就在图书馆的右边。

妈妈: 我还要去美术室找你的老师，从图书馆到美术室怎么走？

丽青: 美术室在图书馆的楼下。美术室就在楼梯的附近，往右拐就看到了。

Answers

a. ii **b.** ii **c.** iii **d.** ii

6 ✏️ Writing

If students find that they have answered all the questions and haven't met the minimum word count, they should think of more questions to answer and include the answers in their writing, together with more detail.

Sample writing

今天的天气非常好，晴天有太阳。我跟小明和小冰一起去动物园参观。我们先在市中心碰面，然后一起坐地铁，十五分钟就到了动物园。我们看到很多动物，有老虎、狮子、熊猫等。老虎和狮子长得很威武，熊猫很可爱。小明喜欢猴子，觉得它们很聪明，小冰喜欢胖胖的兔子。我最喜欢袋鼠，因为它们跳起来特别漂亮。

7  Speaking

If your school does not have any conservation clubs or activities, tell students they can imagine the activities based on what they've learned in this unit.

Sample answers

a. 学校环保小组将会举办垃圾回收和绿化环境等环保活动。

b. 回收利用垃圾可以节约能源，避免很多的浪费。

c. 绿化环境活动最主要是种树来美化我们的环境。

d. 环保小组以后还会举办两场节约能源的演讲，请有名的专家来跟我们一起讨论环保的问题。

Further differentiation

Put students in small groups. Give each group a different weather report or weather map (from a newspaper clipping), and ask them to script (or even film) a mock weather report in Chinese.

 Make sure you give students a straightforward weather report.

 Sometimes forecasters comment on how the weather may affect an upcoming outdoor event. Students can add such a segment to their weather report if they so wish.

Assessment suggestion

 Students should design a leaflet on recycling rubbish. It should cover:

• 什么是垃圾回收利用？

• 可否举一些垃圾回收利用的好例子？

• 处理垃圾时要注意些什么？

Assessment suggestion

Students should give a presentation on an environmental issue that concerns them. It could be overpopulation, waste disposal, exploitation of resources or any form of pollution. They should cover these three points:

1) the environmental issue

2) the cause of the issue

3) any solutions.

UNIT OBJECTIVES

- Practise greeting people and holding polite conversations in different situations.
- Share information and your views on a range of cities and countries.
- Learn about some interesting traditions and festivities from around the world.

- Describe and discuss different modes of transport and transport-related issues.
- Share your experiences of dealing with lost property.

7.1 预习 Unit introduction

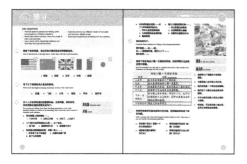

Prior knowledge

Since this unit is about people, places, and customs from around the world, students will have plenty of opportunities to practise and consolidate what they have learned in Units 3–6 (e.g. describing and discussing food and drink, travel and holiday arrangements, natural and manmade features in both local and foreign places). You should therefore ensure that students can recall vocabulary to do with these areas.

Icebreaker activity

Using the sentences provided on the worksheet "Where in the world…" on the CD-ROM, play a matching game with the class by asking students to match up the sentences with the correct countries. Select volunteers to read out the sentences, replacing 这个国家 with the name of the country.

Lesson activities

  Reading

This should be a straightforward activity as students should recognise these country names from previous units. You may also want to take this opportunity to teach students names of other countries.

Answers

a. v **b.** iv **c.** i **d.** ii **e.** iii

 Students could make a sentence about each of these countries, like those in the icebreaker activity. If they want to write about the people of the country, remind them to add 人 after the country name.

  Reading

Say each character slowly and clearly to help students write out the pinyin and work out the tone.

Answers

a. traffic / jiāo tōng **b.** aeroplane / fēi jī

c. train / huǒ chē

d. underground or subway train / dì tiě

e. car / qì chē **f.** bicycle / zì xíng chē

  Listening

Remind students to jot down the pinyin for the answer options to help them listen for the answers in the recording.

Transcript

a. 我是海伦，现在和家人一起住在上海。我常常坐地铁去学校，可是我不喜欢坐地铁，因为上海地铁的人太多了。

b. 我是马克。上个星期妈妈来中国看我，我带她去西安参观了兵马俑。我们是从北京坐很快的火车去的，只要五个小时就到了西安。

c. 我是米娜。今年夏天我和家人去了美国的北部旅游。在那里我们坐了火车。我们坐的火车不是很快，在火车上就可以看到外面美丽的风景。

d. 我是本杰明，刚刚去了新加坡。回来的时候在新加坡国际机场里买了很多东西，包括几件衣服和两本书。

e. 我是日晴。明天是周六，天气很好，是晴天。我跟同学们要去森林公园骑自行车。

Answers

a. iii **b.** ii **c.** iii **d.** iii **e.** iii

  Writing

See if students can articulate the differences between the first and second sentences. (The first focuses on the mode of transport; the second on the location of travel.)

Sample writing

我们是坐飞机去北京的。
我们从北京是坐火车去上海的。
在苏州旅游的时候，我们乘坐了小船。
我们觉得坐小船很有意思。

 You could give students more adjectival stative verbs to expand their vocabulary: 舒适 (shū shì; comfortable); 悠闲 (yōu xián; relaxing); 忙碌 (máng lù; busy); 拥挤 (yōng jǐ; crowded).

  Reading

If there is time, encourage students to give reasons for the false statements.

Answers

a. 对

b. 错 (九点的火车)

c. 错 (海边小镇－海蓝多)

d. 对

e. 错 (吃当地有名的海鲜餐)

f. 对

  Speaking

Walk around the classroom and listen to students' conversations. Provide support as necessary.

Answers

a. 我住在土耳其的伊斯坦堡，这是一个大城市。

b. 城市的郊区有飞机场，也有很多火车站。

c. 城里的交通很方便，有地铁也有巴士。

d. 我每天坐地铁上学，有时候妈妈会开车带我去学校，但是路上车子太多，常常塞车，所以我喜欢坐地铁上学。

Further differentiation

Ask students to create their own holiday itinerary based on the one in Activity 5.

 Students create a two-column table showing times and brief descriptions of the activities.

 Students should create a three-column table including time, brief descriptions of activities, and some extra information for each (e.g. remember to bring passport, tickets, sunscreen).

7.2 问候方式 Ways of greeting people

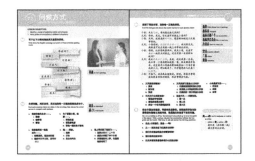

Icebreaker

Discuss the various ways people greet each other. If your class is culturally diverse, ask students to share how they greet one another in their culture.

Lesson activities

  Reading

 Before the activity, show students *An introduction to China and the Chinese language* from the BBC Bitesize website. This short video includes some simple greetings, tones and writing in Chinese.

Say each character slowly and clearly to help students write out the pinyin and work out the tone.

Answers

a. How are you? / nín hǎo ma

b. Thank you / xiè xie

c. Don't mention it / bù yòng xiè

d. You are welcome / bù kè qi

e. I am sorry (or excuse me) / duì bù qǐ

f. It's all right (or never mind) / méi guān xì

g. Greetings, teacher / lǎo shi hǎo

h. Good morning / zǎo ān

i. Good evening / wǎn ān

j. See you again (or goodbye) / zài jiàn

Language and culture

As with other cultures, the Chinese have different ways of greeting and addressing people depending on the situation.

- Among friends, people often say 喂. (This is also what people say when they pick up the phone.)

- 最近身体好吗? This is often used at the start of a conversation to show concern for the person to whom you're speaking.

- 吃过饭了吗? This is used around mealtimes.

- 你去哪里啊? Similar to "What are you up to now?" in English, this is a normal greeting on encountering a friend.

- It is considered polite when addressing a Chinese person to add honorific titles like 先生, 女士 or the job position such as 老师 for teacher and 医生 for doctor before his/her surname. When greeting someone in a position of respect, people normally say 好 after their job title. First names are used between family members, good friends and well-acquainted colleagues.

 Give students the opportunity to practise different greetings in pairs. Students could act out scenarios in front of the class to make the context clear.

 Listening

Remind students to jot down the pinyin for the answer options if it helps them to listen out for the answers in the recording.

Transcript

a. 陈先生, 您好。认识您我很高兴, 我们可以去附近的咖啡馆坐一坐, 再聊一聊。

b. 小海。谢谢你带我参观了你家乡的美术馆, 太有意思了。为了谢谢你, 我请你吃饭吧。

c. 对不起, 我的中文不太好。请您再说一遍, 我刚刚没有听明白。

d. 太晚了, 我得回家了。如果晚了, 我就坐不上十五路公共汽车了。

e. 老师, 对不起我迟到了。因为今天早上我乘坐的火车晚了二十分钟。

Answers

a. ii **b.** i **c.** ii **d.** iii **e.** i

 Reading

Ask two volunteers to read the dialogue, so the class can look through the text together. Remind students to go through the questions and answer options, noting key words that will help them look for answers (a. 现在; b. 怎么认识; c. 麦可的; d. 为什么; e. 次)

Answers

a. ii **b.** i **c.** ii **d.** iii **e.** i

 Speaking

Encourage students to use their imagination and expand on their answers where they can. You can show students some of the sample answers so they understand how to do it.

Sample answers

a. 您好, 我就是安迪。

b. 通常一个半小时, 但是今天飞机误点, 我从北京坐了三个小时才到西安。

c. 我们先去酒店吧, 我想先洗个脸, 再去吃饭。

d. 这是我第三次来西安。以前来都是工作, 没有时间玩。这一次一定要好好玩玩。

e. 这次来西安, 我最想看兵马俑, 也想去华清池, 还想到处看看西安这个古城, 尝尝西安有名的小吃。

Further differentiation

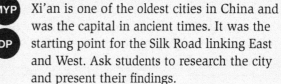 Xi'an is one of the oldest cities in China and was the capital in ancient times. It was the starting point for the Silk Road linking East and West. Ask students to research the city and present their findings.

Students can create a leaflet covering: the location; why the city is famous; attractions; regional foods; the best time to visit; how tourists can get there (from Europe, for example).

 Students can create a poster listing 5 facts about Xi'an.

Homework suggestion

Give students the following scenario: A Chinese teenager has just met a French exchange student, who is visiting Beijing, at the airport.

Ask students to write a short dialogue to imagine what the they would say to each other, including:

- an appropriate greeting and response

- one thing the French student would like to do/ see in Beijing

- one suggestion by the Chinese teenager on what the French student should do.

7.3 国家与城市 Countries and cities

Lesson activities

  Reading and Speaking

Go through the pen strokes of each of the characters with the class. Pay particular attention to students' pronunciations as they say the continents out loud.

Answers

red continent: 北美洲; orange continent: 南美洲; blue continent: 欧洲; brown continent: 非洲; yellow continent: 亚洲; purple continent: 大洋洲; beige continent: 南极洲.

 **Reading and Speaking**

Before the activity, select a few volunteers to say the names of the countries out loud – correct their pronunciation as necessary.

For part b, ask students which preposition (在) they need to include in order to make a sentence meaning "Korea is in Asia".

Answers for part a

a. 韩国   **b.** 加拿大   **c.** 印度尼西亚   **d.** 德国

e. 西班牙   **f.** 马来西亚   **g.** 新西兰   **h.** 新加坡

Answers for part b

a. 韩国在亚洲   **b.** 加拿大在北美洲

c. 印度尼西亚在亚洲   **d.** 德国在欧洲

e. 西班牙在欧洲   **f.** 马来西亚在亚洲

g. 新西兰在澳洲   **h.** 新加坡在亚洲

③ 📖 Reading

Remind students to read the questions and identify the key words in each one to help them look for the answers (a. 什么地方 means the student should look for a position; 主要语言 means to look for a main language; b. 气候 means to look for information about climate; c. 暑假……两个活动 means to look for two summer holiday activities; d. 还可以……做什么 means to look for an additional activity).

Answers

a. 德国在欧洲中部，主要语言是德语。

b. 德国的气候是夏热冬冷，四季分明。

c. 暑假的时候，大卫常常跟朋友去山里或森林徒步和露营。

d. 冬天可以去德国南部山区滑雪。

 **Listening**

Remind students of the importance of understanding the questions and the answer options before listening to the recording, since the answer options in the activity may be paraphrasing what is in the recording. For example, question a refers to weeks as 周, but in the recording 星期 is used.

a. 今年夏天爸爸妈妈要带我去日本旅游。我们计划去那里玩两个星期。

b. 我想去世界上很多国家看一看，今年圣诞节我计划去欧洲的法国和德国看一看那里有名的传统圣诞节市场。

c. 我去过美国、英国、巴西、澳洲和日本，但是还没有去过非洲。明年暑假我会和朋友一起去非洲看那里有趣的动物。

d. 这是我第一次去南美洲。从中国北京坐飞机到南美洲里约需要一天半左右的时间，时间太长了，非常累。

Answers

a. ii **b.** iii **c.** i **d.** iii

 Writing

While it is not necessary for students to include measure words or adjectival stative verbs in their answers, it is good to encourage them to do so.

Sample answers

一条河流、一座桥、一些绿绿的树、一条船、很多建筑

Homework suggestion

Ask students to write a short paragraph (60–80 characters) about a country they plan to visit. They need to include the stative verb 计划 in their writing, and explain what they plan to do whilst there.

7.4 世界名城 Famous cities around the world

In pairs, students look at the 6 pictures of famous cities in Activity 1. Student A chooses one of the landmarks and makes a sentence starting with a time phrase, e.g. 明年秋天，我想去北京的故宫。Student B completes Student A's sentence with a reason, starting with "因为……", e.g. 因为北京的秋天天气不冷也不热。Student B then chooses a different landmark and they repeat the exercise, taking turns until they have worked through all 6.

Lesson activities

1 **Reading**

Before the activity, ask students if they know what the landmarks are called in English (a. Big Ben; b. Eiffel Tower; c. Sydney Opera House; d. Gateway of India; e. Forbidden Palace; f. Statue of Liberty). Then, go through the Chinese names, writing them on the board with the pinyin. (See page 145 for more about how these names are translated.)

Answers

a. iii. 伦敦 (大笨钟)   **b.** vi. 巴黎 (铁塔)

c. v. 悉尼 (歌剧院)   **d.** ii. 孟买 (印度门户)

e. i. 北京 (故宫／紫禁城)   **f.** iv. 纽约 (自由女神像)

---

2 **Reading**

Students should be able to translate most of the terms into English, having learned them in previous lessons.

 If necessary, you can write the answers jumbled-up on the board and turn this into a word-matching activity.

Answers

Scale/ size	Global position	Location	Features
large small medium	in the world international capital city	east/ west/ south/ north seaside central part	modern/young ancient/ traditional energetic/popular attractive/eco-friendly busy/lively

Speaking

 If necessary, write out the following sentence patterns as prompts:

- [country] 的 [city] 是 一个 [feature] 的城市。
- [city] 是 [country] [feature or position] 的城市。
- [city] 在 [country] 的 [location]。

Sample answers

a. 北京是中国的首都。

b. 英国的伦敦是一个繁忙的国际都市。

c. 里约在巴西的东南边。

d. 意大利的罗马是一个吸引人的城市。

e. 东京是日本最大的城市。

 Ask students to use the remaining words in the table from Activity 2 to describe one city further, e.g. 北京是中国的首都，位于中国北部。北京有许多历史悠久的古迹，也有很多年轻人喜欢去的百货商店，它是一个有传统的现代城市。

  Listening

Since this is a long recording, pause it according to where each question is to give students time to note down the answer.

Transcript

韩国釜山是亚洲著名的旅游城市，不仅有干净的沙滩和美丽的夜景，这里还有最有名的历史悠久的传统市场。因为市里大多数的景点在地铁站附近，因此乘坐地铁是最方便的。釜山每年十月初还会举办釜山国际电影节，这个活动已经举办了二十多年了。参加活动的电影人很多，因此十月去釜山你会见到很多著名的电影明星。

Answers

a. iii b. iii c. iii d. ii

  Reading

Explain to students what each blank represents:
a. something that describes a period of time; b. a location; c. a distance; d. a stative verb for giving an opinion; e. an adjectival stative verb to describe the city; f. something to do with transport; g. an adjectival stative verb linked with 方便; h. a verb–noun compound.

Answers

a. 五年   b. 东边的   c. 很远   d. 觉得

e. 现代化的   f. 地铁   g. 快   h. 买车

  Writing

 Write out some of the sentence structures covered in Activities 2 and 3 as prompts for students who need support with this task.

Sample writing

威尼斯是我去过最棒的一个旅游城市，因为威尼斯非常美丽，威尼斯的建筑古老而有特色。它跟其他的城市很不一样，公共交通工具不是汽车也不是地铁而是船只。我喜欢走在古老窄小的巷子，坐在圣马可广场上喝咖啡，我觉得浪漫极了！

 You can re-use the sample writing by turning it into a true-or-false activity: create a set of statements to go with the passage, ask students to read it and decide which statements are false, giving their reasons.

Assessment suggestion

Give students the following heading: 一个热闹的城市。Ask them to describe (in writing) some qualities of a lively city.

 Students list three features/qualities as separate sentences.

 Students write a coherent paragraph, using the language structures from this lesson.

Homework suggestion

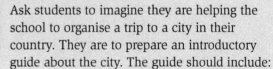 Ask students to imagine they are helping the school to organise a trip to a city in their country. They are to prepare an introductory guide about the city. The guide should include:

- 城市在国家哪里？
- 那是一个怎么样的城市？
- 那儿的公共交通是怎么样的？
- 有什么景点？

7.5 各地的传统习俗 Traditions and customs from around the world

Icebreaker activity

Find and show students video clips of festivals from around the world. Ask them to name/ guess which countries they are from in Chinese, as well as suggest 2–3 adjectival stative verbs to describe what they see.

1 Reading

This activity provides an opportunity for students to revise reading and saying dates in Chinese. Also, ask them what 一般, 通常, 之间 mean in English.

Answers

a. Between March and April every year

b. Between 13 and 15 April every year

c. February every year

2 Reading

Point out the common features found on a poster promoting a social event: 活动 (activity); 地址 (address); 问询处 (contact information); 时间 (time); 交通方式／停车场 (travel information/parking); 门票 (tickets).

DP Encourage students to give reasons for the false statements.

Answers

a. 对   b. 错 (在新湖公园里)

c. 对   d. 错 (周日提早在下午五点结束。)

e. 对   f. 对 (门票免费)

3 Reading and Speaking

Explain to students what each blank represents: a. an indication of time; b. a location; c. a stative verb; d. an adjectival stative verb to describe the music festival; e. a conjunction or connecting word; f. an adjectival stative verb to describe something; g. a stative verb; h. a stative verb; i. a noun; j. an adjectival stative verb.

Answers

a. 每年   b. 英国   c. 举行   d. 最受欢迎的

e. 除了   f. 各种各样的   g. 参加   h. 住在

i. 票价   j. 免费

Local festivals

MYP In groups, students introduce a festival in their local area or, failing that, a festival they have participated in. You could provide questions to guide them.

4 Listening

Remind students to jot down the pinyin of the answer options first to help them to listen for the answers.

Transcript

a. 马德里是西班牙的首都，位于西班牙的中部，是一座历史文化旅游名城。

b. 在这里每年的5月15日的那个星期，马德里都会举行圣伊西德罗节。这是一个可以了解西班牙民俗传统的节日。

c. 在5月15日这一天许多马德里的大人们、小孩们都会穿传统民族服装，跟着音乐跳传统的西班牙舞蹈。

d. 在节日期间还会有精彩的斗牛表演、免费的音乐会、美食小摊和儿童游乐场等娱乐活动。

e. 因为参加活动的人非常多，马德里市区的交通会十分拥挤，所以建议游客们最好坐地铁或走路前往活动地点。

Answers

a. iii b. iii c. ii d. i e. i

See how many adjectival stative verbs students can identify in the recording (传统，精彩，免费，多，拥挤).

Explain that bullfighting is a cultural tradition in Spain, but acknowledge that some people find it distasteful. Encourage students to use language to express their opinions, and introduce some words they could use to describe bullfighting, e.g. 过时的 (outdated), 残忍 (cruel).

  Writing

Remind students they are writing a postcard to a friend so should keep the tone fairly informal and friendly, and, since they are writing about a past event, they need to use the appropriate tense in their writing (e.g. using 了 after a verb). Encourage them to use adjectival stative verbs to describe the festival, too.

Sample writing

上个月我参加了一个春季音乐节。这个节庆在捷克的首都布拉格 — 一个古老又美丽的城市。节庆中有许多音乐节目，最主要是古典音乐，也有爵士乐；还有歌剧和舞蹈。我觉得这个节庆很棒，我听了好几场音乐会，我最喜欢的是大提琴独奏表演。

Further differentiation

Turn the sample writing from Activity 5 into a reading comprehension activity. Ask students:

- 音乐节在哪儿举行？
- 音乐节在哪一个季节举行？
- 音乐节有哪些音乐节目？

 Provide multiple answer options for students if necessary.

 Ask students to write out their answers in full sentences.

Homework suggestion

 Students design an itinerary for a multi-city trip, giving the date, location, means of transport, and any special local festivals/sights to visit. Remind students to consider a reasonable route.

 Students can fill in the details of their itinerary using the worksheet "A multi-city trip" on the CD-ROM.

 Students fill out the itinerary, but then write a leaflet of 120 characters to describe in more detail what tourists can expect to do/see at each location.

7.6 在国际机场 At the airport

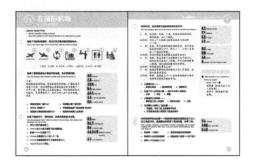

Lesson activities

1 **Reading**

Go through the signs with the class before the activity to check they are interpreting them correctly. (Note: picture D is showing a piece of baggage being checked in, *not* baggage reclaim.)

Answers

a. vi **b.** vii **c.** iv **d.** ii **e.** i **f.** iii **g.** v

---

Remind students that some of these terms are nouns (海关，卫生间，服务台), and some are verbs (到达，出发，转机，办票).

2 **Reading**

Remind students to read the questions first so they know what they need to look for in the text message.

Answers

a. 妈妈在机场接机等林阿姨。

b. 林阿姨从香港来。　　**c.** 因为香港下大雨。

d. 晚了一个半小时。　　**e.** 妈妈要他们先吃饭。

f. 他们大约八点十五分回家。

---

3 **Listening**

This is a challenging activity, since it requires them to check the accuracy of the statements aurally in order to find what errors there might be. If necessary, repeat the recording 2–3 times or read the transcript out slowly.

Remind students that statements b and c apply to the second part of the recording, while statements d and e apply to the third part.

Transcript

a. 前往马德里的林萍女士，请您马上到机场马来西亚航空售票处，您把护照忘了。

b. 旅客朋友们，欢迎乘坐OUP8112次从北京前往马德里的航班。现在我们的飞机已经起飞了。请您坐在您的座位上。本次航班全程禁止吸烟。

c. 乘坐OUP6886次航班的旅客们请注意了，21号登机口已经开始登机，预计半个小时后起飞。

d. 旅客们晚上好，我们的飞机马上就要到达伦敦希思罗机场了。如果您是外国客人，入境前，请您填好入境卡，方便入境。

Language and culture

In the above recording, the two consecutive 1s (e.g. OUP8112) are pronounced as "yāo yāo". This practice is used by native Chinese speakers to distinguish 1 (yī) from the similar-sounding 7 (qī). See Unit notes in 11.4 for more detail.

Answers

a. 错 (她把护照忘了。) **b.** 错 (是从北京飞马德里。)

c. 对 **d.** 对

e. 错 (已经开始登机，预计半个小时后起飞。)

f. 对

Sample answers

a. 我要去香港。 **b.** 我要双程票。

c. 中午十二点以后的航班都可以。

d. 什么航班都可以，我要最便宜的。

e. 经济舱就可以了。

 Give students these additional sentences to ask and answer to develop their conversations further: 您喜欢靠窗口还是靠走道的位子？您是否要订特别餐？您打算怎么付款？现金还是信用卡？还有什么需要我为您服务的吗？

Homework suggestion

 Ask students to write a dialogue between two people based on one of the following scenarios. They need to resolve the issue in their scenario.

- Two friends are going on holiday. They arrive at the airport by taxi. At the check-in counter one realises they have left their passport in the taxi.

- Two friends are returning from their holiday. They are waiting for their bags in the luggage reclaim area but one never arrives.

Select a couple of interesting dialogues and get students to act them out.

4 **Reading**

To help students engage more with this activity, they could read out the dialogue in pairs before answering the questions. Walk around the classroom listening to students' conversations and providing support as necessary.

Answers

a. ii **b.** iii **c.** i **d.** ii

 Ask students to identify the grammar structures in the dialogue that indicate (1) something has already happened and (2) something is happening (Answer for 1: the use of 了；Answer for 2: the use of 还在).

7.7 公共交通 Public transport

Icebreaker activity

Ask students how they travel to school and why they choose that method. List the different methods of transport and find out which is the most popular.

5 **Speaking and Writing**

Remind students to make notes of what their partners are saying – this will help them complete part b.

Lesson activities

1 Reading

Go through the pictures with the class first so students are familiar with the Chinese names of the different modes of transport before they read the sentences.

Answers

a. v **b.** i **c.** iii **d.** ii **e.** iv **f.** vi

Students could translate the sentences into English.

2 Reading

Before the activity, ask students to skim the reading passages and list the modes of travel mentioned. (Answer: 走路，坐船，开车，坐地铁)

 In addition to identifying the false statements, students should also give reasons for them.

Answers

a. 错 (米娜住在一个古老的小镇，交通是靠走路和坐船。)

b. 对 **c.** 对 **d.** 错 (他坐地铁上班。)

3 Listening

Remind students to jot down the pinyin of the answer options if it helps them to know what to listen out for.

Transcript

a. 您好。是蓝天出租车公司吗？我刚刚坐了你们公司的一辆黑色出租车，我把我的背包忘车上了，背包里有好几本书。您帮我问一问。谢谢了。

b. 旅客们大家好。非常抱歉因为现在北京国际机场很忙，我们飞机降落的时间大约会晚二十分钟。

c. 亲爱的旅客朋友们，很抱歉现在我们的火车停了，因为火车前方的铁路出了小事故，通知说铁路上出现了两头牛。

Answers

a. i **b.** ii **c.** iii

 Ask students to also give: the colour of the rental car in the first clip (黑色), the name of the airport in the second clip (北京国际机场), and the reason for the accident in the third clip (铁路上出现了两头牛).

 4 Speaking

Walk around the classroom listening to students' conversations and providing additional support as necessary.

Sample answers

a. 您好，我去郑州。 **b.** 我要单程票。

c. 我要买软卧票。 **d.** 中午十二点那班火车。

e. 我要买四张票，我们都是学生，可以打折吗？

5 Writing

The strokes animation from the MGDB online dictionary is useful for showing students the sequences of writing individual characters.

6 Writing

Remind students they are writing a diary entry, so they should include some common features of a diary entry (e.g. date and weather), and remember to use language appropriately to share their feelings.

Sample writing

星期三 大风大雨

昨天从伦敦坐飞机到郑州，在北京转机。但是正好碰到北京大风大雨，所有的飞机都不能飞了。我就买了从北京到郑州的软卧火车票。平常只要五个小时就可以到，但是因为天气不好，我们坐了九个小时！在火车上，有两个阿姨跟我们住在同一间软卧车厢，她们给了我们很多美味的小吃。

Spring Festival travel season: 春运

 Explain to students that every year, just before Spring Festival, train stations across China become incredibly busy as people prepare to travel home for the holidays. Look for a suitable video online to show students just how busy it gets!

Explain that native speakers use the term "春运" to refer to this busy period.

Ask students if they have ever experienced similar travel chaos during the public holidays, and ask them to suggest some suitable adjectival stative verbs to describe the situation.

Students could make a poster listing some pros and cons of travelling home during Spring Festival (or an equivalent important festival back home).

Homework suggestion

 Ask students to write a paragraph of 80–100 characters describing a memorable journey made by public transport.

7.8 哪种交通工具最好？ Which mode of transport is the best?

Lesson activities

Reading

1

Ask students to identify which of the sentences are passive (a) and which are active (the rest). How do they know? (Answer: 被 is used in passive sentences.)

> **Answers**
>
> **a.** v **b.** iv **c.** i **d.** ii **e.** iii

2   Listening

Remind students that sometimes the questions or true-or-false statements in a listening activity may not appear in the order in which the events are mentioned in a recording, so students should always read the statements (or questions) first to get some context.

Transcript

天空岛是我市的一个没有污染的自然风景保护区。

在岛上游客们可以看到很多特别的鸟。

这个岛上没有汽车。在岛上参观你只能走路或者骑自行车。

每天开往天空岛的游船是每小时一班。

但是今天天气预报报道，明天下午两点前后开始将有大风，为了游客安全，游船公司决定明天中午十二点以后开往天空岛的所有游船都停开。

> **Answers**
>
> **a.** 对 **b.** 对
> **c.** 错 (可以看到很多特别的鸟。) **d.** 对
> **e.** 对 **f.** 错 (明天下午两点前后开始有大风。)
> **g.** 对 (明天中午十二点以后所有游船停开。)

3 Writing

For part a, point out that 污 on its own means "filth and dirt", while 染 means "to stain" or "to dye". Together, these characters conjure up an image of spreading filth, which is basically what pollution is!

For part b, students' posters could include phrases such as: 污染的世界，没有污染的人生，让我们一起走路或骑自行车上学。

4 Reading

Remind students to use appropriate language to begin their answers. For example, questions b and c are both 为什么 (why) questions, so students need to start their answers with 因为 (because).

> **Answers**
>
> **a.** 电车 **b.** 因为电车是最便宜、最方便、最环保的公共交通工具。
> **c.** 因为一方面怀旧，另一方面可以悠闲地欣赏多彩多姿的城市景观，是很特别的旅行经验。

5 Speaking

Encourage students to give reasons when answering the questions, not just one-word answers. Tell students to make notes of their conversation as they can re-use the notes for their homework.

> **Sample answers**
>
> **a.** 我住的城市在上下班的时间常常堵车。
> **b.** 我们学校周围的交通很忙，我每天早上都要提早出门才不会迟到。

c. 学生们和老师觉得不是很安全，因为路上的车子实在太多了。有些司机不遵守交通规则。

d. 除了不安全，路上车子太多还会造成空气污染的问题。

e. 我觉得学校、学生、家长还有当地政府应该多宣传交通安全的概念，让学校周围更安全。

Cultural spotlight

Go through unfamiliar vocabulary as necessary (竞争者, 出口国). Ask students if they have travelled on a high-speed train before. Encourage those who have to share their experience, and those who have not/wouldn't want to to say why.

Sample answers

a. 英国有高铁。我觉得高铁最大的好处就是促进交通，可以减少大家花在旅途上的时间，可以很快地从一个城市到另一个城市。缺点就是高铁会造成许多环境的污染和噪音的污染，我希望科学家能够发明更好的方法来减少这些污染，让大家可以更方便地旅行。

b. 在我居住的地方，很多人开始使用混合动力汽车，听说开这样的车比较环保，可以减少一些汽油的污染。

Homework suggestion

 Students use their notes from Activity 5 as the basis for a poster promoting road safety in their neighbourhood. They can either use pictures and brief sentences to illustrate good and bad practice, or just list the traffic rules.

7.9 失物招领 Reclaiming lost or stolen property

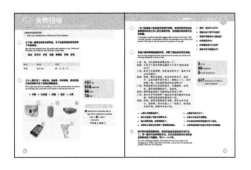

Lesson activities

  Reading

Here is an opportunity to practise character recognition. Remind students that a radical is a component in a Chinese character, which indicates either a meaning or a sound of the word. For example, ask them to consider why 脑 and 背 both have 月 (肉) as their radical. Note: explain that 月 does not mean "moon" here – it is best to write the characters on the board for students to see the subtle difference in the pen strokes.

Answers

物品	拼音	部首
现金	xiàn jīn	现＝王；金＝金
信用卡	xìn yòng kǎ	信＝亻；用＝用；卡＝丨
手机	shǒu jī	手＝手；机＝木
电脑	diàn nǎo	电＝田；脑＝月
照相机	zhào xiàng jī	照＝灬；相＝目；机＝木
护照	hù zhào	护＝扌；照＝灬
背包	bēi bāo	背＝月；包＝勹

  Listening

The pinyins noted down by the students for Activity 1 will help them with this listening activity.

Transcript

a. 我是米娜。我的钱包不见了。钱包里有信用卡。

b. 我是本杰明，我的五百元美元现金找不到了。

c. 警察您好，我是约翰。我的手机被小偷偷走了。

d. 先生您好。我是志军。我等了一个小时都没有看到我的行李箱，是不是还没有到这里。

e. 我是小美，你有没有看到我的照相机？我找不到我的相机。

Answers

a. iii **b.** v **c.** iv **d.** ii **e.** i

  Speaking

This is a good opportunity for students to revise some air-travel-related vocabulary from previous lessons. Walk around listening to students' conversations. Provide support as necessary.

Before the activity, students can complete the "Lost property form" worksheet (on the CD-ROM) and use their notes as prompts for the conversation.

Sample answers

a. 您好，我是李约翰。

b. 我昨天晚上从希思罗出发，飞来北京。

c. 我的行李箱是黑色的，上面有一条红带子。

d. 我的行李箱是中等大小。

e. 我的行李箱里面有衣服、皮鞋还有一些书。

f. 我的手机号码是0123456789。

4 Reading

Remind students to give reasons for the false statements if they can.

Answers

a. 对	b. 错 (钱包不见了。)	c. 对
d. 对	e. 错 (她还去了外语教室。)	
f. 错 (她在外面的餐厅吃的。)		g. 对

h. 错 (她正在跟妈妈发短信，下课后找不到钱包的时候再给妈妈打电话。)

 In pairs, students re-read the dialogue in Activity 4. They should jot down all the things Xiaomei has lost, then take turns role-playing Xiaomei and her mother, having a new conversation about these lost items. Go around listening to the role-plays and select a few pairs to act out their dialogues to the class.

5 Writing

Remind students they are writing a diary entry so they need to adopt an appropriate tone. Ask them some questions as prompts:

a. 你昨天什么时候去游泳的?

b. 你什么时候发现手表不见了?

c. 你的手表有什么特点?   d. 你要怎么去找回手表?

Sample writing

4月17日 星期一 下雨

昨天早上十点的时候我到中央游泳池去游泳，游完泳在更衣室的时候，我想看看时间，就发现手表不见了。手表是爸爸送给我的生日礼物，所以我很担心。我立刻去找服务人员，他们友善地告诉我，有人在卫生间找到我的手表了。失而复得，我觉得特别开心。

Language and culture

失而复得 (shī ér fù dé) means to have lost then found something (失去后又得到). This is a common idiom used after someone has found something precious which they thought was lost.

Homework suggestion

Ask students to write an email of 120–150 characters to their parents, explaining that their luggage went missing on a school trip, what was in their luggage, how they responded and whether or not any of the missing items were recovered.

7.10 复习 Progress check

Lesson activities

1 Reading

For extra revision, ask students for the meanings of all the answer options before doing the activity.

Answers

a. i b. iii c. iii d. i e. ii

2 Reading

You may want to provide a world map for students as reference for this activity. Students should also give reasons for the false statements.

Answers

a. 对   **b.** 对   **c.** 错 (纽约在美国的东部。)

d. 错 (澳大利亚的首都是堪培拉不是悉尼。)   **e.** 对

 **3** **Writing**

Ask students to include measure words in their list.

Sample answers

一部手机; 两本书; 一支笔; 一把牙刷

 4 **Writing**

This activity requires students to use appropriate adjectival stative verbs to describe each mode of transport.

If necessary, you can turn this into a word-matching activity by writing a selection of adjectival stative verbs or reasons on the board, then ask students to pick a suitable one for each mode of transport.

Sample writing

a. 自行车 – 自行车又便宜又方便, 而且是最环保的交通工具。自行车可以带你去许多汽车到不了的地方。

b. 摩托车 – 摩托车比汽车便宜而且容易停车, 骑摩托车的时候看起来很酷!

c. 出租车 – 出租车很方便, 没有开车和停车的困扰, 只要花点钱立刻到达目的地。

d. 公共汽车 – 宽敞明亮、便宜又方便, 没有开车和停车的烦恼。

e. 船 – 宽敞舒适, 没有城市汽车的噪音, 跟大自然一起旅行。

DP
MYP Students carry out a comparison of the impact of different methods of transport on the environment by answering these questions:

a. 那一种交通工具排出的废气最多?

b. 那一种交通工具发出的噪音最强?

c. 如果我们只有自行车一种交通工具, 我们的世界会变成什么样子? 你喜欢这样的世界吗? 为什么?

Encourage students to give reasons for their answers and say how people could reduce the impact of transport on the environment.

 **5** **Reading**

This is a good activity for checking students' understanding of grammar and word order. Note: for b and c there are two ways of re-ordering the sentences.

To make the activity easier, you can break the sentences up into fewer fragments.

Answers

a. 在台北的市中心, 走路是最好的旅行方式。

b. 我们打算周末骑自行车去植物园。

周末我们打算骑自行车去植物园。

c. 去年夏天我们是坐船去西班牙的。

我们去年夏天是坐船去西班牙的。

d. 伦敦城里的公共汽车上有免费的网络。

 6 **Listening**

Remind students to read the questions first so they get a sense of what they need to listen out for.

Transcript

女海关: 您好。欢迎来到中国北京。请把您的护照给我。您从哪里来?

男旅客: 我从美国纽约来。

女海关: 您来北京做什么? 旅游、学习还是工作?

男旅客: 我来北京大学上大学, 学习汉语。

女海关: 这是您第一次来北京吗?

男旅客: 不是的, 两年前我来北京参加过中文夏令营。

女海关: 您在北京呆多久? 住哪儿?

男旅客: 我会呆六个月, 住在大学的国际学生公寓。

女海关: 您的手提袋里有什么?

男旅客: 有手机、电脑、钱包和一件衣服。

女海关: 给您护照。希望您在北京生活愉快!

Answers

a. i   **b.** iii   **c.** ii   **d.** i   **e.** i

Writing

Depending on the ability of your class, you could use the sample writing below to turn the activity into a reading comprehension, and ask students to answer the questions in the Student Book using information in the passage rather than composing their own article.

Sample writing

台湾有很多公共交通工具，例如：火车、高铁、捷运、公车和计程车等等。我认为公共交通可以带给人们很多方便，也可以节省能源有益环保。交通公司如果提供便宜的票价以及频繁的班次，就可以吸引很多人。政府如果提供一些折扣，再加上一些宣传，就可以鼓励更多人来乘坐公共交通工具。来台中旅行，最好坐公共汽车，因为这里的观光景点多数都有公车可抵达；另外，旅程前段两公里以内都是免费的。

Speaking

Walk around the classroom listening to students' conversations. Provide support as necessary.

Sample answers

a. 我去过世界上很多有名的城市，例如巴黎、柏林、罗马、布拉格等等。

b. 我最喜欢巴黎，因为巴黎的建筑非常美丽，有悠久的历史还有很浪漫的文化气息。

c. 如果你来巴黎玩，除了去看一些有名的名胜古迹，我推荐你到巴黎的郊外去看看莫内的花园 (Monet's Garden)。因为在那个花园里，你可以感受到为什么莫内能够画出那么多美丽的画。

d. 在巴黎旅行，坐火车和地铁都非常方便及便宜。

e. 我以后很想去中国，我特别想去南方的三亚，一方面想去那儿看看几个好朋友，另外一方面我听说三亚的空气是全中国最好的，我想去那里呼吸新鲜的空气。

Further differentiation

 Explain that in China smog (雾霾) is a major environmental concern. Show them some photos or videos of a smoggy day in Beijing.

 Students can list 4 or 5 ways that smog can affect people living in the city.

 Students write a report on what can be done to reduce air pollution.

Assessment suggestion

Ask students to imagine that they have just returned from a short holiday abroad staying with a relative. They now need to write a thank-you letter that:

- uses language correctly to greet the relative and thank them for looking after them
- says what they liked best about where they stayed
- says which cultural activity they enjoyed most during the holiday and why
- tells the relative they may have left behind a personal item and asks them to help look for it
- signs off appropriately.

UNIT OBJECTIVES

- Describe and discuss a variety of extracurricular activities.
- Describe and discuss what happens on a school exchange programme.
- Share your experiences of organising and taking part in volunteering activities.

- Describe and discuss your preparations for university.
- Share your hopes and plans after university graduation.
- Share facts and opinions about vocational education.

8.1 预习 Unit introduction

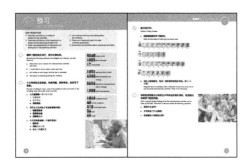

Prior knowledge

The focus of this unit is education, so students will have plenty of opportunities to practise and consolidate what they learned in Units 1–2 (in particular, talking about school subjects and activities, personal hobbies and interests), as well as to practise talking about the future. Ensure that students are able to recall vocabulary to do with these areas.

Icebreaker activity

Ask students to call out the names of extracurricular activities/clubs offered by your school – and any others they wish were available. You may need to help students with the Chinese names. Keep the list on the board for use later on in the lesson.

Lesson activities

1 Speaking

Students should do this activity in pairs, writing down their translations before reading them out. Where a sentence contains a time expression, remind them of the word order: time → place → event/action.

Where students have come up with different translations, go through these as a class and point out which are incorrect and why.

Sample answers

a. 妈妈要我为下学期选两项课外活动。

b. 明年我想上一门网络课程。

c. 我哥哥的大学生活过得很愉快。

d. 爸爸很喜欢参加周末的义工活动。

2 Listening

Remind students to read the questions and all the answer options carefully, jotting down their pinyin, before starting the activity.

Transcript

小文：劳拉，你交了大学入学申请的表格吗？

劳拉：还没有，小文。我还在想要读哪个专业。你呢？

小文：我早就交了。我想读计算机学。

劳拉：为什么你对这个专业特别感兴趣？

小文：我觉得电脑科学和网络世界很有趣。我以前参了不少和网络有关的课外活动，例如网络校际交流。我还去了老人院做义工，教老人上网呢！

劳拉：希望你申请成功！

小文：谢谢！我现在很期待未来的大学生活。你快填好申请表格，我们一起进大学吧！

Answers

a. i b. ii c. i

3 Writing

For part a, ask students for the meaning of each radical – they should recognise all except for 夕 (evening).

For part b, you can use the list of activities students wrote for the icebreaker activity as prompts.

Sample answer for part b

我最喜欢的课外活动是话剧社，因为我喜欢演戏。

4 Speaking

Remind students to give their reason when answering question c. Listen to students' conversations and provide support as necessary.

Sample answers

a. 我叫李露西。　　b. 我今年参加了划船社。

c. 我觉得划船社很棒，一方面可以锻炼身体，另一方面可以亲近大自然。

Further differentiation

Find and show students some pictures of after-school clubs or activities in your school. Ask them to choose a picture and write one or two sentences describing what is going on.

 Give students pre-written sentences with blanks and some alternatives from which to choose the correct terms.

 Students choose a picture and write a sentence describing what is happening, plus another sentence saying whether it is something they have done, and whether they enjoyed it.

8.2 课外活动 Extracurricular activities

Icebreaker activity

Ask students if they have done any volunteering or community activities out of school hours. If they have, ask them to mime the activity (in pairs if necessary) for the rest of the class to guess what it is. Write out the Chinese translation of any unfamiliar activities on the board for students to learn. Leave the list on the board as it will come in handy later on in the lesson.

Lesson activities

1 Reading

Even if students don't understand every single character in each vocabulary term, they should recognise enough verbs and nouns to match the terms with the correct pictures. Prompt students by asking them to find the verbs (给/讲，发，清洁) in each term. Point out that 义卖 is a noun, but 卖 on its own means "to sell".

Answers

a. i 给老人讲故事　　b. iii 发传单

c. iv 义卖　　d. ii 清洁沙滩

2 Reading

Remind students to read the questions first, noting the key words to help them look for the relevant answers:

a. 以前参加过 asks about the past; b. 今年打算参加 asks about the future; c. 邀请谁 asks who to invite.

Answers

a. 他以前从来没有参加过社区服务活动。

b. 去老人院给老人讲故事、清洁沙滩、发健康知识的传单和义卖筹款。

c. 他要邀请日晴、汤姆、小明一起参加。

 You can also re-use the diary entry to create a true-or-false activity for students.

3 Listening

Remind students to read the questions carefully before listening to the recording. The first two questions are asking for activities that the speakers haven't taken part in (没有参加). Some students may find the last question challenging, as the recording lists activities Zhijun is doing with other friends, but the question specifically asks for two activities Zhijun is doing *with* Sammy.

Students may not be familiar with the term 书法 from question a. Explain it means "calligraphy". Show them some pictures or videos of people doing Chinese calligraphy if there is time.

Transcript

心美：志军，你去年参加了哪些课外活动？

志军：心美，我去年参加了很多课外活动，例如：摄影、爬山和画画。你呢？

心美：我去年和前年参加了歌唱协会和跳舞协会。我学跳舞和唱歌学了两年了。今年想试一试参加不同的活动。

志军：我今年打算参加一些社区服务活动，例如：去老人院给老人讲故事、清洁沙滩、发健康知识的传单。不如我们一起参加吧，好吗？

心美：好啊！我觉得去老人院给老人讲故事比较有意义。我们一起去吧！

志军：好吧，我和你一起去老人院。小明和我一起清洁沙滩。他参加这个活动参加了两年。汤姆会和我一起参加发传单和义卖这两个活动，他参加这两个活动参加了六个月。

心美：唔…我也想试一试参加义卖活动，那我们就一起参加这两个活动吧。

志军：好的。

Answers

a. iii 书法　　**b.** iii 摄影　　**c.** ii 两年

d. i 义卖和去老人院给老人们讲故事。

Speaking

Students can use the list of volunteering and community activities from the icebreaker to help them with this speaking activity.

Sample answers

a. 我今年参加了社区数学协会 (community maths club) 的活动。

b. 我想试一试帮助小朋友们学习数学。

c. 我参加这个活动已经三个月了。

This activity provides a good opportunity to consolidate students' understanding of the use of past, present and future tense. After they have discussed and answered the questions in pairs, ask students (as a class) how they would answer the questions if they were asked what activity they would like to do *next summer* and for how long they would like to do it.

Writing

Again, students can refer to the list from the icebreaker for ideas for this activity. Remind students they are writing an email to a friend, so they need to include elements such as the greeting and sign-off.

Sample answer

吉姆你好，

今天我们全班同学到郊区的一个孤儿院 (orphanage) 去了。我们跟那里的孤儿 (orphans) 一起唱歌跳舞，我们还教他们学英文。我们带了很多点心送给孩子们。我觉得这个活动很有意义，晚上回到家，我特别感谢爸爸妈妈，觉得自己很幸运。以后我还要再参加这样的活动。

志军

Assessment suggestion

 In pairs or groups of 3–4 students design a new school club, using the "Design a new school club" worksheet from the CD-ROM.

They need to discuss an idea for a new club or society. It could be to promote a hobby or a social or environmental cause. Students should consider:

- 为什么你想组织这个协会？
- 这个协会的目的是什么？
- 这个协会叫什么？
- 协会会员在那里能做什么？
- 活动在哪里举行？
- 协会经费从 (running costs) 哪里来？

Explain that you will be listening to the discussion and encouraging participation. This is an opportunity to assess students' verbal skills.

Students can design a poster promoting the club and give a short presentation, with each member of the group reporting on one aspect of their plan. Students can vote for the most appealing new club.

Homework suggestion

 Ask students to find out about the work of one local charity or community organisation, and write a short paragraph covering:

- 这个慈善机构／组织叫什么?
- 他们的目的是什么?
- 他们会举行什么活动?

8.3 校际交流 Going on a school exchange programme

Lesson activities

1 Reading

To pick the correct mode of transport, students need to be aware of the distances between the places mentioned. If necessary, show them a map of China.

 For scenario iii, draw students' attention to the sentence "我买不到机票". Ask how they think this affects their answer.

Answers

i. c   **ii.** b   **iii.** a

2 Reading

Use this activity to revise language for describing past and future events. After students have read the passage, ask them if it is about a past or future event – how do they know? (Answer: the use of 打算). Encourage them to give reasons for the false statements.

Answers

a. 对   **b.** 错 (他会坐飞机去。)

c. 对

d. 错 (他会和那儿的学生一起唱中国的京剧。)

e. 对   **f.** 对   **g.** 错 (汤姆也很期待。)

3 Listening

Before the activity, remind students to study the questions and pictures, and jot down the pinyin of the answer options if it helps them to listen for the answers in the recording.

Transcript

志军：玛莉，你想去哪儿参加校际交流活动?

玛莉：啊, 志军, 我想去中国的学校和那儿的学生交流，当一个交换学生。

志军：为什么你要去那儿当交换生?

玛莉：因为我想了解中国文化，所以我要去和那儿的人交流。

志军：你会住在宿舍还是酒店里?

玛莉：我会住在学生宿舍里，方便和那儿的学生交流。

志军：你会去那儿多久?

玛莉：大约一个星期吧!

志军：你坐什么交通工具去?

玛莉：我坐飞机去。

志军：你到了那儿会做什么?

玛莉：我会表演戏剧和跳舞给那儿的学生看。

志军：除了表演之外，你还会做什么?

玛莉：我还会去那儿学中文。

Answers

a. iii   **b.** i   **c.** ii   **d.** ii

 For extra practice, re-use the transcript and turn it into a reading comprehension activity by adding your own questions.

4 Speaking and Writing

For part a, walk around the classroom and listen to students' conversations; provide support as needed.

For part b, ask students which two features they need to include when writing an email or a letter to parents (answer: they need to use the correct opening and ideally sign off using 敬上 to show respect).

 If necessary, you can use the sample answer below as a basis for a gap-filling activity.

Sample answer

爸爸妈妈好，

我今天坐地铁到上海中学参加校际交流活动。这几天我会跟同学们一起住在学校宿舍里。今天我拿到了节目单，我们早上会学中文，下午做许多文化活动，例如书法、画画、太极拳、做中国菜等等。我觉得活动安排得很充实，每一天都很忙。

儿子 敬上

 Find and show students a video clip of "Joy Dancing Beijing", an annual international youth art exchange event that began in 2012. It gathers young performing groups from all over the world to showcase their native culture. After the video, have a class discussion on whether a dance extravaganza is a good way to bring cultures together.

Homework suggestion

 Students devise a five-day cultural exchange programme for some students from China visiting their school. They need to prepare a leaflet in Chinese giving a brief description of the school facilities; a timetable outlining the activities (2 each day) and a brief description of each activity.

8.4 做义工 Volunteering

Lesson activities

1 Reading

This is a good activity for checking understanding of grammar and word order. Note: for c and d there are several ways to re-order the sentences.

 To make the activity easier, join up some of the fragments yourself first, so there are fewer fragments for students to re-order.

Answers

a. 玛莉计划带同学去参加社区服务活动。

b. 心美、小明和玛莉都会做义工。

c. 心美带同学去老人院，负责帮老人打扫卫生。

　心美负责带同学去老人院帮老人打扫卫生。

d. 小明带同学去沙滩，负责清洁。

　小明负责带同学去沙滩清洁。

　小明负责带同学去清洁沙滩。

e. 玛莉负责义卖活动。

2 Reading

Point out that because the text is in note form and the sentences very short, it is especially important to pay attention to the punctuation to see where one sentence ends and another starts.

Answers

a. 四人参加　　　　b. 三人不参加

c. 一共十七人

d. C班的同学参加了清洁沙滩和义卖的活动。

e. 去参加义工活动的时间。

  For extra practice, re-use the text in a true-or-false activity, making up your own statements.

3 Listening

Start by asking students to look at the photos and the statements below, and tell you which activity is represented in each (a. storytelling; b. charity sale; c. beach cleaning).

For the listening activity itself, students need to write down the name of the contact person for each activity.

Transcript

a. 约翰：我想带同学参加清洁沙滩活动，我得先和学校的老师联系。

　问：约翰想带同学参加清洁沙滩活动，他得先和谁联系？

b. 海伦：我想组织义卖活动，然后邀请同学参加。我得先和慈善机构的职员联系。

　问：海伦想组织义卖活动，她得先和谁联系？

c. 小华：我想带同学去老人院给老人讲故事。我得先和老人院联系。

问：小华想带同学去老人院给老人讲故事，他得先和谁联系？

Answers

a. 学校的老师   **b.** 慈善机构职员

c. 老人院职员

4 Speaking

Ask students how they know if the questions listed require them to talk about past or future events. Encourage students to use their own activities when giving their answers.

 Encourage students to give reasons when answering question a.

Answers

a. 我今年会参加一个陪老人散步的义工活动。

b. 我打算跟我的好朋友丁卡、天伟、尼玛一起去参加。

c. 这个活动是由学校的爱心慈善社团负责计划和组织的。

5 Writing

While students can design posters about activities mentioned in recent lessons, encourage them to think of new activities using vocabulary they already know: 陪老人散步 (walking with elderly people), 清洁街道活动 (cleaning the streets), 陪孩子读书 (reading with children), 慈善糕点义卖 (charity bake sale).

Sample answer

陪老人散步

*把阳光与爱心带给孤单的老人

*陪老人散步、聊天、下棋

*每周六早上10:00在校门口集合

主办单位：爱心慈善社团

联系方式：丁卡（手机：987654321）

微信：爱心慈善社团

Assessment suggestion

Give students the reading comprehension worksheet (on the CD-ROM) to complete. There are two versions for ability-differentiation purposes.

Homework suggestion

 Students research their favourite charity and prepare a presentation for the class. They should consider:

- 这个慈善机构叫什么？
- 为什么你喜欢这个机构？
- 机构的目标是什么？
- 机构举行什么活动？
- 你可以怎样支持这个机构？

8.5 大学专业 University fields of study

Lesson activities

1 Reading

Students should be able to work out 医学 is the study of medicine based on the character 医; they should also work out 心理学 means psychology easily since 心, meaning "heart", is also related to thinking and feeling, while 理 means "reasoning" or "theory".

Answers

a. iii   **b.** i   **c.** iv   **d.** ii

 Students can practise writing the characters by making sentences using the structure: 我想读…… or 我不想读…….

Language and culture

Point out the nuance between 科 (subject) and 系 (faculty/department/studies). The latter is more commonly used when talking about higher education.

  2 **Reading**

Encourage students to give reasons for the false statements.

> **a.** 错 (她做的是了解同学打算读的大学专业的调查。)
> **b.** 对 **c.** 对 **d.** 错 (都想读工程。)
> **e.** 对 **f.** 对 **g.** 对 **h.** 错 (最多,有十四人。)

Carry out a survey of what students want to study or do after finishing school. Write the results on the board and ask students to make sentences from them.

  3 **Listening**

This activity combines multiple-choice with gap-filling: make sure students read the sentences and the answer options carefully first. They can jot down the pinyin of the answer options to help listen for the answers.

Transcripts

a. 问:你为什么想读医科?

丁卡:因为我想研究医学,我希望将来可以帮助很多病人。

问:丁卡为什么想读医科?

b. 问:你为什么读工科?

天伟:因为我想进大学的工程系,我希望将来可以建大楼。

问:天伟为什么想读工科?

c. 问:心美,你哥哥打算读中国大学的哪一个专业?

心美:因为哥哥希望以后能伸张正义,所以他打算读中国大学的法律系。

问:心美的哥哥打算读中国大学的哪一门专业?

d. 问:你不想读医科吗?

娜依玛:我不想读医科,我想读法律。

问:娜依玛想读哪一科?

e. 问:你正在读什么学位?研究什么?

汤姆爸爸:我正在读博士学位,研究心理学。

问:汤姆的爸爸正在读什么学位?他研究什么?

Answers

a. ii, iii **b.** i, iii **c.** ii **d.** ii **e.** i, v

  4 **Speaking**

Start by reading the questions together, and ask students to tell you how they know question a is to do with the present (use of 现在) while questions b and d are to do with the future (use of 将来／想).

Sample answers

a. 我现在读的是理科。

b. 我将来想在大学读电脑工程。

c. 因为我喜欢用电脑帮人们解决问题。

d. 我将来读完学士,我还想读硕士,然后我想先做些工作再去读博士。

  5 **Writing**

Before the activity, ask students to tell you what they need to include and what tone they should adopt when writing a diary entry.

Sample writing

十月三日 星期一 下雨
我现在心情很恶劣,因为刚刚跟妈妈吵了一架。我现在读的是文科,我对政治和经济都特别有兴趣。但是妈妈认为我的性格比较适合读教育,将来当老师。所以当我告诉她我要去大学读政治外交的时候,她立刻反对。我希望妈妈能够好好听听我的想法。

Cultural spotlight

Ask students why they think the ancient Chinese particularly valued the study of literature (文学), history (历史), poetry (诗歌), and philosophy (哲学). Do students agree these subjects are still valuable in today's society?

Further differentiation

Use the sample writing in Activity 5 to reinforce students' understanding of adjectival stative verbs.

 Students underline all the adjectival stative verbs in the diary entry.

 Students rewrite the diary entry, using different subjects and adjectival stative verbs.

Homework suggestion

Students compile a list of pros (好处) and cons (坏处) of a person going to college or university straight after secondary or high school.

8.6 入学申请 Applying to university

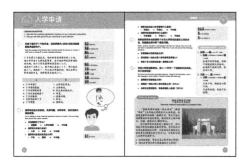

Icebreaker activity

Ask students what factors are important in a university or college application. Write their suggestions in Chinese on the board. Do they think it is the same for all subjects? Is it harder to get into some universities or colleges than others? What about vocational or creative courses?

Avoid alienating students by emphasising too much traditional academic subjects. (Vocational training is covered separately in Lesson 8.9.)

Lesson activities

1 Reading

Students need to be sure that the sentences not only make sense grammatically but are also logical and accurate according to what they have read in the passage.

Answers
a. i **b.** vi **c.** v **d.** ii **e.** vii **f.** iv **g.** iii

2 Listening

Remind students to read the questions and answer options first. They can jot down the pinyin of the answer options if it helps them listen for the correct answers.

Transcript

丽莎：安迪，大学考试的成绩怎么样？

安迪：还可以。你呢，丽莎？

丽莎：我也是。你想申请读哪一个专业？

安迪：我想读工程。我刚刚交了入学申请表了，现在正在等待去面试。

丽莎：我想申请读心理系。我昨天去了大学参加面试了。

安迪：太好了。你的面试怎么样？

丽莎：我觉得我的面试很顺利。因为在面试前有认真准备，所以我对这次的大学申请很有信心。我相信只要肯认真准备，就有机会进大学。

安迪：说得好，丽莎。对了，听说娜依玛明天就要参加大学面试了，她有点害怕，她还说如果不能通过这次面试，就不能进大学。你知道吗？

丽莎：安迪，你叫娜依玛不用担心。听说她成绩不错，只要她认真准备，就有机会通过面试。

安迪：对，只要肯认真准备，就不用怕！

Answers
a. ii **b.** i **c.** ii **d.** ii **e.** ii

3 Speaking

Before the activity, ask students how they know whether the questions are to do with past, present or future events. (Answer: terms like 刚才 and 了 indicate the speaker is referring to a past event.)

 You may want to write on the board a list of emotions (e.g. 有信心，紧张，认真，顺利，怕，担心，用功) to help students construct their answers.

Sample answers
a. 我觉得刚才的面试进行得很顺利，虽然我有点紧张。
b. 我对这一次的大学入学申请很有信心。
c. 这次面试我准备了六个月，我很认真。

4 Writing

Remind students they are writing a text message so they need to write concisely.

Sample writing

妈妈，我的面试很顺利，不用担心！我对这次大学入学申请很有信心，以前准备了的面试题目考官都问了。如果这次面试成功，真要感谢您和爸爸，因为您们一直陪我准备考试。丽莎

Cultural spotlight

Go through new vocabulary with students: 招生 (admissions), 主要渠道 (main channel), 省 (province), 直辖市 (municipalities), 综合 (integrated/combined), 状元 (top scorer in a public exam). Also explain that 清华 and 北大 are names of two top universities in China. (Note: the English name for 北大 is Peking University, not Beijing University.)

To encourage further discussion, show students a video clip (in English) *High School in China: inside of Chinese high schools*. This gives an overview of two top-performing high schools in China. Discuss with the class:

a. Is it a good idea to only choose between liberal arts or science in the final years of high school, in preparation for university?

b. What do they think of the statement "a nation's future is determined not on the battlefield, but rather in every classroom"?

c. Would they like to study under a high school system like the one in China?

Further differentiation

Students write some tips for their classmates on interview preparations and techniques. This is an opportunity to revise vocabulary from earlier units (e.g. home and school life, health and wellbeing).

Students can write a list of dos and don'ts for people about to attend a university interview.

Students should also write a few sentences to explain why each point should be followed.

Homework suggestion

Students use their imagination to write a short personal statement saying why they want to study a particular subject at a particular university or college. It doesn't matter whether or not it is true!

8.7 大学生活 Life at university

Icebreaker activity

Ask students what they are most looking forward to about university/college life. Write their reasons on the board in Chinese.

Lesson activities

 1 Reading

Use this activity to remind students of some of the differences between Chinese and English word order.

For students who are struggling with this activity, write out the correct answers in Chinese on the board (but jumbled up) to make it easier.

Answers

a. France (法国), not America (美国): 吉姆去了**法国**的大学当交流生。

b. A doctorate (博士), not a master's degree (硕士)：小强打算将来读**博士**。

c. Dance society (舞蹈协会), not the Green Society (绿色协会)：读大学的时候，静儿参加了**舞蹈协会**。

d. Living with his parents (跟父母住在一起), not in a dormitory (住在学校宿舍)：家明读大学时跟父母住在一起。

e. Revised at home (在家里温习), not in the library (图书馆)：读大学的时候，丽莎每天在家里温习。

 2 Reading

Encourage students to give reasons for the false statements.

Answers

a. 错 (只有一年多)

b. 错 (静儿参加了舞蹈协会和绿色协会。)

c. 错 (他常和中国室友交流。)

d. 错 (他每天都去图书馆。)

e. 错 (他打算将来当医生。)

f. 对

g. 错 (他去了美国的大学。)

After the activity, ask a few students to say whose university life from the passage they envy most, and explain why.

3   Listening

Remind students to read the questions and answer options first. They can jot down the pinyin of the answer options if it helps them listen for the answers.

Transcript

菲菲：小强，你去了美国一个多月了，还好吗？

小强：还不错。我觉得在美国当交流生很有意思。这里的老师和同学都很好。啊，菲菲，听说你最近读书很用功，将来有什么打算？

菲菲：我正在读法律，要是成绩好的话，我毕业以后就会去英国或美国读硕士。你呢？将来有什么打算？

小强：我下一年可能到中国或日本当交流生。还没有想到毕业以后的打算。等回来再说吧！不过，我爸爸说要是我毕业以后不读硕士的话，就会考虑让我去找工作。

Answers

a. i b. ii c. ii d. i

4   Speaking and Writing

For part a, students can either list what they want to achieve academically or list some extracurricular activities they would like to try.

For part b, students can refer to the reading passage in Activity 2 for ideas.

Sample answers

a. 学西班牙语、学习吉他、参加义工队、交很多朋友。

b. i 我很期待大学生活。

ii 考上大学之后，我会参加吉他协会、慈善协会和外语协会等等课外活动。

iii 考上大学之后，我打算到巴黎去当交流生，好好学法语。

iv 考上大学之后，我打算先住学校宿舍，再跟一些好朋友一起租房子住。

Homework suggestion

Tell students to imagine they have just started their first term at college. Unfortunately, they are finding their course pretty challenging, and they are missing home terribly! Ask students to write an email to their family, explaining how they are feeling and why they are homesick.

8.8 网络课程 Online learning

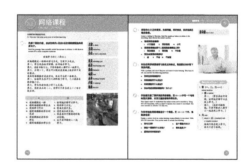

Icebreaker activity

Ask students if they have ever learned anything (e.g. a new skill or language) using an app or via an online program (if they haven't, ask them to say what people might want to learn online); ask them why people might or might not use apps to learn new things. Write their ideas on the board, and translate them into Chinese for future reference.

Lesson activities

1   Reading

The reading passage contains a fair amount of new vocabulary, so it is best to go through it with the class first.

Answers

a. ii **b.** i **c.** vi **d.** v **e.** iii **f.** iv

Compare the reading passage with the students' suggestions from the icebreaker activity – what similarities and differences are there between the two lists?

  2 **Listening**

Remind students to read the questions first to get a sense of what to listen for. They can also jot down the pinyin of the answer options to help them listen for the answers.

Transcript

劳拉：小文，听说你爸爸在读网络课程，他觉得怎么样?

小文：爸爸白天上班，只能在晚上学习，他觉得网络学习很方便。他也觉得网络课程很有趣。因为在网络上的同学年龄都不一样，所以大家分享的看法也很不一样。劳拉，你也想读网络课程吗?

劳拉：我还在考虑。网络学习是很方便。但是，它也有一些缺点。第一，网络课程没有真正的互动，我还是喜欢和同学面对面交流。第二，我喜欢在大学环境下学习，因为可以和同学多一点儿情感交流，可以交到真正的朋友。

小文：是的，网络课程有优点，也有缺点，没有最好的课程，只有最适合自己课程，对不对?

劳拉：小文，你真聪明!

Answers

a. i **b.** ii **c.** iii

  3 **Speaking**

Refer students back to the ideas gathered during the icebreaker activity for inspiration.

Sample answers

a. 我听过也上过网络课程。

b. 我认为网络课程最大的优点就是很方便，在任何地方、任何时候都可以学习。

c. 网络课程的缺点是因为跟老师和同学没有实际的互动，有时候学习的效果不是很好。

d. 我还是会考虑读网络课程，因为我每天很忙，放学后没有时间去其他地方上课。

  4 **Writing**

Remind students they are writing an email to a friend, giving them their opinion about something so the email needs to be friendly but informative.

Sample writing

小文你好，

我最近在读一个写作的网络课程，我觉得很方便，任何时候任何地点我都可以学习。老师录了很多教学影片，我有空的时候就看影片，写作业。不过网络课程也有一些缺点，我只能跟老师通过电邮讨论学习上的问题，没有面对面互动的机会。希望以上意见对你有用!

大明

 For extra practice, use the sample writing above as the basis for a reading comprehension activity. Devise your own list of questions for students to answer.

  5 **Writing**

Students can refer to the list of online learning ideas from the icebreaker for inspiration for their poster.

Start by asking students what makes a good poster (clear description of the activity being promoted; information about date, venue, cost; contact details).

Sample writing

网络课程：学习如何制作多媒体演示

对象：十年级以上的同学

课程时间：共四课，每课一小时。所有同学都有指定的网上导师，通过电邮与同学讨论学习上的问题。

费用：免费

联系人：电脑协会陈老师

Homework suggestion

Ask students to review an app or online program that teaches Chinese and write a report including a list of the program's pros and cons, with reasons.

8.9 职业培训 Vocational training

Icebreaker activity

If your school offers vocational courses, list them on the board (in English and in Chinese). Have a class discussion to find out which courses students would be most interested in and why.

Lesson activities

  Reading

Start by going through the pictures with students – see if they can work out their meanings in English. Next ask if they can guess the meanings just by looking at the characters. Expect students to recognise characters like 老 (old/the elderly), 建筑 (building/architecture), 健康 (health) and 美 (beauty). Explain what the character combinations represent. For example, 养 means "to look after or support", so 养老 means "to look after the elderly". 容 is to do with one's facial expression or complexion, so 美容 means "to beautify one's complexion".

Answers

a. iv **b.** i **c.** ii **d.** iii

  Reading

This passage contains a lot of new vocabulary, so it is advisable to go through it together as a class first. Encourage students to give reasons for the false statements.

 You could write a simplified version of the passage and turn it into a gap-filling activity, to help reinforce students' learning and understanding of the new vocabulary, verbs and adjectival stative verbs.

Answers

a. 错 (没有读大学的学生可以参加学徒培训计划。)

b. 错 (在培训的过程中，学生要学习和不同行业有关的技术。)

c. 对   **d.** 对

e. 错 (现在受学生欢迎的课程有传播和媒体行业、健康和美容行业、建筑行业、养老服务行业等等。)

f. 错 (三至四年)   **g.** 错 (政府提供津贴)

Take this opportunity to check students' understanding of some grammar features:

- Ask them to find an example in the passage where the sentence is describing two actions being done at once (一边学习，一边工作).

- Ask them to find an example where the sentence is describing something being put in place for the sake of something else (为了......而......).

- Ask them for the meanings of 等等, 通常.

- Ask them to explain the difference between 要 and 会.

3   **Listening**

Remind students to read the questions first so they know what to listen for. They can also jot down the pinyin of the answer options.

Transcripts

a. 问：你打算参加什么计划？

丽青：我打算参加学徒培训计划。

问：丽青打算参加什么计划？

b. 问：你每个星期要做什么？

小文：我每个星期要做实习工作。

问：小文每个星期要做什么？

c. 问：你每个星期要读什么？

森姆：我每个星期要读技术培训课。

问：森姆每个星期要读什么？

d. 问：你想参加什么课程？

阿健：我想参加传播和媒体行业课程，因为我将来想当记者。

问：阿健想参加什么课程？

e. 问：你想参加什么课程？

露西：我想参加养老护理行业课程，因为我希望将来可以帮忙照顾老人。

问：露西想参加什么课程？

f. 问：你想参加什么课程？

国华：我想参加建筑行业课程，因为我将来想建大楼。

问：国华想参加什么课程？

Answers

a. i **b.** i **c.** ii **d.** ii **e.** ii **f.** iii

 **4** **Speaking**

Go around the classroom listening to students' conversations and providing support as necessary. Encourage students to give reasons when answering question a.

Sample answers

a. 我对养老护理学徒培训课程感兴趣。

b. 参加了计划之后，我每个星期将会到养老院实习。

c. 我要培训两年。

 **5** **Writing**

Remind students that they are asked to make notes (笔记), so they don't need to write in full sentences. However, the content of their notes should still cover the questions raised in the Student Book.

Sample writing

- 刚刚看到学徒培训计划，高中毕业生都可以参加，参加之后每星期要到相关的机构一边工作一边学习。
- 受欢迎的行业：工程、电脑、美发、电子商务。
- 培训期：两年 (政府提供津贴)。
- 应该赶快报名参加!

Assessment suggestion

In no more than 150 characters, students explain whether they would prefer to go on an apprenticeship/vocational programme or go to university when they finish school, giving two reasons.

Homework suggestion

Students imagine they are a teacher responsible for running some new vocational courses in their school. They have been invited by the school radio station to promote the new courses. Students should write a one-minute dialogue between the teacher and the interviewer.

8.10 复习 Progress check

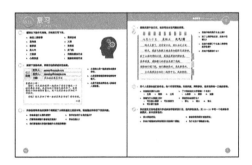

Lesson activities

 **1** **Reading**

This should be a fairly straightforward activity. For extra practice (and to check students' pronunciation), ask students to read out the phrases in Chinese.

Answers

a. storytelling for the elderly / to tell stories to old people

b. to clean the beach   **c.** to hand out leaflets

d. charity sale

e. faculty of medicine or medical studies

f. faculty of law   **g.** to travel by train

h. to travel by plane   **i.** faculty of engineering

j. communication and media industry

k. the faculty of psychology

l. health and beauty industry

2 Reading

Encourage students to give reasons for the false statements as well.

Answers

a. 错 (心美和她的同学一起去。)　　b. 对

c. 错 (她还会再去参加清洁沙滩活动。)

 Students can also draft a reply as Xiaoming, answering Sammy's questions.

3 Speaking

Encourage students to give reasons for their answers. Listen to students' conversations and look out in particular for incorrect use of grammar. Provide support as necessary.

Sample answers

a. 我会参加一些跟我的学习很不同的课外活动。

b. 我平时会在自己的房间温习，因为我读书的时候喜欢安静。

c. 我打算将来去南美洲的巴西当交流生。

d. 我会住在学校的学生宿舍，这样上课比较方便。

e. 我打算在大学的时候做一些冒险的事，例如去爬喜马拉雅山。

4 Reading and Writing

Remind students to read the questions first, so they know what they need to pay attention to. Encourage students to write in full sentences.

Sample answers

a. 她是坐飞机到上海去的。　b. 她住在学校的宿舍。

c. 她表演了戏剧还唱了歌。

d. 她很期待和上海的同学一起学中文。

 For extra practice, students can rewrite the diary entry, replacing the location, method of travel, accommodation, and activities with their own ideas. If necessary, provide a list of suggestions for them to choose from.

5 Listening

Remind students to read the questions first. Select a few volunteers to read out the answer options to check students' pronunciation.

Transcript

a. 问：你现在读什么科?

吉姆：我读理科。

问：吉姆现在读什么科?

b. 问：你将来想在大学读哪一个专业?

丁卡：我将来想在大学读医科。

问：丁卡将来想在大学读哪一个专业?

c. 问：为什么你想读工科?

汤姆：因为我希望将来可以读工程系。

问：汤姆为什么想读这个专业?

d. 问：你将来读硕士还是读博士?

菲菲：我将来会读硕士。

问：菲菲将来读什么?

Answers

a. ii　b. ii　c. iii　d. ii

 Ask students to write down a logical reason for each speaker's response in the recording.

6 Writing

For this activity, encourage students to use new language features they have learned in this unit, for example: 第一、第二 and 试一试.

Sample writing

大卫你好，

我觉得读大学和学徒培训计划各有好处。

大学有不少优点：第一，可以增长你的知识，激发你的思想。第二，可以让你认识一些志同道合的朋友。

学徒培训计划也有优点，因为它可以让你了解工作岗位需要的知识与技能。你一向喜欢电脑，我建议你试一试参加电脑方面的培训计划，也许会帮你将来找到好的工作。

我期待你的回复。

菲菲

Further differentiation

In 2015, the BBC made a documentary called *Are Our Kids Tough Enough? Chinese School* about a social experiment where a group of British students spent a month being taught by educators from China. Select a few suitable clips of the documentary on the internet and show students.

Students list pros and cons of the style of education shown in the documentary. They can comment on its impact on students' wellbeing, their exam performance, or the lives of the teachers.

Students write a short paragraph explaining whether and why they believe a more regimented style of schooling will prepare them better for school exams or life in university.

Assessment suggestion

 Ask students to complete one of the following:

1. Write a script for a speech entitled "为什么我喜欢做义工". The speech should cover: where they volunteer; the purpose of the organisation; what they do as a volunteer; why they enjoy helping there.

2. Tomorrow you have a college interview. Write a diary entry to say where you are going tomorrow, what will happen and how you are feeling.

事业和就业
CAREERS AND EMPLOYMENT

UNIT OBJECTIVES

- Discuss and compare different career options.
- Describe your dream job.
- Describe what people do on work placement.
- Discuss and compare gap-year activities.
- Describe the steps people take when job hunting.
- Learn what to say during a job interview.

9.1 预习 Unit introduction

Prior knowledge

This unit requires students to discuss past and present experiences as well as future plans, so do ensure they are comfortable using the correct tenses when writing/speaking. Students should be familiar with the names of a range of occupations (e.g. teacher, doctor, nurse, police, athlete, chef, care-home worker, shop assistant, bank clerk, lawyer). Revise them with students if necessary.

Be aware that some students may not feel comfortable talking about what their parents or guardians do for a living – do not insist that they share information with the rest of the class.

Icebreaker activity

Have a class discussion about some unusual jobs students have encountered. What did they involve? Encourage students to describe them in Chinese if possible. Write any new vocabulary on the board for future reference.

Lesson activities

1   Reading

This is a straightforward activity, as students will have come across all of the terms in previous units.

Answers

a. vi **b.** v **c.** i **d.** vii **e.** viii **f.** iii **g.** ii **h.** iv

2   Listening

Go through the questions and the answer options with the class. Select students to read them out so you can check their pronunciation. Explain any unfamiliar vocabulary. Remind students they can jot down the pinyin of the answer options to help them listen for the answers.

Transcript

a. 我是海伦，小的时候我很喜欢坐飞机，那时候我想当一名航空服务员。

b. 我是马克。我们家里开了一家餐馆，爸爸希望以后我做厨师，在自己家的餐馆工作。

c. 我是米娜。我们在中国北京旅游的时候参加了一个慈善活动，在那里我们看到了中国香港著名的电影演员周星驰。

d. 我是本杰明，在机场我把我的背包忘在了一个咖啡馆里，找不到了，还好机场的警察帮我找到了。

e. 我是日晴。今年夏天我打算和两个好朋友一起去咖啡馆做短期服务员。

Answers

a. iii **b.** iii **c.** i **d.** i **e.** iii

 You could re-use the transcript for a true-or-false activity. Create your own statements: students can give reasons for the false ones.

3   Writing

For part a, the strokes animation from the MGDB online dictionary is useful for showing students the sequences of writing individual characters.

For part b, ask students what part of speech these missing characters are (they are verbs). See if students are able to choose the correct verbs without help.

Answers

a. 想 **b.** 做 **c.** 训练 **d.** 想 **e.** 读 **f.** 当

Language and culture

When it comes to describing someone's occupation in everyday Chinese, 做 and 当 can be used interchangeably, in that broadly speaking both mean "to work as". However, there are differences in terms of the characters' meanings. While 做 means "to act/work (as)" or "to be", 当 actually means "to take responsibility" or "be in charge of". A good way to remember the difference is to learn the idiom: 敢做敢当, which is used to describe someone who is not only willing to take action (做) but is also willing to accept responsibility (当) for it.

4  Reading

DP Remind students to read the statements first. This will help them to find what they are looking for. Encourage them to give reasons for the false statements.

Answers

a. 对	**b.** 错 (广告没有提电脑老师)
c. 对 (5–12岁的小学生)	**d.** 对
e. 对	**f.** 错 (发邮件)

Further differentiation

Students share their experiences of doing a part-time job, holiday job, or volunteering.

 Students write a couple of sentences to say what they did, when they did it, and for how long.

 Students imagine they have just started a new holiday job or volunteering position. They write a diary entry about their first day, and whether they enjoyed it.

9.2 职业选择 Choosing your career

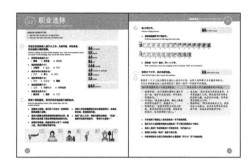

Lesson activities

1  Listening

Before the activity, go through all the jobs listed in the answer options with the class; make sure students are familiar with the pronunciation.

Transcript

a. 我叫苏菲。我们家有六口人。我的爸爸是一位建筑师。

b. 妈妈是一名导游，常常去不同的地方。

c. 爷爷以前是农民，现在已经不工作了。

d. 哥哥喜欢动物，他是一名兽医，给小动物们看病。

e. 姐姐的英文很好，在中学当英文老师。

f. 我现在在餐馆做服务员。

Answers

a. iii **b.** iii **c.** i **d.** i **e.** iii **f.** i

2  Reading

Before the activity, check that students know what each of the pictures represents (a. 飞机上的服务员，b. 作家，c. 兽医，d. 导游，e. 农民). This activity is about word association – students are expected to pick out the key vocabulary in each description and use it to work out what occupation it is describing.

Answers

a. iii **b.** iv **c.** v **d.** i **e.** ii

 Get students to make up sentences for these occupations: 建筑师，老师，演员，警察.

Writing

For part a, point out the meanings of the radicals of both characters (贝: shell/cowry; 金: gold) – both are money related. Ask students what part of speech 赚钱 is. (It is a verb–noun combination.)

For part b, ask students to write a sentence giving their own point of view on the importance of earning money/earning a living.

Sample answer for part b

赚钱固然重要，但金钱不能买来幸福！

 Ask students to translate the sample answer sentence.

Reading and Speaking

This reading passage contains different points of view about a subject.

 The layout of the passage may be confusing to some students. You may need to tell students to read the bulleted list on the left before reading the list on the right.

Students can either write their answers or you can select students in the class to answer the questions verbally.

Answers

a. 工程师、教师和护士都是让人快乐的职业。

b. 三个让老师快乐的理由：第一，和孩子们在一起让老师觉得快乐。第二，看到学生们学习进步，老师也觉得很开心。第三，老师帮助学生理解问题的时候也会觉得高兴。

c. 当老师的两个缺点：第一，老师忙的时候，周末和晚上都要工作。第二，老师也感受到学生考试的压力，学生考不好时，就会认为自己教得不好。

d. 开心、高兴

e. 我觉得找工作一定要做一份自己喜欢的职业。人们通常会努力做自己喜欢的工作，不怕辛苦也不觉得无聊，这样也可以把工作做得好。

Assessment suggestion

This follows on from Activity 4. Ask students to write 100–120 characters expressing their own views on whether or not teaching is a happy profession. They should not repeat any reasons from the passage.

Homework suggestion

Ask students to choose an occupation from the following list, then write 3 advantages and 3 disadvantages of it: 科学家, 建筑师, 音乐家, 记者, 护士, 演员

9.3 我的梦想工作 My dream job

Lesson activities

Writing

Before students begin the translation task, ask what part of speech the missing words are (a. adverb, b. adjectival stative verb, c. measure word, d. location noun, e. action verb).

Answers

a. 将来   b. 成功   c. 名   d. 市中心   e. 开

Listening

Go through the questions and answer options with the class before playing the recordings to students.

Transcript

a. 我是米娜的姐姐。星期六和学校放假的时候我都会去市区的一家时装店做兼职售货员。时装店里星期六是最忙的时候，因为周六有很多人逛街。

我现在在读时装设计，希望以后成为时装设计师，所以我觉得在时装店工作对我以后找工作会有帮助。

b. 我是康纳，来自苏格兰的爱丁堡。现在是剑桥大学历史专业的三年级学生。

在暑假里我通常都会做兼职。剑桥城因为有世界著名的剑桥大学和美丽的康河，每年特别是夏季有很多游客来这里参观，所以兼职工作很容易找。

我最喜欢的兼职是给游客们一边划船一边讲剑桥的历史和英国文化。我喜欢遇到来自世界各地的不同的人。

Answers

a. ii **b.** ii **c.** i **d.** iii **e.** iii

 Play the recordings again, and ask:

- 根据录音A，为什么周六是店里最繁忙的一天？
- 根据录音A，在时装店工作对姐姐有什么好处？
- 根据录音B，康纳喜欢一边划船一边做什么？
- 根据录音B，每年什么时候有很多游客到剑桥？

Language and culture

The people who first transliterated Cambridge into Chinese are said to have come from the Fujian and Guangdong area (闽粤一带). The pronunciation of 剑 in Fujian and Cantonese dialects is similar to "Cam", and the name 剑桥 is used to this day. In his poem 再别康桥, early 20th-century writer Xu Zhimo (徐志摩) referred to Cambridge as 康桥, since 康 in Mandarin sounds more similar to "Cam". This latter transliteration is not used often today. That said, the River Cam is more commonly referred to as 康河!

3 📖 Reading

Take time to read this long passage with students before the activity. Ask volunteers to translate a sentence each to check understanding. Go through any unfamiliar vocabulary and sentence structures. Ask:

- Is Naima's work experience a past or future event? How do they know?

- Name two tasks Naima had to do during her work experience.

Answers

a. 对   **b.** 错 (她打算读历史和英文。)

c. 错 (律师楼在市区，离地铁站很近，坐十五分钟地铁就到。)   **d.** 对

e. 错 (她觉得这次实习对她的未来非常有帮助，给了她非常宝贵的工作经验。)

4 📖 🗨 Reading and Speaking

Go through the advert with the class before students discuss the questions in pairs. Ask them to say why this is a good advert or not. Is there anything else job hunters might like to know about the job that isn't mentioned in the advert?

Sample answers

a. 这份广告是招聘一名导游。

b. 我觉得这份工作挺吸引人的，因为地点在风景优美的巴厘岛，工作时间不长，工作内容基本上就是陪客人玩。

c. 这份工作必须会游泳和潜水，还必须会说中文和英文。

d. 我梦想的好工作的年薪是六位数，年假最少二十天，工作地点在一个漂亮的海岛上。

e. 我希望以后在国外工作。

f. 我最想做的工作是电脑动画设计师，因为我喜欢做些让自己也让别人都开心的有趣工作。

Further differentiation and assessment suggestion

Students complete the reading comprehension worksheet from the CD-ROM. There are two versions of the worksheet for ability-differentiation purposes.

Homework suggestion

 Ask students to prepare a short presentation about a well-known public figure whose job/work they admire. They need to cover:

- 那人做什么工作？   • 那人在哪儿工作？
- 说出三样那人令你敬佩的原因。

9.4 职业计划 Planning for my future career

Lesson activities

1 📖 Reading

Even though half of the vocabulary in this activity is new to students, they should be able to work out the meanings by studying the characters. For example, 牙医

means "dentist" since 牙 means "teeth" and 医 means "doctor" or "to heal"; 摄影师 means "photographer" since 摄影 means "to take photos".

Answers

a. iv **b.** v **c.** viii **d.** i **e.** x

f. ii **g.** ix **h.** vii **i.** iii **j.** vi

 In pairs, students choose 3 occupations from the list, and use the structure 我(不)喜欢做一名 …… 因为 …… to explain to each other whether or not they are interested in those occupations. For example, 我不喜欢做一名运动员，因为我不喜欢天天做运动。

2 Speaking

Remind students they need to use appropriate language (e.g. 现在, 以前, 将会) to indicate whether the sentence refers to a past, present or future event.

a. 他现在是一名中学教师。

b. 我现在教历史，但是我以前在大学读英语。

c. 她将会去马来西亚工作。

3 Listening

Before the activity, go through the pictures so students are clear what they represent (i. courier/postal worker; ii. photographer; iii. architect; iv. lawyer; v. swimmer).

Transcript

a. 我是玛莉。我喜欢拍照片，而且大家说我拍得不错。我以后要做摄影师。

b. 我是迪伦。我觉得快乐比赚钱更重要。我不喜欢压力大的工作，我中学毕业后可能会做一名邮递员。

c. 我是娜依玛，因为爸爸是律师，他希望我长大了也做律师。我也觉得律师工作不错。

d. 我是小亮。我从小就喜欢游泳，游得很快，经常参加各种游泳比赛。我希望以后成为游泳运动员。

e. 米娜：我是米娜。我喜欢画画，中学还学了手工设计，在大学我要读建筑学，毕业后我要做建筑师，设计很多新房子。

Answers

a. ii **b.** i **c.** iv **d.** v **e.** iii

4 Reading

Ask students to go through the statements before they read the conversation. For extra practice, put students in pairs and ask them to read out the dialogue. Encourage students to give reasons for the false statements.

Answers

a. 对 **b.** 错 (她还不知道怎么办。)

c. 错 (她小时候学过画画。)

d. 错 (她的老师说她可以做建筑师。)

e. 错 (米娜想试一试表演。) **f.** 对

5 Speaking

Tell students they can make up their plans if they are not sure yet what career they want to pursue. The important thing is to give logical answers.

Sample answers

a. 我将来想做旅行作家，因为我喜欢写作也喜欢旅行。

b. 这个工作可以在国内也可以在国外做，因为要到处旅行。

c. 要是有时间的话，我还打算多学几门外语，这样可以帮助我更了解各地文化，写作得更好。

d. 我的父母很支持我的决定，他们送我去上一些写作的课程，而且还帮我付学费。我很感谢他们。

Cultural spotlight

Go through the passage with the class, explaining any new vocabulary to students (创业基地: business-startup hub; 经济特区: Special Economic Zone; 加工: processing; 出售: to sell)

 Find and show students a video entitled *Learning tour in Shenzhen 2015: welcome to the Silicon Valley of hardware*, produced by Innovation is Everywhere. This video looks at some of the innovations that have come out of Shenzhen in recent years, and contains interviews with businesspeople and inventors. Ask students to make notes during the video, and select a few volunteers to repeat in Chinese some of the reasons given by the interviewees as to why Shenzhen is a good place for innovation.

Homework suggestion

Students write a paragraph of 80–100 characters using the sentence structure: 我有兴趣成为一名…… 因为…….

中文	拼音	英文
动物园	dòng wù yuán	Zoo
博物馆	bó wù guǎn	Museum
音乐节	yīn yuè jié	Music festival
银行	yín háng	Bank
汽车工厂	qì chē gōng chǎng	Car factory
咖啡馆	kā fēi guǎn	Coffee shop
医院	yī yuàn	Hospital
电视台	diàn shì tái	TV station
健身中心	jiàn shēn zhōng xīn	Gym
农场	nóng chǎng	Farm

9.5 实习经历 Work experience

Icebreaker activity

If students have done or will do work experience this academic year, have a group discussion about their placements. They can share what they most and least enjoyed, or what they want to gain from it. Write the names of job titles and places of work in Chinese on the board for students to learn.

If students are not doing work experience, discuss what they might like to do if they had the opportunity.

 **Reading**

Lesson activities

This activity serves as a kind of revision since students should recognise these places from previous units.

 If necessary, read out the Chinese name of each place slowly to help students work out the spelling and intonation.

2 🔊 Listening

Go through the pictures before playing the recordings so students know the workplaces they represent (i. in a gym, ii. in a hospital, iii. in a photographic studio, iv. on a farm, v. in a café).

Transcript

a. 我是杰西卡，我很喜欢骑马，我也会照顾马。最近我在一个农场实习，帮忙照顾马和羊。

b. 我是大海。我特别爱运动，希望以后做体育方面的工作。这个夏天放假我在我家附近的健身中心教人们做健身训练。

c. 我是阿得。我今年十五岁了，来自印度尼西亚。以后我想做一名咖啡师，做出印度尼西亚最好喝的咖啡。今年暑假我在雅加达的一家咖啡馆做兼职，一边工作，一边学做咖啡。

d. 我是日晴。我的爸爸妈妈都是医生，他们希望我以后也做医生。最近我在爸爸工作的医院里帮忙照顾生病的小朋友。

e. 我是本杰明。我喜欢拍照片和摄像。我希望以后在电视台或杂志社工作。这个星期一我刚刚开始在当地的电视台帮忙，跟着摄影师学拍照。

Answers

a. iv **b.** i **c.** v **d.** ii **e.** iii

3 📖 Reading

Read the advert with the class first. You can either ask volunteers to read out sentences in Chinese, or ask them to translate a sentence into English.

You may need to explain that 在校大学生 means students who are in the middle of their university studies. (在校 = in the middle of school)

Sample answers

a. 将培训两年

b. 培训地点在伦敦

c. 可以选择去中国的大城市，例如北京和上海的新生代银行工作。

d. 新生代银行在培训期间会提供很有吸引力的年薪和年假，努力在工作与生活中帮助学生。

e. 培训在每年六月到八月开始。

f. 希望未来去中国工作的最后一年的在校大学生，或者刚刚毕业的大学生。

4 Writing

For part a, start by displaying 申请 on the board, and ask a volunteer to write them again on the board. Ask the class if the volunteer's pen-stroke order was right. Then, show students the strokes animation from the MGDB online dictionary for the correct sequences of writing those characters.

For part b, encourage students to choose a workplace in a foreign city to write about – use this as an opportunity to practise country and city names.

Sample answer

我想申请去肯尼亚的医院实习，体验一下不同的文化生活。

5 Speaking

Remind students the activity requires them to talk about past and future events. As you listen to students' conversations, pay attention to any incorrect use of adverbs/time expressions and provide support as necessary.

Sample answers

a. 这几天我在各部门做一些简单的工作：影印、会议记录等等。

b. 我觉得你们的单位的工作效率很高。

c. 我希望将来的工作地方类似贵单位，所以来这里实习。

d. 我以前没有做过这方面的工作。

e. 我计划未来五年能在这一个行业做得很出色。

f. 我希望能够多参与一些实际的工作。

6 Writing

You can simplify the task by turning the sample answer below into a gap-filling activity. Either provide multiple answer options or ask students to fill in the blanks using their own words.

Sample writing

我在一家大书店工作实习，我每天要负责把新书上架，有时候要帮客户找书，有时候也帮忙收银。书店的老板和同事都很友善，常常帮助我。我在那里学到了分类整理，也学了如何跟陌生的客户相处，帮助他们解决问题。我觉得中学生应该做实习，体验职场生活。

Homework suggestion

Students pick one of the workplaces from Activity 2 and write about it. Include the following:

- 为什么有些人会选择在那个地方实习？

- 在那个地方做实习生你需要做哪些工作？

- 你会在那个地方学到哪些新的东西？

9.6 空档年 Taking a gap year

Lesson activities

1 Reading and Speaking

This activity checks students' understanding of nouns and verbs. Listen to students' conversations to check that they are able to articulate the differences.

Answers

a. iv (其他的都是跟工作有关的动词)

b. i (其他的都是职业)

c. i (其他的都是职业)

d. i (其他的都是职业)

e. i (其他的都是职业)

f. iv (其他的都是名词)

 Ask students to come up with an additional term for each of the categories. For example, category a is "verbs to do with work", so 赚钱 (to earn money) would fit.

  Writing

Go through the list with the class to make sure students understand what each verb means. Remind students not to just read the few characters before and after each blank; they need to read the whole sentence to get the full context.

Answers

a. 发生 **b.** 上 **c.** 找 **d.** 做 **e.** 去 **f.** 认识

g. 有 / 发生 **h.** 读

  **Listening**

Ask students to read the questions and the answer options first, jotting down the pinyin if that helps them listen for the answers in the recording. Remind them that what they hear may not match the answer-option phrases word for word.

Transcript

a. 我是日晴。如果有机会，我想我也会做空档年的。我想我可能会去非洲做义工，在那里我可以教小学生中文和英文。

b. 我是迪伦。我爱运动，上大学以前我会先做空档年。我想去澳大利亚旅游，去看那里奇怪特别的动物，在澳洲东海岸学习冲浪。

c. 我是米娜。中学毕业以后，我不打算立即上大学。因为我对中国历史感兴趣，所以我想去中国的很多古老的城市看一看。我最想去西安。

d. 我是家明。我想快点上大学，读完大学找工作。我不会做空档年，因为我觉得太浪费时间了。

e. 我是心美。我很想试一试空档年。中学毕业后我想去台湾生活一年,但是爸爸妈妈不支持我的想法，他们说上大学更重要。

Answers

a. iii **b.** ii **c.** i **d.** i **e.** iii

 **Reading**

Depending on the ability of your students, either ask them to read the passage by themselves, or read it as a class. You could ask volunteers to read out sentences in Chinese or you read them out yourself first, and ask students to translate them into English.

Answers

a. 空档年的活动一般有三类：义工、旅游和工作。

b. 空档年的好处：第一，参与环保的义工活动丰富了他们的生活。第二，尝试新东西，了解不同的文化。第三，学会独立，了解自己。

c. 有的年轻人选择工作，一方面赚取学费，另一方面在工作中学会独立。

d. 选择旅行的学生可以尝试一些不同的活动：例如去美国的夏威夷冲浪、在英国南部海港学习航海、在台湾骑自行车环岛旅行等等。

 Find and show students a short online video entitled *China Gap Year Fall 2015 – Nanjing University of Finance and Economics*. As they watch, ask them to jot down, in Chinese, the different activities the students participate in. If there is time, show them *Favorite Experience – NUFE Gap Year Spring 2016* and ask them to list, in Chinese, three memorable experiences given by the interviewees.

 **Speaking**

Listen to students' conversations and provide support as necessary. Encourage students to use vocabulary learned in previous units (e.g. to do with travelling, hobbies, interests), as well ideas from the video they just watched.

Sample answers

a. 在我的国家没有空档年。

b. 如果有，我要做空档年，我会选择旅行。

c. 我会去世界各地旅行。

d. 我希望通过旅行可以体验各种各样的文化。

e. 我会学一些简单的法语和西班牙语为我的旅行做准备。

f. 我的朋友都认为我很有勇气。

g. 我的父母都很支持我的想法，他们愿意给我财力帮助。

Assessment suggestion

DP Turn the transcript from Activity 3 into a true-or-false reading comprehension exercise by writing your own statements.

Homework suggestion

Students imagine they are about to start their gap year and that this is their last night at home. They write a diary entry describing their feelings as they embark on their adventure.

9.7 个人技能 My personal skills

Lesson activities

1 Reading

Students should recognise these terms from previous units so it shouldn't take too long to complete this task.

Answers

a. iii	**b.** v	**c.** ii
d. i	**e.** iv	

After the activity, ask students what they think these terms have in common. (Answer: they are all skills employers look for.) Can they think of any more?

2 Writing

Start by going through the verbs with the class, asking what each one means. Remind students to read the whole sentence to get the context, to help them choose the most appropriate verb to fill in the blank.

Answers

a. 说 **b.** 用 **c.** 开 **d.** 做 **e.** 教 **f.** 擅长

Students can make additional sentences using each of these verbs.

3 Listening

Get students to read the answer options first, and group them as verbs, jobs, places, directions, events. They should then read the sentences in the Student Book, and decide which category each blank is likely to be. Students can jot down the pinyin to help them listen out for the answers. Remind them that what they hear in the recording may not match the sentences in the Student Book word-for-word, so they should listen to the end of each clip before filling in the blanks.

Transcript

a. 有的学生不爱说话，所以在暑假里他们有的做兼职导游，有的做兼职售货员，因为这些工作帮助他们更好地和人交流。

b. 暑假里的工作机会很多，有的是在博物馆组织活动，有的是在音乐节帮忙，这些工作锻炼了学生们的组织能力。

c. 小亮是家里的独生子，从小想要什么东西，想做什么事情，父母都会给他。为了让小亮更有爱心，他的爸爸今年会带着他一起去中国西南的山区小学做义工，给山里的孩子们上英文课。

Answers

a. i 导游 ii 售货员 iii 交流

b. iv 博物馆 v 音乐节 vi 组织

c. vii 西南 viii 给

4   Reading and Writing

Part a checks students' understanding of the features of an email and the order in which the elements should appear. It is a good opportunity to revise ways of greeting people.

For part b, ask students to read the questions first and note the key words in each one to help them work out what to look for in the text: a. 什么工作感兴趣; b. 读……专业; c. 什么教课经验; d. 教……科目; e. 语言; f. 形容自己.

Answer for part a

To: 张教授

尊敬的张教授：您好

我的名字是康纳，我来自英国。我今年刚刚从剑桥大学历史专业毕业。我以前在英国的游学夏令营里教过中国学生。除了教英文，我还可以教英国历史。我是一个工作认真努力的人，热爱教师工作，能很好地和学生交流，而且我还会说一点汉语。我在您学校的网站上看到你们需要两个英文老师。我对这个工作很感兴趣。

请您把工作信息用邮件发给我，可以吗？非常感谢！期待您的回复

祝好。

康纳 六月一日

Answers for part b

i. 康纳对英文老师这个工作感兴趣。

ii. 他大学读了历史专业。

iii. 他曾经在英国的游学夏令营里教过中国学生。

iv. 他可以教英文和英国历史。

v. 他会说英文和一点汉语。

vi. 他说他是一个工作认真努力的人，热爱教师工作，能很好地和学生交流。

 **Writing**

Take this opportunity to explain the features of a formal letter, in terms of how to address the recipient [1]; ways of greeting someone [2]; introducing who you are and the purpose of this letter [3]; giving examples of the skills you have [4]; and how to sign off [5]. You could copy the sample answer as an example to show the class.

Sample writing

[1] 尊敬的领导：

[2] 您好！

[3] 我是爱心中西医学院的应届本科毕业生。结合中医和西医，帮助病人解除痛苦，一直是我的梦想。

[4] 我在大学里不仅上了西医的课程，还做了中医的训练，我的成绩都是优等。我在实习期间，病人对我的评论是有耐心、有责任感。我在学校参加了许多社团，我擅长与团队相处。贵医院中西医并重，正是我理想的工作地点。

[5] 随信附上我的个人简历，希望能够与您面谈。
此致

敬礼

求职人：李大文

2017年7月1日

Language and culture

When writing a formal letter or email in Chinese, it is important to consider the position of your recipient. If the recipient is in a senior position, or superior to you, for example a teacher or advisor, then it is especially important to use the appropriate words to start and end the letter. In a formal letter, never address the recipient by his or her first name. It is best to use the recipient's surname and his or her job title. For example:

尊敬的王经理钧鉴

尊敬的李老师钧鉴

When ending a letter or email, it is polite to use 敬上 (yours truly) or 谨上 (your sincerely) after your own name.

6 ⬤ ✎ **Speaking and Writing**

Remind students that the answers to questions i, ii and v will need to be logical depending on the type of training the student playing the manager has in mind.

Listen to students' conversations and provide support as needed.

Sample answers

i. 培训完了可以在许多科技公司 (tech companies) 找到工作。

ii. 培训需要六个月的时间。

iii. 培训的地点在伦敦，我们公司总部。

iv. 你可以上培训公司网页，下载申请表格，把填好的表格送给公司的人事部就可以了。

v. 你必须具备撰写编程语言(programming language) C++能力。

Homework suggestion

 Students pick one occupation from the list below and write a paragraph to explain why they would be good at it, mentioning any relevant personal skills.

售货员、司机、老师、作家、
工程师、农民、建筑师、厨师

 Students write 2 important skills associated with each occupation in the list.

9.8 找工作 Job hunting

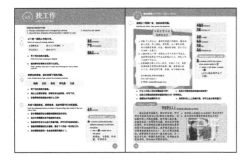

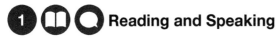

Lesson activities

1 📖🗨 Reading and Speaking

For part a, students may be able to guess the meanings as they will recognise some of the characters, e.g. 网站 (website), 报纸 (newspaper), 广告 (advert), 认识的人 (people I know), 参加 (attend), 会 (meeting). You can go through the pronunciation once they have worked out the meanings.

For part b, students can discuss the benefits in English but encourage them to use Chinese if they can.

Answers

a. 上招聘网站 – visit recruitment sites

看报纸上的招聘广告 – read the recruitment section in newspapers

问认识的人 – ask people you know

参加招聘会 – attend a recruitment fair

b. 各种方式的好处：

上招聘网站 – easy to search jobs by location or salary

看报纸上的招聘广告 – easy to look up many jobs at once

问认识的人 – you may come across something that isn't advertised publicly

参加招聘会 – you can talk to employer and find out more about the companies you're interested in

2 📖✏ Reading and Writing

Students should recognise these character traits from earlier units. Ask a few volunteers to read their answers for part b out loud. The others then suggest a suitable occupation based on each student's answer. The person then reveals what job they chose for themselves. Repeat with other volunteers.

Answers

a. 热情 warm/enthusiastic; 友好 friendly; 亲切 kind/approachable; 有礼貌 polite; 认真 serious/hard-working

b. 我的个性热情亲切而且认真。

c. 我觉得我的个性可以做慈善事业募款的工作。

3 🔊 Listening

Ask students to go through the statements first. Encourage students to give reasons for the false statements.

Depending on students' ability, you may want to give them clues to what to listen for. For example, in clip a, they should focus on the skills; in clip b, the number of teachers required; in clip c, the contact method, and so on.

Transcript

a. 夏令营要找两名音乐老师，要求能和小朋友很好地交流，擅长唱歌和跳舞。

b. 四川大学外语系需招聘五名外籍英文老师，年龄在二十五岁到六十岁之间,最好能听得懂一些中文。

c. 农业中心需要招聘一名农业工程师，如果您喜欢在户外工作，对这个工作有兴趣，请打农业中心电话 013-987654。

d. 警察局现招聘一名社区警察，要求爱说话，对人亲切。从本月二十一日开始上班。

e. 历史博物馆找秘书人员一名，要求会熟练地使用电脑，擅长做会议记录，最好会说西班牙语。

Answers

a. 对

b. 错（老师年龄在二十五岁到六十岁之间）

c. 对

d. 错 (从本月二十一日开始上班)

e. 错 (说西班牙语不是一个先决条件)

4 📖 Reading

Before reading the advert, go through the questions with the class. Ask students to point out the key words in each one, which will help them look for the answers: a. 年龄; b. 三种语言; c. 两点好的待遇; d. 兼职; e. 联系.

 If students find this activity challenging, you can turn it into a gap-filling exercise by writing a brief summary of the advert, leaving some blanks for students to fill in.

Answers

a. 十八岁以上

b. 普通话、粤语和英语

c. 免费住宿和每年免费去国外旅游一趟

d. 免费午餐、晚餐，但不提供住宿

e. 可以跟马经理联系：可以打他的手机或是给他写电子邮件

Cultural spotlight

Go through the passage, explaining any new vocabulary. Ask students if they are familiar with business etiquette in their own culture, and discuss what differences there are between their culture and Chinese culture.

Further differentiation

Find a selection of short job adverts from newspapers or recruitment websites. Copy and print them out for students.

 Students choose a job advert and translate it into Chinese as best they can.

 After the translation task, students should draft a reply to that advert in Chinese, saying why they would be the ideal candidate for the job and mentioning their personality, skills and past experiences.

Homework suggestion

Students imagine they are job hunting and have spent all day looking at recruitment websites. They need to write a diary entry which should include:

- 有没有在招聘网站上找到工作?
- 是什么类型的工作?
- 写好了个人简历吗?
- 有没有信心公司会回复?

9.9 面试 Job interviews

Lesson activities

1 🔊 Listening

For part a, go through the vocabulary and make sure students know their meanings before you play the recording.

Part b provides a good opportunity to check students' knowledge and understanding of Chinese character pen strokes. Ask students to complete the task themselves first before going through the answers as a class.

Transcript

a. 面试，面试 **b.** 机会，机会

c. 网络，网络 **d.** 面试官，面试官

e. 招聘，招聘 **f.** 申请表，申请表

g. 简历，简历 **h.** 报纸，报纸

Answers

词语	听力先后顺序	根据比划多少
招聘	5	3 (21)
面试	1	4 (17)
简历	7	4 (17)
申请表	6	2 (23)
面试官	4	1 (25)
报纸	8	7 (14)
网络	3	6 (15)
机会	2	8 (12)

2 Listening

Ask students to read the statements first, if necessary jotting down the pinyin to help them with the listening activity. Encourage students to give reasons for the false statements.

> If students struggle to listen to a recording of this length, turn the transcript into a gap-filling activity. Students follow the transcript when listening to the recording, and write in the missing words. To further simplify the activity, provide multiple answer options for each blank.

Transcript

两周前，我收到一封招聘广告的邮件。邮件说一家汽车工厂需要一名工程师。

我对那个工作相当感兴趣，就给汽车工厂发了个人简历。没过几天我就收到他们的电子邮件，要我参加面试。我很开心，但是也很紧张。

面试那天我穿了一套蓝色的西装，希望面试官对我有好的印象。那天他们问了我关于大学和工作经验的一些问题，还好都不是很难的问题。

我觉得那天的面试是成功的，因为第二天他们就打电话给我告诉我："那份工作是您的。"

Answers

a. 错 (他收到招聘广告邮件。) **b.** 对

c. 对 **d.** 错 (他很紧张。)

e. 对

f. 错 (他们问了关于大学和工作经验的问题。)

g. 对

3 Writing

To give students some context for this activity, explain that the words should form phrases that people are likely to hear when they attend a job interview.

> For some students, it may be better if each sentence is broken into fewer fragments, e.g. 您大学读的是 / 请您说一说 / 什么专业/?

Answers

a. 请您说一说您大学读的是什么专业？

b. 您毕业后去了哪个公司工作？

c. 您为什么想来我们的公司工作？

d. 您有什么问题吗？

e. 谢谢您来参加我们公司的面试。

4 Reading

This activity should be relatively straightforward.

Answers

a. iii **b.** i **c.** ii **d.** iii **e.** i

> To provide extra writing practice, create additional comprehension questions and ask students to write answers in full sentences.

5 Speaking

Listen to students' conversations, providing support as necessary.

> Give students 3–4 questions from the list to answer instead of the full set.

Answers

a. 我是本杰明，大学的专业是电脑科技。

b. 我最大的优点是我很忠诚而且认真负责。我会好几种电脑语言，我可以制作网站和app。

c. 我最不擅长的是绘图。

d. 我打算在电脑公司工作，设计许多解决人类生活问题的机器人。

e. 在工作中我觉得最重要的是能够看到客户的需要，解决问题。

f. 我喜欢跟团队脑力激荡 (brainstorming)，但是在做实际工作的时候，我喜欢单独工作，不受打扰。

g. 我喜欢滑雪、旅行，也喜欢看电影、吃美食。

h. 我希望我的年薪是六位数。

Assessment suggestion

Show students the BBC Bitesize video *Business and work in Beijing*. The video covers formal introductions in business situations, as well as ways to talk about the work people do. In groups of 4–5, students devise a short sketch demonstrating the consequences of good and/or bad business etiquette in an interview, perhaps using some questions from Activity 5. The groups can take turns to perform their sketch, with students voting for their favourite. You can also record the performances to assess students' verbal skills.

Homework suggestion

Students can write a simple CV in Chinese, using the "My CV" worksheet from the CD-ROM. They can also refer to the CV in Lesson 9.10: Activity 5 for inspiration.

9.10 复习 Progress check

Lesson activities

1 Reading

This activity revisits some common occupations and job titles covered in the unit. Check students' pronunciation by asking volunteers to say each one out loud.

Answers

a. iv **b.** ix **c.** i **d.** x **e.** ii

f. viii **g.** v **h.** iii **i.** vi **j.** vii

2 Listening

This activity checks students' ability to listen and to write down different occupations.

Transcript

a. 我叫小安。我觉得和小朋友一起很快乐，我希望将来能成为一名小学的老师。

b. 我叫丽丽。我从小就喜欢唱歌和跳舞，现在我也在学习音乐。将来我想成为一名唱跳歌手。

c. 我叫阿军。我特别爱玩游戏，也喜欢制作游戏。我想将来成为一名创造网络游戏的电脑工程师。

d. 我叫小娜。我觉得警察很酷，他们让我们住的地方更安全。我希望将来做一名警察。

e. 我叫大文。我画画画得很好，中学的时候还在学校里举办了自己的个人画展。以后我想做一名有名的画家。

Answers

a. 小安 = 小学老师   **b.** 丽丽 = 唱跳歌手

c. 阿军 = 电脑工程师   **d.** 小娜 = 警察

e. 大文 = 画家

Ask students how they know the clips are about people's future plans (Answer: the speakers use terms like 希望, 将来, 我想成为, 以后我想做).

3 Listening

Ask students to read the questions and answer options first to get a sense of what the recording might be about, and jot down the pinyin for the answer options.

Transcript

-最新暑假短期工作机会-

文化教育协会 北京办公室招聘暑假短期工两名。

时间为8月1日到10月1日，一共两个月。

适合在读大学的大学生。

工作内容为翻译文件。

感兴趣的大学生需要会流利的中文和英文，擅长用电脑。

申请时间在7月15日以前。

有兴趣的大学生请发送中英文简历到文化协会的电子邮箱。

Answers

a. i **b.** iii **c.** iii **d.** iii **e.** ii

4 ✏ Writing

Check students understand the meanings of these words by asking what part of speech they are (verbs).

Answers

a. 想 **b.** 打算 **c.** 当 **d.** 开 **e.** 看

5 📖 Reading

Remind students to read the questions before they look at the CV, and identify the key words so they know what to look out for: a. 什么工作; b. 大学专业; c. 哪些国家工作过; d. 2013年到 2015: 两个活动(设计网站); e. 除了网站设计……, 其他技能; f. 爱好.

Encourage students to write full sentences.

Answers

a. 网站设计的工作

b. 计算机专业

c. 英国和中国

d. 大学生戏剧节和伦敦唐人街新年活动

e. 摄影、会说流利的中英文

f. 艺术设计、摄影、旅游

DP You can re-use the CV to create a true-or-false activity for students by writing out your own set of true-or-false statements.

6 💬 Speaking

Remind students to refer to the CV in Activity 5 in order to answer questions a to e. However, for question f, they can use their own imagination.

Sample answers

a. 你好, 我是尼克。

b. 我在大学主修计算机，擅长网页设计。因为喜欢旅游，就副修了观光。

c. 我曾为英国伦敦唐人街新年活动设计网站及广告，也为英国文化会上海办公室做过网站设计。

d. 我会说流利的中英文，还懂摄影。

e. 我喜欢艺术设计、摄影、旅游。

f. 除了在国内工作，我希望也能有国外的工作经验，拓展国际视野，让我的工作能解决顾客需求，提供更专业更优质的服务。

7 ✏ Writing

Students should be familiar with the CV-writing format. To avoid repetition, ask them to create a new persona and write their CV.

Further differentiation

Give students the reading comprehension worksheet from the CD-ROM to complete. There are two versions of the worksheet for ability-differentiation purposes.

Assessment suggestion

MYP In groups of 4, students discuss the following questions:

- 在你居住的地方，你们觉得哪一个职业是最让人快乐的职业? 写三个原因。

- 哪一个是你们觉得最差的职业? 写三个原因。

Each group then presents to the class a summary of their discussion. You can record the presentations for assessment purposes. Keep a list of the jobs mentioned, so the class can vote for the most and least happy jobs.

UNIT OBJECTIVES

- Discuss and compare the seven continents.
- Learn about China's National Day and how people celebrate it.
- Learn about popular cities and tourist attractions in China.
- Discuss issues relating to international air travel.

- Discuss and compare different ways of organising a holiday.
- Discuss and compare cities and landmarks from around the world.
- Discuss and share information on ecotourism.

10.1 预习 Unit introduction

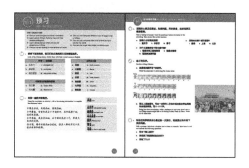

Prior knowledge

Students should know the names of a number of countries and major cities. They should be able to talk about holidays, transport, and different cultures, make comparisons, and be familiar with environmental issues.

Icebreaker activity

To get students familiar with saying the names of the continents in Chinese, divide the class into two groups. Each group takes a turn giving a city name and the other group should reply with the continent where the city is located.

Lesson activities

1  Reading

Before the activity, ask students how they prefer to travel and when they normally have their longest holiday. Also ask what continents they have visited, and hold a vote on the most popular places for holidays.

> **Answers**
>
> **a.** iii **b.** i **c.** ii **d.** vi **e.** iv **f.** v **g.** viii
> **h.** vii **i.** x **j.** ix **k.** xii **l.** xi

2 📖 Reading

This is a straightforward gap-filling activity consolidating students' grasp of vocabulary from Activity 1.

> **Answers**
>
> **a.** 北美洲 **b.** 欧洲 **c.** 自由行
>
> **d.** 绿色旅游 / 跟团游 **e.** 黄金周

3 🔊 Listening

Remind students to beware of traps in the questions. For example, question b asks where Tom plans to go on holiday. In the recording, Sammy mentions two destinations, Beijing and Shanghai, but students must not be misled by this. They should listen for Tom confirming his holiday destination.

Transcript

心美：汤姆，你去中国游学差不多一个月了，最近还好吗？假期有什么计划？

汤姆：还不错，下星期一是中国的国庆节，一共有七天假期，我还在想着去哪儿旅游呢！

心美：太好了。听说在中国，人们把这几天假期叫做黄金周，他们会在假期去不同地方旅游和购物，在北京、上海这些大城市里，人特别多。对了，你打算去哪儿旅游？

汤姆：我打算去香港。我对这个城市特别感兴趣。

心美：为什么你对这个城市感兴趣？

汤姆：听说香港是购物天堂。我想去那儿购物！

心美：希望你有一个愉快的旅行！到了香港，你要寄明信片给我啊！

汤姆：谢谢！没问题！

> **Answers**
>
> **a.** i **b.** i **c.** ii

Writing

For part a, the strokes animation from the MGDB online dictionary is useful for showing students the sequences of writing individual characters.

For part b, first practise writing a selection of holiday activities with students, and then help them to link the activities with 黄金周.

Sample writing for part b

黄金周的时候有一周的假期，我们全家打算去三亚的海边旅游。

Speaking

Remind students that the three questions here all use 了 sentence patterns. You may need to give them a quick recap. Walk around listening to students' conversations and providing support as necessary.

Sample answers

a. 我最近去了土耳其旅行。

b. 我是自由行。

c. 我在土耳其参观了许多名胜古迹，也吃了很多当地的美食。

Class travel fair

Students each choose a country and prepare a presentation. Encourage them to talk about or show pictures of the national costume, speciality food and/or local crafts. Place a large world map on the wall and ask students to mark their countries on it. Encourage them to compare countries in the same continents.

Further differentiation

 Ask students to write answers to the same questions in Activity 5, but to add in time phrases and give more information. For example, 暑假我去了法国。圣诞节的时候我去了香港。

 Ask students to add even more information to their sentences, such as means of travel, accommodation, reasons for going, etc.

10.2 七大洲 The seven continents

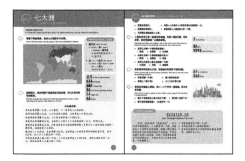

Icebreaker activity

Students can complete the "In which continent would you find...?" worksheet (on the CD-ROM) to refresh their knowledge of names of countries and continents.

Lesson activities

Speaking

Ask students to say what continent they come from. Extend this to include celebrities, sportspeople or politicians.

 You could use the different continent colours from the map to further help students. For example, write Asian cities in yellow, European cities in blue, and North American cities in pink.

Reading

Start the activity by asking students some general "most" questions, such as the largest and the smallest continents. You could then ask students to find out which countries are the largest, smallest, hottest, coldest, wettest, where people live longest, etc. This could also be developed into homework for students to research their own "most" categories.

Answers

a. 对   b. 对   c. 错 (南美洲比欧洲大。)

d. 错 (欧洲是人口密度最大的一个洲。)   e. 对

Listening

Using the transcript as a guide, ask students some questions first. For example: 哪一个是世界上最大的洲？

Transcript

小明：志军，你知道在七大洲中，哪一个是世界上最大的洲？

志军：我知道，亚洲最大。

小明：真聪明。第二大呢？

志军：欧洲有很多国家，是欧洲吧？

小明：当然不是，非洲才是第二大的洲。

志军：是吗？我看非洲和欧洲差不多。

小明：才不是呢！非洲面积约3000万平方千米，欧洲只有大约1000万平方千米，差远了。对了，我再考考你，世界上最小的是哪一个洲？

志军：我知道。是大洋洲，对吧？

小明：对，大洋洲面积只有大约900万平方千米。

Answers

a. i **b.** iii **c.** i

 **4** **Speaking**

Remind students to use the 过 pattern for past experiences.

Sample answers

a. 我生在亚洲，去过北美洲、南美洲、非洲和欧洲。

b. 我没有去过大洋洲和南极洲。

c. 英国位于欧洲。

d. 肯尼亚位于非洲。

 Go through the speaking questions with students and give them some example answers.

 **5** **Writing**

Students are asked to write a speech here. Remind them to use the questions as a guide to link the beginning, middle and end of their speech. Encourage students to add in some of their own opinions too.

Sample writing

从大小来看，亚洲、非洲和北美洲是世界上最大的三个洲。亚洲是最大的一洲，它比非洲大，非洲又比北美洲大。从财富来看，过去北美洲最富有，因为强大的美国在北美洲。非洲最贫穷。近年来亚洲因为中国繁荣的经济，也变得强大起来。

Cultural spotlight

Ask students if they know what 希腊人 means (Greeks). Ask students to name as many countries in Asia as possible. Write their names on the board in Chinese, to increase students' vocabulary.

Homework suggestion

Ask students to write about an adventure through different continents. They may make up their own stories or describe a famous explorer's journey.

10.3 国庆黄金周 Celebrating China's National Day

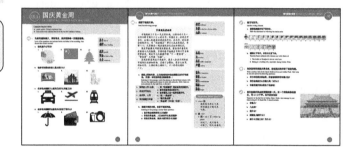

Lesson activities

 **1** **Listening**

First ask students to describe what each picture represents. Then tell them that they are about to hear a radio broadcast. There will not be any pauses, so they should take as many notes as they can while listening.

Transcript

以下是北京电台的广播

一年一度的国庆黄金周将于明天开始！

除了在各百货公司购物、去天安门广场看阅兵和升旗仪式之外，很多市民都会和家人朋友外出郊游。

由于人多车多，交通繁忙，提醒各位听众朋友多坐地铁，尽量别开车。这样既环保，又方便。

十月是北京的秋天，是赏花的好季节。外出郊游的朋友们，千万别忘了带相机。

另外，由于天气干燥，在外面别忘了多喝水。

Answers

a ii **b.** ii **c.** iii **d.** iii

2  Reading

 For part a, you could make flashcards using the phrases (e.g. use red cards for phrases in the left-hand column, and white cards for phrases in the right-hand column). Ask students to match them one-by-one to see which pairings work best grammatically.

Answers

Part a

a. ii **b.** iii **c.** i **d.** v

Part b

i.   国庆黄金周有连续七天的假期。

ii. 国庆黄金周的时候，很多人会去不同城市或郊区旅游。

iii. 国庆黄金周的时候，很多大城市例如北京、上海的街上特别挤，堵车情况特别严重。

3 Writing

For part a, draw students' attention to the composition of each character: 繁 is made up of top and bottom parts, and the top part is also made up of two parts, left and right. 忙 is made up of left and right parts.

You can also discuss the radicals and their implications for each character. For example:

The radical for 繁 is 糸 (糹), which means "silk", indicating something that is wound up.

The radical for 忙 is 心 (忄), which means "heart". Point out that the two parts of 忙 mean "heart" and "dead".

For part b, remind students to pay attention to the sentence order when translating – the location tends to come first.

Answers for part b

i. 上海的交通总是很繁忙。

ii. 北京是一个繁忙的城市，特别是在国庆黄金周期间。

 Ask students to write a couple more sentences, either to support the first sentence or about other busy cities they have visited.

4 Speaking

Ask students if they go on holidays with their family. If so, where do they normally go? What transport do they use, and why? Remind students to use the correct verb-noun compounds. For example:

坐车、坐船、坐飞机 (if you're a passenger)
开车、开船、开飞机 (if you're the one behind the wheel/controls)
骑马、骑摩托车、骑自行车

Sample answers

a. 今年的国庆黄金周，爸爸妈妈带我到泰国去玩。

b. 我们是坐飞机去的，因为这是最快的方式。

c. 我很喜欢国庆黄金周，因为每年爸妈都会带我们去玩。

5 Writing

If your students are not overly familiar with Golden Week, take this opportunity to discuss with them what families and friends do together at this time.

Sample writing

明天我们要去天安门看升旗典礼，五点就出发，我会带国旗还有照相机。因为天安门广场关闭不准车辆进入，所以最好坐地铁。

 Students could write about their weekend plans instead. You could provide a "ready-made" structure, for example:

明天我们要去＿＿＿＿看足球。＿＿＿＿点＿＿分出发。记得要带＿＿＿＿和＿＿＿。我们打算坐＿＿＿＿去，因为＿＿＿＿＿＿。

Language and culture

The national anthem is sung regularly at primary and secondary schools in China, usually as part of a flag-raising ceremony.

Assessment suggestion

Show students the video *2016 China's National Day Flag-rising Ceremony in Tiananmen Square Beijing* [00:00–04:38], produced by China Plus. The National Day flag-raising ceremony in Tiananmen Square is the biggest annual ceremony in China. Then ask students to prepare a presentation on a popular national event in another country.

Homework suggestion

Show students the video *Best parts of the Beijing 2008 Olympics | Highlights* [00:00–01:30], produced by the IOC's Official Olympic Channel. Then ask them, as homework, to write about a memorable sporting event for their country.

10.4 假期的旅游活动 Things to do on holiday

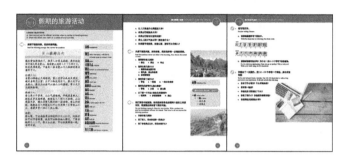

Lesson activities

Reading

 For some more information on Huangshan (Yellow Mountain), show students the CCTV video 六集纪录片 《大黄山》 第一集 人间仙境 [00:00–02:00]. Then discuss the following questions (answers and timings of clips shown in brackets):

Q1: 黄山距离东海多远？ (400 公里 [00:53])

Q2: 黄山是以谁命名？ (黄帝 [01:12])

Q3: 黄山有哪五绝 ("five pinnacles")?
(奇松 "peculiar pine trees", 怪石 "spectacular rocks", 云海 "sea of clouds", 冬雪 "winter snow", 温泉 "hot springs" [01:19])

Q4: 黄山有哪三项桂冠(honours)?
(世界文化遗产、世界自然遗产、世界地质公园 [01:44])

Answers

a. 这是旅行社的宣传广告。

b. 三天。

c. 第一天可以先到风景区，建议去的景点有：翡翠谷和九龙瀑布。第二天可以去爬山，登山以后可以住山上的宾馆。第三天下山后回机场。

d. 黄山高二千多米，山上气温偏低，早晚温差较大，旅客应多注意保暖。

e. 登山前，可以住在景点附近的家庭式旅馆，这样不但可以节省旅费，而且可以和当地人聊天。

2   Listening

Inform students that they are about to hear a conversation about planning a holiday and they should take note of the destination, preparations and holiday activities.

Transcript

小明：丽青，国庆黄金周快到了。在这七天的假期里，你要去哪儿旅游？

丽青：我会和哥哥一起去中国泰山观光旅游。

小明：到了那儿，你们会做什么？

丽青：虽然很多人去泰山观光的时候会买很多纪念品，但是我和哥哥不喜欢购物，我们只去那儿看风景和爬山，我们还会拍一些照片，到时候我一定会发给你看的。

小明：先谢了！那你做好准备了吗？

丽青：早就准备好了！听说山上的商店不多，我会多带几瓶水和一些食物。

小明：你们会带什么爬山装备？

丽青：导游会给我们爬山头盔，我只要多带一双爬山鞋就可以了。对了，小明，你在黄金周假期会去哪儿旅游？

小明：爸爸妈妈会带我去北京旅游。妈妈说北京烤鸭特别好吃，她会带我去吃烤鸭。爸爸说故宫博物馆很有趣，我们全家都会一起去故宫博物馆参观。

丽青：真好！不过听说北京堵车问题很严重，对吧？

小明：对，我们会早点出门，不用担心。丽青，希望你在泰山玩得开心。

丽青：谢谢小明，你也是。

Answers

a. i **b.** ii **c.** iii **d.** iii **e.** iii

3  Speaking

To prepare for the speaking activity, ask students to create an itinerary for a forthcoming holiday in China. It should include a destination, the tourist attractions there, and the activities available.

Sample answers

a. 我要去苏州旅游。

b. 我要去参观苏州园林和丝绸博物馆。

c. 除了参观景点之外，我还想吃吃苏州的点心，买一些苏州的丝绸。

4 Writing

For part a, the strokes animation from the MGDB online dictionary is useful for showing students the sequences of writing individual characters. Ensure students pay attention to the spacing of each character.

For part b, remind students to keep their answer succinct as the word count is only up to 30 characters.

Sample writing for part b

旅游时我喜欢观光，因为可以多多了解当地的文化。

5 Writing

Point out the use of 了 sentence patterns here. Encourage students to use more complex sentence structures such as 因为……，所以……。

Sample writing

我去年圣诞节的时候去了法国的阿尔卑斯山，我和家人一起去的。因为要去滑雪，所以我准备了滑雪的衣物。我们在那儿天天滑雪并且吃了很多法国美食。这些都是我最喜欢的活动。我觉得这次的旅游景点很棒，希望很快能够再去。

Homework suggestion

Ask students to write guidelines for a class field trip to a destination of their choice. They may follow the format of the text in Activity 1.

10.5 中国的旅游业 Tourism in China

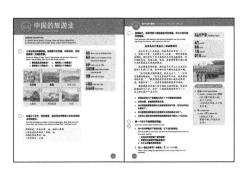

Lesson activities

 **1** Listening

First go through the pictures with students and find out whether they have been to the places and how much they know about them. Point out these places on a map of China.

Transcript

小华：米娜，你想去哪儿旅行？

米娜：我想去中国旅行，但是还没想好去哪儿。

小华：我也想去中国旅行。你打算去北京吗？那儿有很多古迹，是一个观光的好地方。

米娜：我去过北京了，我参观过北海公园和故宫，还拍了不少照片呢！

小华：我也去过北京，我还登上了长城哩！米娜，如果你想参观古迹，你也可以去西安参观兵马俑。我去年去过西安，那里的兵马俑比我还高两头。

米娜：真有趣，不过我这一次不想去大城市，想去一些乡村地区观光。

小华：那么你可以去桂林。听说桂林的七星岩很有名，那儿的风景一定很美。

米娜：我以前去过桂林的七星岩了。我想到了！我会去拉萨参观布达拉宫，我还没坐过青藏铁路的火车呢！

小华：我不喜欢坐火车。我还是喜欢坐飞机去中国的大城市玩，既方便，又快捷。我打算下次去上海。

Answers

a. ii, iii, vi　**b.** i　**c.** iv　**d.** v

2 Listening

Remind students to read the questions first, so they know what to listen out for. They should pay attention to 过, which refers to past experiences, and 打算, which refers to future events, in the recording.

Transcript

See Activity 1.

Answers

a. 故宫　**b.** 桂林　**c.** 西安兵马俑　**d.** 布达拉宫

3 Reading

Help students to identify the key words/phrases in each statement and the corresponding sentences in the text. Compare them to judge whether the statement is true or false. For example:

Statement a: 记者在天安门广场看到大约五十个中国游客在照相。

In the text: 记者来到北京的天安门广场，这里人不多，大约五十人左右，一群外国游客在照相。

Statement d: 来自美国的游客喜欢北京是因为北京的景点太多了。

In the text: 我觉得在北京买东西比我们老家更便宜，我爱北京！一名来自美国的游客高兴地说。

Answers

a. 错（一群外国游客在照相。） **b.** 对 **c.** 对

d. 错（美国游客觉得在北京买东西比美国老家便宜。） **e.** 对

4 Speaking and Writing

You may like to use this chart to help students carry out their surveys. Encourage them to pay attention to the similarities and differences between each interviewee. If not many students have been to China, they can just carry out the survey about other countries/cities.

姓名	去过的城市	去过的景点	为什么喜欢这些景点？

Sample writing

Part a

a. 北京、上海、成都、重庆。

b. 北京的长城，上海的城隍庙，成都和重庆之间的长江三峡。

c. 长城很壮观，城隍庙很热闹，长江三峡很美丽。

Part b

很多同学都去过中国，大部分的人都去过首都北京和上海这样的大城市，也有些人去了西安和成都。大家都喜欢北京历史悠久的长城，觉得长城非常雄伟；也喜欢上海的城隍庙，觉得那里很热闹。去过西安的同学很喜欢兵马俑，觉得它很壮观；去过成都的同学有的人喜欢那里可爱的熊猫，也有的人觉得长江三峡的风景真是太美了！

Assessment suggestion

Students should choose a city of interest and give a group presentation about it, including pictures.

Students should include in their presentations how and why the city they have chosen has become a popular tourist attraction.

Homework suggestion

Students write a paragraph to say which of the places in Activity 1 they would most like to visit and why.

10.6 旅游备忘录 A checklist for international travel

Icebreaker activity

Put students in pairs and ask each of them to prepare a list of things to pack when travelling abroad. They should then compare their lists to find out which items they both chose and which are different. Get them to explain their choices.

Lesson activities

1  Reading

Go through the pictures and ask students if they would pack each item when travelling. If not, ask them why.

Answers

a. viii **b.** iv **c.** ii **d.** ix **e.** i **f.** vi **g.** iii

h. v **i.** vii

2 Reading

This is a Q&A about international travel guidelines. You may like to put students in pairs to read the text before asking them to work out if the statements are true or false.

Answers

a. 对　**b.** 对　**c.** 对

d. 错 (手提行李总重量不超过5公斤。)

e. 错 (必须找问询台的服务员。)

3 Listening

Inform students that this conversation is between a mother and her son; hence, the tone is more relaxed and there may be some colloquial expressions.

Transcript

a. 志军：妈妈，我们什么时候要到机场？

妈妈：飞机晚上七点起飞，我们要提早两小时到机场，我们应该在下午五点到机场。

b. 志军：妈妈，到了机场以后，我要先去买东西。我想寄存行李,我应该找谁帮忙？

妈妈：不用担心，你可以请行李寄存台的服务员帮忙。

c. 志军：哎呀，妈妈，我忘了买礼物给心美，过了安全检查以后还可以买东西吗？

妈妈：别担心。过了安全检查以后，我们还可以在机场的商场购物。

d. 志军：哎呀，妈妈，我肚子好疼。机场有厕所吗？厕所在哪儿？

妈妈：当然有，不过我不清楚厕所在哪儿，你忍一下，我去问询台问一问服务员吧！

Answers

a. ii　**b.** iii　**c.** i　**d.** ii

Language and culture

哎呀 is a very common Chinese interjection, and it can be used in many ways:

1. when encountering someone or something unexpected: 哎呀！你怎么也在这儿上班？

2. to express confusion: 哎呀！你到底怎么了？

3. to express anxiety: 哎呀！火车已经进站了，他怎么还没来呢？

4. to express shock/pain: 哎呀！我肚子好痛！

5. to express a nice surprise: 哎呀！她怎么长得这么漂亮了！

4 Speaking

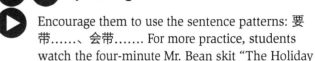

Encourage them to use the sentence patterns: 要带……、会带……. For more practice, students watch the four-minute Mr. Bean skit "The Holiday Suitcase". Ask them what is in the suitcase.

Students do a voice-over in Chinese for the video.

Sample answers

a. 我出国旅行要带的个人卫生用品有牙膏、牙刷、洗面乳、洗脸毛巾等等。

b. 我会带一些止痛药和感冒药以防万一。

c. 出国旅行我一定会带护照和驾照。

d. 我还会带手机和我的个人电脑。

5 Writing

Students can create a basic bullet-point checklist.

Sample writing

出国旅游备忘录:

个人用品	卫生用品 －牙膏、牙刷、洗面乳、洗脸毛巾、面霜 药品 －止痛药、感冒药、胃药 换洗衣物 －三件T恤、两条牛仔裤、七双袜子、七件内衣裤、两件洋装、一双运动鞋、一双皮鞋、一双海滩鞋、一顶草帽 个人用品 －隐形眼镜、一般眼镜、太阳眼镜
其他东西	手机、个人电脑、充电线、充电宝、转换插头
机场注意事项	准备重要证件－护照、电子机票、旅馆预定确认
	随身行李中的化妆液体装在100毫升的小瓶，并装在透明的袋子里。

If time allows, go through any unfamiliar words in the chart with students to increase their vocabulary.

6 🗨 Speaking

Review the directions (东南西北) with students before asking them to carry out the speaking activity.

Sample answers

a. 北京在地图上的北方。

b. 布达拉宫在地图上的西方。

c. 桂林在西安的南方。

d. 从北京去黄山比从上海去要远。

Assessment suggestion

Students give a presentation about three essential things they always pack whenever they travel, giving their reasons – they can include more interesting things than socks!

Homework suggestion

Give each student a copy of the "Packing checklist" worksheet (on the CD-ROM) to complete. Remind them that their answers will need to make sense depending on the destination and time of year they have chosen.

10.7 自由行还是跟团游?
Self-guided or package tours?

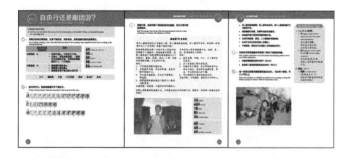

Icebreaker activity

 Show students the video *"你不知道的日本" 第2集* [00:00–03:00], produced by 日本当地省力省钱跟团游. Then discuss the following questions (answers and timings of clips shown in brackets):

Q1: 自由行的最大好处是什么? (自由 [00:24])

Q2: 自由行的缺点是什么? 为什么? (交通有些麻烦,

因为旅行时时间很宝贵, 日本的交通费不便宜, 而且语言不通。[00:27])

Q3: 影片中跟团游一日游的费用多少钱? (9900日币 [01:27])

Q4: 跟团游的好处是什么? (方便 [01:33])

Lesson activities

1 🔊 Listening

Look over the table with the students before the listening activity, so they are sure of what gaps they need to fill.

Transcript

汤姆: 日晴, 寒假就快到了。听说你会和爸爸、妈妈去旅游。你们会跟团游还是自由行?

日晴: 我们还没决定。听说跟团游比较方便, 不用自己计划行程。我妈妈说她比较喜欢参加旅游团, 因为很方便。她觉得自由行要自己安排行程太麻烦了。

汤姆: 也对。不过, 跟团游行程没有自由, 又不能选择团员, 如果碰到麻烦的团员就不好了, 而且在每个景点的停留时间也不多, 我觉得还是自由行好。

日晴: 对, 我爸爸的看法也一样。但妈妈说自由行不安全。如果是跟团游, 一般旅行社的交通、住宿安排等都经过把关, 自己未必熟悉当地的情况, 风险比较高。

汤姆: 是啊。在外地旅行的时候, 如果没有导游, 有紧急事情要自己解决, 未必能应付得了。

日晴: 到底我们跟团游好, 还是自由行好呢?

汤姆: 我也不知道, 还是让你的爸爸妈妈决定吧。

Answers

a. 跟团游　　b. 方便　　c. 安全　　d. 自由行

e. 自由　　f. 团员　　g. 停留时间

2 ✏ Writing

Ask students to highlight the radical for each character and try to remember it.

You can also ask students what they think of package tours.

 Ask students to write a few sentences expressing their opinion of package tours.

Sample writing

我滑雪的时候喜欢跟团游，因为比较方便，旅行社会做好所有的旅行安排，我可以安心地滑雪就好了。

3 Reading

Remind students to read the statements first to identify the key words/phrases before reading the passage. Note that the middle sections of the reading passage are actually split into two columns – make sure students don't just read across the width of the page.

Answers

a. 错（每个人喜爱的旅行方式都不一样。）

b. 错（跟团费通常包括交通费用。）　　**c.** 对

d. 错（自由行的机票、签证、住宿通通由自己安排。）

e. 对　　**f.** 对

Divide students into two groups to have a debate: "Which is better – package or self-guided holidays?" Ask them to use the reading text as reference. Then hold a class poll to see how many prefer package holidays and how many prefer self-guided holidays.

4 Speaking

Before putting students in pairs for the speaking activity, you may like to hold a group discussion around the following questions:

你最近去哪儿度假？跟谁一起去？

是自由行还是跟团游？

你觉得好玩吗？为什么？

Sample answers

a. 滑雪度假的时候，我喜欢跟团游，因为旅行社做了所有的安排，方便很多。至于其他的旅游，我喜欢自由行，因为这样可以看到更多的当地文化。

b. 我的家人比较喜欢自由行，因为我们可以选择自己喜欢的行程和旅游方式。

5 Writing

Remind students to use the 因为 sentence pattern to explain their reasons.

Sample writing

我喜欢跟团游，因为旅行社安排了行程、旅馆和交通工具，不用操心，也不用浪费时间。

我喜欢自由行，因为我喜欢自己规划行程和旅游方式，可以自由地旅行，也不用受团体的限制。

Homework suggestion

Ask students to imagine they are on a package tour abroad. They should write a postcard telling their parents about the tour and commenting on its pros and cons.

10.8 世界著名地标 Famous landmarks around the world

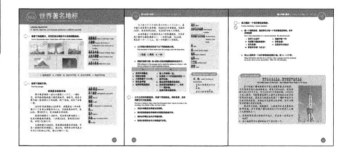

Lesson activities

1 Reading

Explain to students the three approaches used when translating English names into Chinese:

a. a pure phonetic translation (known as transliteration), such as 纽约, 埃菲尔, and 伊丽莎白女王, etc.

b. a translation of the meaning, such as 白宫, 自由女神, etc.

c. a combination of sound and meaning, such as 牛津, 剑桥, etc.

You may also like to discuss Big Ben's Chinese translation with students: 大笨钟 (large cumbersome clock)! Go through the names of some other famous landmarks and places with students. Ask them which translation approach has been used in each case.

Answers

a. iv　**b.** v　**c.** ii　**d.** iii　**e.** i

Drag-and-drop game

Design a PowerPoint or interactive whiteboard drag-and-drop game for students to play to revise continents, countries and landmarks. A sample layout is given below:

亚洲　北美洲　欧洲　非洲　南美洲　大洋洲　南极洲

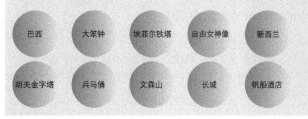

巴西	大笨钟	埃菲尔铁塔	自由女神像	新西兰
胡夫金字塔	兵马俑	文森山	长城	帆船酒店

2  Reading

This activity is good for revising numbers in Chinese. Ask students to rewrite the numbers they see in the passage using Chinese characters.

> **Answers**
>
> **a. i.** 标志 = 地标　**ii.** 闻名 = 著名　**iii.** 一共 = 共有
>
> **b. a.** ii　**b.** iv　**c.** i　**d.** v　**e.** iii

3 Listening

Ask students to note the key words in the statements before listening to the recording, which will help them to judge whether each is true or false.

> **Transcript**
>
> 小文：玛莉，听说你刚从法国巴黎回来，有没有上埃菲尔铁塔玩呀？
>
> 玛莉：当然有，埃菲尔铁塔是巴黎著名的地标，到巴黎玩的人都会去。埃菲尔铁塔有300多米高，还好我们可以坐电梯上去。
>
> 小文：我爸爸刚去了迪拜的帆船酒店，它是迪拜有名的地标。爸爸说这个酒店也很高，也有300多米，我想它和埃菲尔铁塔应该差不多高。
>
> 玛莉：真厉害。对了，听说你下个星期去纽约，你知道纽约有名的标志是什么？
>
> 小文：当然知道，是自由女神像。听老师说，它是法国在1876年送给美国的100周年礼物，有46米高。但我去年在埃及看过的胡夫金字塔高约140米，比自由女神像更高！
>
> 玛莉：哇！世界上这么高的地标还真多。

Answers

> **a.** 错（它是美国著名的地标。）　　**b.** 对
>
> **c.** 对　　**d.** 错（埃菲尔铁塔比自由女神像高很多。）

4 Speaking and Writing

You may like to make two sets of cards: one set with photos of famous landmarks, and another set with a couple of basic facts about the landmarks.

Ask students to pair up each photo with its relevant facts. They can then choose one pair of cards as the basis for their presentation.

> Students include in their presentation at least three more facts from their own research on the landmark.

> **Sample answer**
>
> 台北101是位于台湾台北市信义区的摩天大楼，楼高509.2米（1,671英尺）。1999年动工，2004年12月31日完工启用。大楼内拥有全球第二大的阻尼器（仅次于上海中心大厦），也是全球唯一向游客开放参观的巨型阻尼器、以及全球起降速度第二快的电梯（仅次于上海中心大厦）。台北101原是全世界最高建筑物，2007年被位于迪拜的哈里发塔所超越。台北101外观上和竹子一样一节一节，象征节节高升。自2004年底起，以烟火及灯光秀作为主题举办跨年活动，每年都吸引了很多观众。

Cultural spotlight

You may need to explain a few words in the text to students, such as 建筑面积, 兴建, 覆盖, 半径范围, 大幅度, 广播, 收听收视, 太空舱, 历史发展陈列馆, etc.

> Students list the similarities and differences between the Eiffel Tower and the Oriental Pearl Radio & TV Tower.

Assessment suggestion

Ask students to complete the "Reading comprehension" worksheet (on the CD-ROM). Two versions of the worksheet are available depending on students' abilities.

Homework suggestion

 Ask students to design a promotional poster for their favourite landmark. They could include the following information on their posters:

- Date of construction
- Landmark's facilities
- What is special about this landmark?

10.9 绿色旅游 Ecotourism

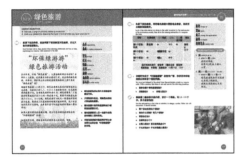

Lesson activities

1 Reading

Explain that in Chinese essay writing there are normally quite a few foreshadowing statements before the final focus point appears at the end of the paragraph or article. Students should pay special attention to the fact that Chinese topic sentences normally appear near the end of a paragraph or piece of writing.

Answers

a. 对

b. 错 (其他环保的旅游方式也是绿色旅游。)

c. 错 (绿色旅游是节约能源和减少碳排放的旅游方式。)

d. 对

e. 错 (环保绿游游的活动是由绿色旅游协会举办。)

2 Listening

Remind students to read the questions before listening to the recording. Tell them it is a radio broadcast. The speech will be more formal, and they will need to take notes as they listen.

Transcript

各位同学:

大家好！欢迎收听校园电台的活动宣传广播。我是绿色旅游协会的大使美美。

为了让更多同学了解绿色旅游，从下星期一十月十七日开始，绿色旅游协会将会在负责老师们的带领下，举办"环保绿游游"绿色旅游课外活动。

第一个活动是远足，由黄老师组织，名额十个。有兴趣的同学到三楼办公室找黄老师报名。

第二个活动是观察昆虫活动，名额十五个，有兴趣的同学请到二楼图书馆找李老师报名。

第三个活动是自行车郊外旅行，有兴趣的同学请到五楼体育馆找陈老师报名，名额二十个。

截止报名日期是十月十日，每个活动报名费不一样，请向负责老师查询。欢迎大家踊跃参加!

Answers

a. 观察昆虫 b. 自行车郊外旅行 c. 李老师

d. 陈老师 e. 3楼办公室 f. 体育馆 g. 15 个

h. 10月10日 i. 负责老师

3 Speaking

Remind students to refer to the table in Activity 2 to help them with this speaking activity.

Sample answers

a. 我想参加自行车郊外旅行。

b. 我要去找陈老师报名。

c. 我要去五楼体育馆报名。

4 Writing

 Tell students that there is no need to write long sentences on posters. All the information they include should be short and to the point: a clear and simple title for the activity, and some basic information, including date, place, fees, etc.

Encourage students to write a slogan for their poster.

Homework suggestion

Ask students to imagine that they are an ambassador for the ecotourism society. They should write a welcome letter to new members, explaining what the society does.

10.10 复习 Progress check

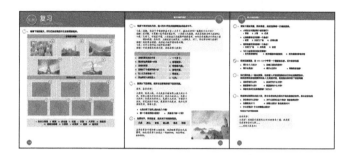

Lesson activities

This activity revisits names of continents and famous landmarks. For extra practice, get students to write out the pinyin and tone of each character as well.

Answers

a. iii **b.** ix **c.** iv **d.** viii **e.** i **f.** ii **g.** xi **h.** x

i. xii **j.** v **k.** vii **l.** vi

Put students in pairs. Make enough copies of the landmarks and continents in the Student Book for each pair to have a landmark and a continent.

One person should introduce the landmark, the city and country where it is located and one special feature. The other person should introduce the continent, its location, some countries and famous landmarks in it.

2 📖 Reading

Put students in pairs and ask them to read the conversation aloud. They can then work out the answers together.

Answers

a. ii **b.** vi **c.** iii **d.** i **e.** iv **f.** v

3 📖 Reading

First, ask some students to read out the questions, and get them to point out the key words. Then ask a more-able student to read the text for the rest of the class.

Answers

a. 心美介绍了世界上最大的三个洲：亚洲、非洲和北美洲。

b. 亚洲是全世界最大的洲。 **c.** 美国位于北美洲。

4 🔊 Listening

Ask students to read the text in the Student Book and guess the answers before listening to the recording. They can then check their answers after listening to it.

Transcript

日晴：志军，你要去哪儿观光旅游？

志军：日晴你好，我打算去中国的黄山观光旅游。

日晴：到了那儿，你会参观哪一些景点？

志军：我会参观翡翠谷和九龙瀑布。

日晴：除了参观景点之外，你还会做什么？

志军：我还会和朋友一起爬山和拍照。

日晴：你会带什么东西去？

志军：我会带头盔、爬山鞋和相机。

Answers

a. 观光 **b.** 参观 **c.** 爬山 **d.** 拍照 **e.** 头盔

f. 爬山鞋

5 🔊 Listening

Remind students to read the questions and note the key words, then use them as the focus of their listening.

Transcript

a. 访问者：小明，你去过中国的哪个城市旅游？

小明：我去过上海。

访问者：小明去过中国的哪个城市旅游？

b. 访问者：心美，你最喜欢北京的哪一个景点？

心美：我最喜欢北京的故宫。

访问者：心美最喜欢北京的哪一个景点？

c. 访问者：丽青，你最喜欢西安的哪一个景点？

丽青：我最喜欢西安的兵马俑。

访问者：丽青最喜欢西安的哪一个景点？

d. 访问者：丽青，为什么你喜欢到西安旅游？

丽青：因为我喜欢参观古迹。

访问者：为什么丽青喜欢到西安旅游？

e. 我喜欢自由行因为我特别喜欢自由，尤其旅行的时候，我喜欢自己订旅馆和行程。

8 Speaking

Here, students have to write a promotional speech to be broadcast. It should be formal and concise. Encourage students to first write out bullet points for each question and then link them together in an organised manner.

Answers

a. ii **b.** i **c.** ii **d.** iii

6 Writing

Remind students that this activity is asking them to write a 备忘录. This should be in the form of a checklist of bullet points and does not require them to write complete sentences. This is a good opportunity for them to display their vocabulary strength.

Sample writing

旅游备忘录

必带个人用品：换洗衣物、泳衣、海滩鞋、阳伞、墨镜、iPad

兑换当地货币：先在机场换一些，再到当地银行换钱

必带药品：感冒药、止痛药、胃药、喉糖等等

必带证件：护照、驾驶执照、电子机票、保险文件

充电器：手机和照相机的充电器和充电宝都要带着

Sample answer

各位同学：

大家好！欢迎收听校园电台的活动宣传广播。我是绿色旅游协会的大使陈小文。我们要举办野外露营和动物救援活动。野外露营是要帮助同学们亲近大自然、保护大自然。白老师负责领队。动物救援是要帮助大家了解动物的需要并且爱护动物。这项活动由王老师负责。野外露营有100个名额，动物救援只有30个名额。有兴趣的同学到学生活动中心报名。露营的报名费是200元，动物救援的报名费是500元。野外露营是在4月的最后一个周末举行，动物救援是在五月的第二个周末举行。报名截止日期都是3月31日。欢迎大家踊跃报名参加！

Further differentiation

 Students give a group presentation on the most visible/important landmark in their city/country.

 Students give a group presentation about the importance of modern landmarks. Are landmarks built to become tourist attractions or vice versa? They should include examples.

7 Speaking

Help students to develop and expand their answers by thinking of all the points in favour of each type of travel and then the disadvantages. For example, the main advantage of a self-guided tour is having "freedom". Guide students to consider in what ways they can enjoy that freedom. But, on the other hand, in order to earn that freedom, what do they have to sacrifice?

Assessment suggestion

Make a recording using the sample answer in Activity 8 and use it as an extra listening assessment. Here are some comprehension questions (answers in brackets).

Q1. 绿色旅游协会的大使叫什么名字？(陈小文)

Q2. 这项活动由谁负责？(王老师)

Q3. 野外露营有几个名额？(100个名额)

Q4. 动物救援的报名费是多少钱？(500元)

Q5. 报名截止日期是什么时候？(都是3月31日)

Sample answers

a. 自由行的好处就是"自由"，可以自由选择住处、行程和想看的景点。

b. 自由行的坏处就是很花时间，因为所有事情都要自己安排。

c. 跟团游的好处是旅行社安排住宿、交通工具和所有的景点，所以很方便。

d. 跟团游的坏处是所有行程都要跟着团体，没有个人自由。

UNIT OBJECTIVES

- Discuss the pros and cons of studying abroad.
- Learn the facts behind some Chinese wedding traditions.
- Understand the history and customs of the Mid-Autumn Festival.
- Understand the history and customs of the Dragon Boat Festival.

- Learn about a range of festivals from around the world.
- Describe and discuss table manners from around the world.
- Share with others your views on social networking.

11.1 预习 Unit introduction

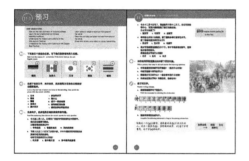

Prior knowledge

Students should have some knowledge of countries, traditions and customs from around the world and should be able to make comparisons and give opinions.

Icebreaker activity

Show students the CCTV video 外国人在中国 洋学生到我家 [00:00–04:19]. Then ask them to answer the following questions (answers and timings of clips shown in brackets):

Q1: 查理是哪一国人? (英国人 [01:04])

Q2: 查理来北京做什么? (学中文 [01:08])

Q3: 查理在中国家庭住了多久? (两个月 [01:15])

Q4: 查理几岁? (24岁 [01:57])

Q5: 查理的中国家庭在北京哪儿? (朝阳区 [02:38])

Q6: 董阿姨特别做了什么菜来欢迎查理? (炸酱面 [03:10])

Lesson activities

  Reading

Ask students whether they have been to these countries, what the capital of each is and if they know any famous landmarks. For example:

你去过德国吗? 德国的首都在哪里? 德国有哪些有名的地标?

Answers

a. 德国 dé guó, Germany

b. 加拿大 jiā ná dà, Canada

c. 日本 rì běn, Japan   **d.** 韩国 hán guó, Korea

e. 泰国 tài guó, Thailand

2 **Listening**

Ask students to read the text first and try to guess any possible matches. Their general knowledge may help them to find some answers. Also instruct them to note the key words in the right-hand column, so they can listen out for them in the recording.

Transcript

a. 我今天在日本的富士山。富士山是日本最有名的山，是一座火山。我现在就在富士山上。

b. 昨天我跟好朋友一起来到了韩国。我们今天要参观民俗博物馆，看韩国传统的面具舞表演，听说很精彩。

c. 我今天上午坐飞机刚刚到德国，晚上就要去音乐厅参加欧洲音乐节。

d. 我在加拿大还要玩三天。我超级喜欢加拿大，因为这里有各种各样的美食。

e. 我上个星期和家人来到澳大利亚度假。我觉得澳大利亚是一个非常特别的地方，这里有很多和别的地方不同的动物。

Answers

a. ii b. iv c. i d. v e. iii

3 📖 Reading

Remind students to read the questions and note the question words, so they know what to look out for as they read.

Answers

a. i **b.** i **c.** iii **d.** ii **e.** ii

4 🗨 Speaking

You may like to make some festival fact cards with information about each festival: the name, date(s), special food, how it is celebrated. In pairs students can discuss the festival card they have been given before turning to the questions in the activity.

Sample answers

a. 中国最重要的传统节日有三个：一是春节，在农历一月一日，通常在阳历一月或二月。二是端午节，在农历五月五日，通常在阳历六月。三是中秋节，在农历八月十五日，通常在阳历九月。

b. 中秋节在农历八月十五日，通常在阳历九月，所以是秋季的节日。

c. 泰国的泼水节又叫宋干节，一般在每年的四月。

d. 我没有参加过泼水节，以后有机会，我想参加。

5 ✏ Writing

For part a, help students to memorise each character by looking at the combination of the individual parts and building an association with the meaning. For example: 特 (meaning: special) = 牛 cattle + 寺 temple = cattle to be offered in the temple.

Answers for part b

a. 国际化 **b.** 世界各地 **c.** 文化 **d.** 一个 **e.** 特别

Further differentiation

 In small groups, students give a presentation about a festival in their home country.

 In groups, students give a presentation comparing two family-reunion festivals in different countries.

11.2 留学经验 Studying abroad

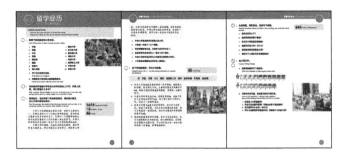

Lesson activities

1 📖 Reading

Ask students to work out the English translations first, remind them that most translations for foreign names work on sound. Most universities are named after the location, which should make it easy for students to match them with the correct countries.

Answers

Part a

a. 中国 China **b.** 美国 America **c.** 日本 Japan

d. 英国 UK **e.** 新加坡 Singapore **f.** 德国 Germany

g. 加拿大 Canada **h.** 澳大利亚 Australia

  i. 悉尼大学 Sydney University

  ii. 多伦多大学 Toronto University

  iii. 慕尼黑大学 Munich University

  iv. 清华大学 Tsinghua University

  v. 哈佛大学 Harvard University

  vi. 南洋理工大学 Nanyang Technological University

  vii. 牛津大学 Oxford University

viii. 东京大学 Tokyo University

Part b

a. iv **b.** v **c.** viii **d.** vii **e.** vi **f.** iii **g.** ii **h.** i

2 🗨 Speaking

 Review the names of academic subjects with students before doing the activity.

Sample answer

我中学毕业以后想上大学读新闻专业。

3  Reading

Instruct students to read the statements and note the key words before comparing them with the text. For example:

b. 大学里一共有<u>三十五个学院</u>。 → There are <u>35</u> colleges in the university.

The text says, 牛津大学由<u>三十八个独立的学院</u>组成。 → The University of Oxford is composed of <u>38</u> colleges.

Hence, statement b is false.

> **Answers**
>
> **a.** 对 　**b.** 错 (十八个学院) 　**c.** 对
>
> **d.** 错 (一百五十多个不同的国家和地区。)
>
> **e.** 对
>
> **f.** 错 (牛津大学的船队世界闻名，文中没有提到赛艇协会的学生人数。)

4  Reading

Tell students that the best way to deal with fill-the-gap questions is to read the text to themselves, trying different options until they feel it reads correctly. They should be able to get the right answers this way most of the time. They can also try the elimination method, deleting the obvious answers and tackling the tricky ones last.

> **Answers**
>
> **a.** i 开始 ii 读书 iii 明白　**b.** i 世界各地 ii 的时候 iii 相处　**c.** i 来 ii 做兼职工作　**d.** i 习惯 ii 打电话

5 Listening

Tell students to read the questions and note the key words, which will help them to work out what to listen out for in the recording.

> **Transcript**
>
> 今天又是星期五了，我来北京已经一个星期了。
>
> 我刚刚给在加拿大的妈妈打了电话。我告诉她来北京以后，我住在北京大学的留学生公寓楼。
>
> 我十分喜欢我住的公寓楼，因为公寓楼很新，很干净，而且楼下有一个篮球场。
>
> 我也告诉她我这几天每天在北京大学的食堂里吃饭。我觉得食堂的饭菜不但好吃，而且也比较便宜。

我还告诉妈妈，北京大学有很多外国留学生，我已经交了几个朋友了，他们有的来自韩国，有的来自马来西亚，有的来自美国。

> **Answers**
>
> **a.** 已经一个星期了。　　**b.** 加拿大
>
> **c.** 他住在北京大学里的留学生公寓楼。
>
> **d.** 他很喜欢他住的公寓楼，因为公寓楼很新，很干净，而且楼下有一个篮球场。
>
> **e.** 他觉得食堂的饭菜不但好吃，而且也比较便宜。
>
> **f.** 他的留学生朋友来自韩国、马来西亚和美国。

6 Writing and Speaking

Ask students to pay attention to the radicals of the characters in part a and study how they are formed. You may also ask students to make sentences with 留学.

Encourage students to expand their answers to part b by adding reasons and comparisons. For example, for ii. encourage students to compare a couple of countries as possible places for study; for iii. encourage them to compare a few subjects for possible study at university and say whether they would choose to study for personal interest or career prospects.

Listen to students' answers and give support as needed.

> **Sample writing**
>
> **i.** 我觉得上大学很重要，因为可以学习更高深的学问并且可以认识更多朋友。
>
> **ii.** 我想去国外留学，我打算去美国或英国。
>
> **iii.** 我打算学电脑科技方面的专业，因为我对这方面有兴趣，将来找工作也比较容易。
>
> **iv.** 我认为出国留学有很多好处，因为可以开拓我的眼界，让我具有国际观。但是不好的方面就是要适应一个陌生的环境和文化。

> **Homework suggestion**
>
> Ask students to imagine they have just arrived in a foreign country to study for a month. They should write a letter to their parents about their studies and life abroad.

11.3 中国人的婚礼 Attending a Chinese wedding

Icebreaker activity

Show students the video 《外国人在中国》 20161001 我的中国婚礼（上）[00:00–05:00], produced by CCTV4. Then ask students the following questions (answers and timings of clips shown in brackets):

Q1. 柏仁睿是哪一国人？(德国人 [00:47])

Q2. 柏仁睿的岳父最爱吃什么？(稻香村的糕点 [01:30])

Q3. 柏仁睿和曹蓉的婚筵是什么时候？(不到一周 [02:27])

Q4. 曹阿姨的拿手菜是什么？(宫保鸡丁 [04:16])

Lesson activities

1 Reading

Ask students to describe the picture, and discuss with them the differences between Chinese and western weddings.

Answers

a. i b. ii c. iii d. i

2 Writing

Remind students of the right order for Chinese when translating English into Chinese: time + place + action.

Sample writing

今天我的表姐结婚了！她看起来真是漂亮。婚礼在市中心的一家大酒店举行。来了一百多个客人，非常热闹。

For extra reading practice, students can complete the worksheet "My cousin's wedding" (on the CD-ROM).

3 Reading

Give students some tips for tackling a longer passage. For example, here there are six sentences in the reading text and seven statements as the questions. It is likely that at least one statement relates to each sentence as the questions will probably be spread through the whole passage. Students should then compare each statement with each sentence to try and find the answers.

Remind students that there are many different terms for "cousin" in Chinese:

Paternal cousins: 堂兄、堂姐、堂弟、堂妹

Maternal cousins: 表兄、表姐、表弟、表妹

Answers

a. 对   b. 错 (他是美国华侨。)

c. 对   d. 对   e. 对   f. 对

g. 错 (这是我第一次参加中式婚礼。)

4 Listening

Emphasise the importance of reading the questions *before* listening to the recording so students know what to listen for.

Transcript

A. 婚宴在哪里办？办婚宴去国际酒店。国际酒店位于市中心城市广场地铁站附近，地理位置方便。酒店内的"龙凤新人堂"在酒店最高层八十八层，可以看到城市全景。酒店环境一流，又大又干净，而且服务周到。

B. "龙凤新人"婚礼服务公司经验丰富，提供婚宴酒店安排，婚车和新婚旅游等服务。您梦想中的婚礼，无论在酒店，还是在户外的沙滩上或公园里，我们都能让您如愿以偿。

Answers

a. iii b. iii c. i d. iii e. i

5 Speaking

You could tell the class about a Chinese wedding you have been to, and then put students in pairs to discuss their wedding experiences.

Sample answers

a. 我参加了一个印度朋友的姐姐的婚礼。

b. 参加的客人非常多，好像有好几百个人。

c. 婚礼在一个大礼堂里举行。

d. 婚礼非常热闹，大家吃得很开心也玩得很开心。

e. 我觉得那场婚礼最令人难忘的部分就是新娘穿的印度礼服非常富丽堂皇。

Cultural spotlight

Teach students the following food names: 枣 (dates), 花生 (peanuts), 桂圆 (longan), 莲子 (lotus seeds), 栗子 (chestnuts).

You may also like to show students photos of weddings you have attended to start the discussion. Different Chinese provinces have different marriage customs. For example, in Guangdong province, when a woman's family is considering her marriage proposal, five dumplings are served to the man. If all five have sweet red bean or sesame fillings, it symbolises that the woman's family has agreed to the marriage proposal. If only three have sweet fillings, the family has some hesitation. If none of the dumplings has a sweet filling, the marriage proposal has been rejected.

 Ask students to compare wedding gifts in different cultures.

Homework suggestion

Students write about a memorable wedding (they can make one up), including the date, location, food and some interesting observations.

11.4 中秋节 Mid-Autumn Festival

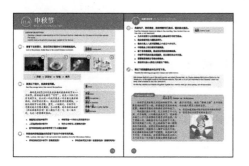

Icebreaker activity

 Show students the BBC Bitesize video *Mid-Autumn Festival in China*. Then ask the following questions (answers and timings of clips shown in brackets):

Q1. 中秋节是庆祝什么？(好收成 [00:19])

Q2. 影片中的中国家庭吃什么庆祝中秋节？(吃饺子 [02:20])

Q3. 吃过饺子以后他们做什么庆祝中秋节？(赏月和吃月饼 [03:50])

You could teach students to say "节日快乐！""Happy Holiday!" and introduce Li Bai's poem《静夜思》:

窗前明月光，疑是地上霜，
举头望明月，低头思故乡。

Lesson activities

1 **Reading**

Begin by asking students to describe what they can see in each picture.

> **Answers**
>
> **a.** iv **b.** i **c.** iii **d.** ii

2 **Reading**

Go through the questions and help students identify the key words to help them find the answers in the text.

> **Answers**
>
> **a.** 东亚各国　　　　**b.** 和月亮有关的节日
>
> **c.** 吃团圆饭、吃月饼、赏月、和家人聊天相聚。
>
> **d.** 因为月饼是圆的，象征团圆。
>
> **e.** 中秋节的新活动是家人朋友聚在一起烧烤，也是一种团圆的象征。

3 **Speaking**

This speaking activity aims to get students to talk about their experience of the Mid-Autumn Festival.

Show student some pictures related to the festival to help them with the activity.

Sample answers

a. 我在台湾过过中秋节。

b. 我在台湾吃过月饼，非常好吃，因为是妈妈亲手做的。

4 Listening

Point out that in this true-or-false activity, the statements can actually be true, false or *not mentioned*.

Language and culture

During war time, soldiers came from all over China with different accents. For the sake of clarity, especially for artillery communications, the pronunciation of some numbers was changed:

0—洞 (dòng)　7—拐 (guǎi)
1—幺 (yāo)　9—勾 (gōu)
2—两 (liǎng)

These pronunciations have remained in use, and are even used by the general public, especially 1 (yāo). Hence, the bus numbers 118 and 511 in the recording are pronounced (yāo yāo bā) and (wǔ yāo yāo).

Transcript

为了庆祝中秋节，从九月三日到十七日，城市广场将在每个星期三晚上举行中秋歌舞晚会。

晚会除了有传统民族舞表演，还会有老人们喜欢的京剧表演。晚会都不需要门票，是免费的。欢迎广大市民参加。

如果您坐地铁，请乘坐"东西三号线"，在城市广场站下车。

如果您坐公共汽车，您可以乘坐306路、118路、511路，在城市广场站下车。

因为中秋节市区的交通会相当拥挤,我们建议大家乘坐公共交通。

Answers

a. 错 (每个星期三晚上举行中秋节晚会。)

b. 错 (地点在城市广场。)

c. 未提及　d. 对　e. 对

f. 对　g. 错 (东西三号线)　h. 对

5 Writing

Encourage students to deal with translating a longer passage by breaking it up into phrases or sentences.

Sample writing

中秋节是最受欢迎的中国古老传统节庆之一。人们在农历八月十五日庆祝中秋节。这个节庆不仅仅只是中国人庆祝，韩国人和其他许多亚洲国家也庆祝中秋节。在这一天家人和朋友会聚在一起吃团圆饭，一起赏月吃月饼。

Cultural spotlight

Go through any unfamiliar words with students to increase their vocabulary. Explain that mooncakes are the main traditional food eaten during the Mid-Autumn Festival. Each region has its own special pastry/fillings, such as:

Yunnan: fresh flowers and ham filling
Sichuan: tea-flavoured fillings and pastry
Hong Kong: sticky rice is used for the pastry, and they need to be kept in the fridge
Taiwan: fluffy, multi-layered pastry

Homework suggestion

Ask students to write a recipe for making mooncakes, with the filling and pastry made to their liking.

11.5 端午节 Dragon Boat Festival

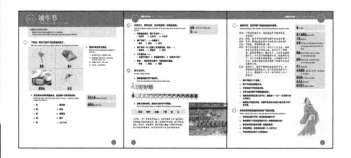

Lesson activities

1 Reading

Ask students what they know about the Dragon Boat Festival, then go through each picture with them, discussing how the items are used during the festival.

Answers

Part a: i. 香包 **ii.** 粽子 **iii.** 雄黄酒 **iv.** 蚊虫

Part b: a. v **b.** i **c.** v **d.** ii **e.** iii

  Listening

This is a gap-filling exercise. Tell students to be aware of the key words near the gaps to help them find the answers.

Transcript

在我住的城市端午节又被称为五月节或夏节。端午节到了，夏季也就不远了。

夏天天气变热，蚊虫越来越多，端午节这一天我们会用中草药洗澡，会做香包驱赶蚊虫。

每一个传统节日都会有传统美食。端午节的美食就是粽子。

去年妈妈从超市买了粽子拿回家吃。但是今年妈妈决定在家里包粽子庆祝节日。

我和妹妹两个人跟着妈妈学包粽子，觉得很有意思。而且我们都觉得自己包的粽子更好吃。

Answers

a. ii **b.** ii **c.** i **d.** iii **e.** ii

  Writing

For part a, tell students that the radical for 比 is the entire character.

For part b, remind students that one simple way to do a gap-filling exercise is to read each sentence a few times, trying all the option words to see which fits best. Students can also analyse the sentences to see whether a subject/verb/object/preposition is missing.

Answers for part b

a. 到 **b.** 让 **c.** 了解 **d.** 举行 **e.** 参加 **f.** 比赛

  Reading

This reading activity is in the form of a conversation. Ask two students to read it out. Note that this passage is quite challenging with lots of new vocabulary.

 Ask students to circle all the new words in pencil. Then ask how much of the text they can

understand without knowing those words. Encourage them to guess! They should then write the pinyin and English translation near each new word in pencil and read the text again. Next they should erase the English translation and read the text a third time. Finally they erase the pinyin and read the text again. If they still struggle, work out a further remedial plan.

Answers

a. 对 **b.** 错 (端午节是纪念屈原。)

c. 错 (粽子是端午节的传统食物。)

d. 对 **e.** 对 **f.** 对

  Speaking

Give students a few minutes to write out some bullet points to answer each question, then get them to use their notes to conduct the interview with a partner.

Sample answers

a. 我听说过端午节也过过端午节。

b. 端午节是纪念爱国诗人的节日。人们吃粽子喝雄黄酒，看划龙舟比赛。

c. 我在伦敦的泰晤士河看过龙舟比赛。

d. 在英国的斯特拉福镇，人们在4月23日庆祝莎士比亚的生日。

e. 每年在莎士比亚生日这一天，英国的斯特拉福镇会举办盛大的游行，剧场会有许多特殊表演，非常热闹。

Homework suggestion

Students imagine they are a reporter, commentating on a river dragon boat race. They should introduce the Dragon Boat Festival, discussing some of the traditions/customs, and then report on the race.

11.6 亚洲国家的节日和习俗
Other Asian festivals and customs

Lesson activities

  Reading

Ask students what their favourite festival is and what they do to celebrate it.

Answers

a. ii **b.** iii **c.** i

  Listening

Remind students to read the questions first and note the key words so they know what to listen for. Tell them to be aware of synonyms; for example, 星期天 is used in a question, which is an equivalent to 周日 in the recording.

Transcript

A. 这个周日——5月10日——就是母亲节了。如果你妈妈母亲节时在新加坡，带她来国际酒店吃海鲜吧，母亲节当天免费送葡萄果汁一瓶。

B. 为庆祝十月的重阳节，文化公园将在这个星期五的晚上举办免费户外京剧表演。时间是十月十四日下午五点到晚上九点。欢迎各位喜爱京剧的老年朋友们参加。当晚文化公园还可以免费品茶。

Answers

a. 母亲节 **b.** 吃海鲜免费送葡萄果汁一瓶

c. 将在星期五的晚上举办免费户外京剧表演

d. 提供免费品茶

e. 时间是十月十四日下午五点到晚上九点。

 Reading

There is quite a lot of new vocabulary in this passage. You may consider the tips suggested in Unit 11.5, Activity 4.

Answers

a. 因为新加坡有华人、欧亚裔、印度裔、马来人等。
b. 开斋节 **c.** 辣肉，马来粽 **d.** 另外一个特色是人们会穿着他们最美丽的传统服装庆祝节日。

Language and culture

The end of Ramadan is known by different names around the world. The name Hari Raya Puasa is mentioned here, as the passage is specifically to do with celebrations in Singapore. Eid al-Fitr is the official term used in the Koran.

 Speaking

For the role-play activity, you may like to advise students to write down some questions first so that they know how the conversation will go.

 Ask students to also write down their answers beforehand so that they don't have to give an impromptu speech.

Sample answers

A: 咱们今天聊聊农历新年。

B: 好的。旧历新年在中、港、澳、台、新、马、印、韩、越、菲等亚洲国家或地区是非常重要的节日之一，而且规定放假。

A: 农历新年以农历计算，农历正月初一的前一天是除夕，放假从除夕开始。在香港人们初五开工，老板会给参加开工的员工红包呢。

B: 是的。除夕全家还会一起吃团圆饭，你家今年吃什么？

A: 我妈妈准备了"剁椒蒸石斑"代表了"年年有余(鱼)"，晚上还会守岁不睡觉，愿爸妈长命百岁。

B: 吃团圆饭时，发红包吗?

A: 当然啰，晚辈向长辈拜完年，长辈就会给未婚晚辈红包。

B: 哈，难怪每年除夕前银行得准备很多新钞呢。

A: 让我们一起向听众拜年吧！

AB一起: 祝大家新年万事如意，恭喜发财，身体健康！

This activity combines gap-filling and multiple choice. Advise students to note the key words in the questions and to use them as the focus while listening.

Transcript

男：父亲节快到了，就在下个星期。你有什么打算？

女：我知道。那天我有事，回不去，但是我已经给爸爸寄了一张贺卡，还给他快递了一份礼物。

男：每年的四月份很多地方的人都会过清明节。你明白清明节的意义吗？

女：我明白。清明节是纪念祖先的节日，那一天家人会聚在一起纪念逝去的亲人。

男：对不起，中午的聚餐我就不参加了，因为这些天是我们的斋戒日。

女：没关系。等你斋戒完了再一起吃饭吧！

Answers

a. iii   **b.** ii   **c.** i

6 **Writing**

Instruct students to write full sentence answers for each question and then to put them in a logical order.

Sample writing

清明节是在4月4至6日，人们过清明节是为了纪念祖先和过去的英雄烈士。清明节吃的传统食物有大葱、青团和枣糕。清明节的时候，人们会去扫墓纪念祖先，也有人会去郊外踏青、放风筝。

Further differentiation

 In groups, students research and give a presentation about how ancestors or past heroes are remembered in their country/culture.

 Students can also compare how past heroes are respected/remembered in China and in their country.

Homework suggestion

Students write an email to a foreign-exchange student inviting him/her to a special festival and briefly explaining the traditions and customs of the festival.

11.7 其他国家的节日 Festivals from other parts of the world

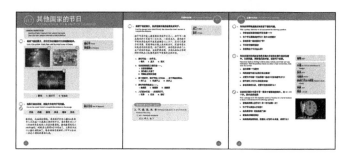

Lesson activities

1 **Reading**

Go through each picture and ask students whether they are familiar with any of the festivals.

Answers

a. ii   **b.** iii   **c.** i

2   **Reading and Writing**

Encourage students to develop the habit of regularly reading Chinese text aloud. This will definitely help them carry out this type of gap-filling activity. They should read the text to themselves, testing the option words for each gap, finding the most suitable ones.

3 **Reading**

Answers

a. 称作	**b.** 最后	**c.** 来自
d. 开始	**e.** 历史	**f.** 传统

Tell students that it is crucial to read the questions and the multiple-choice options first. If they quickly analyse the questions, they can read for the answers and are more likely to get them right.

Answers

a. iii (or i; note that it may depend on whether you are in the northern or southern hemisphere)

b. iii   **c.** i   **d.** ii   **e.** i

Speaking

Before students start their pair work, you may like to mention a fun festival you have been to or use some of the sample answers to give students models to follow.

Sample answers

a. 我参加过的最有趣的节日是威尼斯的嘉年华会。

b. 这个节日每年一月底到二月中在意大利的威尼斯城举行。

c. 我是前年跟几个好朋友一起去威尼斯参加了这个节庆。

d. 在威尼斯嘉年华会的期间，许多人都穿着华丽的古典服装，带着各式各样漂亮的面具在大街小巷走着。剧场里还有许多精彩的表演。

e. 我觉得威尼斯嘉年华会非常有意思，在这里你可以看到许多人很精彩的设计。

 Listening

Explain to students that they will hear a loan word, 派對, which is a direct phonetic translation for "party".

Transcript

史蒂文：玛利亚，这个星期六就是新年了。你打算做什么？

玛利亚：史蒂文你好。我的爸爸妈妈要从马德里飞来上海和我一起过新年，所以我会带他们逛一逛上海。

史蒂文：你会带他们去哪儿看一看？

玛利亚：我会先带他们参观上海的著名景点，比如说外滩，然后去和我在上海认识的西班牙朋友们一起庆祝。我们国家有一个传统，在新年钟声敲响的十二下里，要吃下十二颗葡萄，所以我还得去买葡萄。你呢？新年你做什么？

史蒂文：年末那天的晚上我会和其他留学生一起去外滩公园参加新年派对，听说那里的烟花特别好看。看完了烟花，我们还会一起去跳舞。

玛利亚：新年快乐，也祝你玩得开心。

史蒂文：你也是。

Answers

a. 他们在上海。

b. 他们会先去一些上海的景点，然后去和一些在上海的西班牙朋友们一起庆祝新年。

c. 他会和其他留学生一起去。 **d.** 有放烟花的活动。

e. 他还会和同学一起去跳舞。

Language and culture

Chinese borrows many words from English, such as: 吐司 (toast), 三明治 (sandwich), 披萨 (pizza), 巧克力 (chocolate), 咖啡 (coffee), 可乐 (cola), 起司 (cheese), 巴士 (bus), T恤 (T-shirt), 派对 (party).

 Writing

Ask students to answer each question with one or two complete sentences first and then organise the sentences into a logical order.

Help students to look at the questions carefully and follow their patterns but add in the answers to replace the question words.

Sample writing

番茄战是在西班牙的节庆，在每年八月的最后一个星期三举行。这个节庆原本是当地居民向政府抗议丢番茄，后来变成好玩的丢番茄活动。现在每年都有很多人参加，必须买门票。活动的那一周会有游行、烟火还有美食比赛。如果要参加番茄战，一定要穿轻便的旧衣服和鞋子，并且带着护目镜。

Language and culture

Chinese people like to say and hear auspicious words to bring good fortune, especially during Chinese New Year, weddings and birthdays. It is a way to offer good wishes to acquaintances and friends. Here are some expressions:

For Chinese New Year

恭喜发财 (gōng xǐ fā cái): Congratulations, I wish you prosperity.

岁岁平安 (suì suì píng ān): Peace for every year. (Chinese always say this, especially when someone breaks something, as 岁 shares the same pronunciation as 碎, which means "broken and shattered". It is a Chinese custom to say something auspicious in a negative situation.)

万事如意 (wàn shì rú yì): Everything will be as you wish.

For wedding celebrations

天作之合 (tiān zuò zhī hé): It's a match made in heaven.

百年偕老 (bǎi nián xié lǎo) To grow old together.

For birthday parties (normally for elderly people)

松柏长青 (sōng bó cháng qīng) I wish that you will be like the pine trees which are forever green.

Homework suggestion

Students write a blog post about a special festival they have been to recently, including dates, venue, who they went with and what they did there.

11.8 餐桌礼仪 Table manners

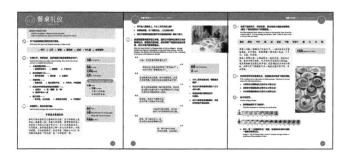

Icebreaker activity

Show students the video *世界各国餐桌文化*, produced by 味全TV, and ask them about table manners in different countries.

Lesson activities

1 Writing

You may like to use pictures or questions to reinforce the vocabulary covered in this activity. For example:

Q1: 中国人通常用什么餐具吃饭？（筷子）

Q2: 美国人通常用什么餐具吃饭？（刀叉）

Answers

a. 筷子 kuài zi, chopsticks

b. 刀叉 dāo chā, knife and fork

c. 谢谢 xiè xie, thank you

d. 请给我 qǐng gěi wǒ, please give me...

e. 说话 shuō huà, to speak

f. 有礼貌 yǒu lǐ mào, to be polite

g. 吃得很快 chī de hěn kuài, eat very fast

2 Listening

For this activity, students will need to correctly identify the bad habit (or problem) each piece of advice is trying to tackle. Each sentence in the activity therefore needs to relate to an action opposite to what the advice says.

Transcript

a. 小亮，吃饭的时候不要那么大声地说话。

b. 欧文，吃饭请用刀叉，不要用你的手。

c. 米娜，慢慢吃饭，不要吃得太快了！

d. 杰克，在爷爷奶奶家吃饭要和他们说"谢谢"和"请"。

e. 新兰，要把饭吃完，不要浪费了。

Answers

a. i **b.** i **c.** i **d.** ii **e.** i

3  Reading

Tell students that the way to tackle short-answer questions is to note down the key words and question words before going back to the text to seek the answers. For example:

a. 在中国人的餐桌上，什么人可以坐在上座？ → Look for people near the key word 上座.

b. 吃饭的时候，为了保持卫生，人们会怎么做？ → Look for actions near the key word 卫生.

c. 短文中讲到吃饭的时候不可以做哪些事情？举两个例子。 → Look for some negative behaviour around the key words 不应该.

Answers

a. 上座给客人或老人坐。 **b.** 用公筷来保持卫生。

c. 吃饭时，不应该敲筷子，发出声音（例如打饱嗝）。

4 Reading

Although this is a reading activity, it may help students to read the conversation out loud in pairs. They may also work out the answers together.

Answers

a. 错（吃完了才说这句话。）

b. 错（在家庭吃饭时也用公筷。）

c. 对 **d.** 对

5   Listening

This listening activity is a dictation test. Point out that there are more option words than will be needed.

 Suggest that for each gap students take a note of the number of characters/syllables they hear in the recording, or jot down the pinyin if they can, before trying to find the answers.

Transcript

英国人吃饭一般都用刀叉和勺子，一般应该是右手拿刀或勺子，左手拿叉。家庭聚餐一般是三道菜，包括开胃菜，主菜，还有甜点。

英国人常常以喝汤作为一餐的开始，然后以甜点结束。吃不同的东西要用不同的餐具。喝东西时不能发出很大的声音！还有嘴里有东西时不要说话。

当你吃完了就要把刀叉一起放到盘子的中间，表示你吃完了。

Answers

a. 刀　**b.** 勺子　**c.** 叉　**d.** 菜　**e.** 甜点

f. 汤　**g.** 餐具　**h.** 不能　**i.** 说话　**j.** 吃完了

6   Speaking

Remind students to be respectful and mindful of different cultural etiquette, especially when travelling abroad.

Sample answers

a. 中国和日本的餐桌礼仪很类似，不过中国人用筷子要用碗或盘子等容器托着，日本人使用筷子时忌把筷子放在碗碟上面。

b. 英国和中国的餐桌礼仪很不相同，基本上这两国的餐具和饮食习惯都很不一样。但是我认为最大的不同是，英国人在餐桌上讲究安静优雅，但是中国人觉得餐桌上安静就太拘束，因此中国的餐桌上大都很热闹。

c. 日本和英国的餐桌礼仪在很多方面很类似，双方都很注重餐桌上要安静，轻声细语。

7   Writing

For part a, remind students to pay attention to the radicals and ask them to think of other words with the same radicals.

For part b, it may be daunting to have to think of 10 dining rules immediately. Help students to think about the different stages of dining: seating arrangements, manners while eating, cutlery etiquette, etc. Then ask them to think of a few rules for each stage.

 Ask students to imagine they are dining with business associates in China. They should consider rules for business etiquette while dining, such as toasting.

Sample writing for part b

十条中国餐桌礼仪：

一、先等老人、上司坐好了之后，等主人请你入座，才可以坐下。

二、等大家到齐了，才可以开饭。

三、等上座的人动筷子了，才可以动筷。

四、口中有食物的时候，不要说话。

五、吃鱼的时候，吃完一边不可翻转。

六、春节吃鱼的时候，不要把鱼都吃完。

七、敬酒的时候，酒杯不可以高过长辈或上司。

八、不可用筷子敲碗盘。

九、不可用筷子在餐盘中挑选食物。

十、不可用筷子指着人说话。

Homework suggestion

Students pick a country of their choice and complete the worksheet "When in Rome" (on the CD-ROM).

11.9 社交网络 Social networking

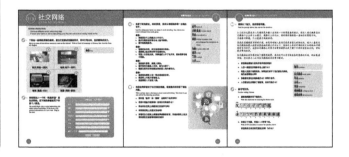

Icebreaker activity

Using the worksheet "My favourite social media app" (on the CD-ROM), students can carry out a survey in their neighbourhood or street to find out which apps their friends and family like to use and why. Select a few people to share their findings in Chinese.

Lesson activities

1   Writing

Remind students that abbreviations are common in the Chinese language. Ask if they have come across any other ones.

> **Answers**
>
> **a.** 网友 = 网络 + 朋友，online friends
>
> **b.** 电邮 = 电子 + 邮件，email
>
> **c.** 微博 = 微型 + 博客，mini blog
>
> **d.** 网游 = 网络 + 游戏，online games

2 Writing

Remind students there is no need to write in complete sentences when filling in a form. The form is asking for some basic personal information. The slightly tricky ones are the last two items: 性格 (personality) and 最新个人计划 (most recent personal plans). Tell students to write something positive about their personalities and something interesting about their future plans to attract friends on social media.

> **Sample writing**
>
> 姓名：王志军　　年龄：16　　性别：男
>
> 居住城市：广州　　家乡：北京
>
> 爱好：中国功夫　　性格：活泼外向
>
> 最新个人计划：打算去欧洲旅行。

3 Listening

Tell students that they won't just be listening for some facts or details, but they have to understand the recording and choose a correct statement out of the three options. It is important to read the questions carefully first and note the key words to analyse the options. For example:

Recording A:

a. 她常在脸书上和朋友分享信息。

b. 她只有周末的时候才会上脸书看看。

c. 她不经常用脸书。

Here students need to listen to find out how often she goes on Facebook. The options will be "very often", "only at weekends" or "very rarely".

A. 我在香港已经留学一年了。我几乎每天都上脸书，和远在巴西的朋友们分享我在香港的生活经历和这个城市的特别的地方。

B. 我不喜欢上社交网，我觉得既浪费时间，又十分无聊，而且对学习一点儿都不好。但是有的人沉迷社交网，如果有一天不上社交网，他们就会觉得非常不舒服。

C. 我在国外留学，我用微信跟家里人视频聊天，虽然家人在中国，我在新加坡，可是因为有微信，我每天都可以和爸爸妈妈说话。

D. 我喜欢在网络上写东西，所以我有一个博客。我常常在博客上写一些有意思，好玩的事情，再上传一些好看的照片，有好多人喜欢阅读我的博客呢。

> **Answers**
>
> **A.** a　**B.** c　**C.** c　**D.** a

Language and culture

The language used on social media by Chinese teenagers is a combination of English, numbers and abbreviations. Here are some examples:

1. 3Q = Thank you. Similar pronunciation to English "thank you" (sān-Q).

2. 你↓到我了！ = You scared me! ↓ means 下 (xià), which shares the same sound as 吓 (to scare).

3. 520 = I love you. Sounds like 我爱你.

4. 88/886 = bye bye (拜拜/拜拜了)

4 Speaking

Discuss whether students use Facebook and Twitter, or other social networking apps, to communicate with their friends. Ask them to share their experience with their partner.

> **Sample answers**
>
> **a.** 脸书是 Facebook，是双向的社交网。推特是 Twitter，是单向追随的社交网。
>
> **b.** 我常用脸书，比较少用推特。我用脸书跟朋友圈交流信息。
>
> **c.** 是的，我在脸书上加入了一些学习小组。
>
> **d.** 我觉得在网上交朋友要小心谨慎，注意安全。
>
> **e.** 我通常会先在网上自己查信息学习新的东西，有时候也会在社交网上跟朋友交流新知识。

5 Reading

Introduce the basic structure for writing a Chinese essay. It is based on four words: 起承转合 (qǐ chéng zhuǎn hé).

起 "open/begin": introduce a concept or an argument

承 "develop": expand on the opening idea

转 "change direction": give arguments from the opposing viewpoint

合 "close": sum up in a conclusion

Ask students to analyse the reading text to see how the above structure has been adopted.

> **Answers**
>
> **a.** 我觉得这篇短文是博客，因为文章的语气是面对一群人。
>
> **b.** 人们一般在社交媒体平台上发表意见，交换信息。
>
> **c.** 这些人不看社交媒体就觉得不舒服。
>
> **d.** 作者喜欢用社交媒体与家人和世界各地的朋友保持联系，另外他也利用社交媒体了解不同的国家和文化，学到新的知识。
>
> **e.** 社交媒体还可以用来组织各种重要的活动，例如慈善活动等等。

6 Writing

For part a, help students to examine the radicals and structures of the two characters and to come up with a way to memorise the characters and their meanings.

For part b, show students the following patterns that can be used with 沉迷 (addiction):

1. 沉迷 + Noun: 他沉迷电脑游戏。
2. 沉迷 + 于 + Noun: 他沉迷于电脑游戏中。
3. 沉迷 + 在 + Noun: 他沉迷在电脑游戏里。

You may like to practise making sentences using 沉迷 with the students orally before the writing activity.

 Students can expand their sentences by giving more detail.

> **Sample writing for part b**
> 我觉得自己很沉迷社交网，因为我每天一定要上社交网好几回。

> **Homework suggestion**
>
> Students write a paragraph about how they and their family members use social media and give their opinion about it.

11.10 复习 Progress check

Lesson activities

1 Reading

Write relevant vocabulary on cards and give one to each student. They should find someone with a synonym for the word on their card. This person can then be their work partner for this lesson.

> **Answers**
>
> **a.** vi **b.** v **c.** i **d.** ii **e.** iii **f.** iv

2   Reading and Writing

Students should work in pairs to fill the gaps. Ask them to try and think of more synonyms.

> **Answers**
>
> **a.** i **b.** ii **c.** iv **d.** iii

3 Listening

Help students to analyse the questions to prepare for the listening activity.

Recording A: From the three questions, we learn that the recording is about a festival, a food related to the festival and a son doing something abroad.

Students should find answers for three key words in the questions: 节日, 食品, 做什么.

Recording B: Reading the questions reveals that the recording is about Dragon Boat Festival and rice dumplings. The questions ask for 1) a restaurant's name and phone number; 2) public transport and stop (to get there); 3) two types of rice dumplings for sale.

Transcript

A. 儿子，下周三是中秋节。今年你会不会回家？你一个人在国外留学，一定要好好照顾自己哦。你那边买不到你爱吃的月饼，所以妈妈给你寄去你最爱吃的"绿健月饼"，一定要好好吃哦。

B. 悉尼城北区大学附近"金龙"饭店端午节可以预订粽子。价格不贵，绝对美味，买过的中国留学生们都说好。肉粽 3.5 澳元一个，豆沙粽 3 澳元一个，买得多可以电话谈，可以便宜点。预订电话 04301239856。你也可以到饭店买，从悉尼大学乘坐68路公共汽车到北区市场站下车，金龙饭店就在公共汽车站旁边。

Answers

a. 中秋节 **b.** 月饼 **c.** 在国外留学

d. 金龙饭店，电话是 04301239856

e. 坐68路公共汽车到北区市场站下车。

f. 肉粽和豆沙粽

4 Reading

Put students in their pairs and ask them to each underline in pencil the words they recognise in the text. They then help one another to underline more words until they can read the whole text.

Answers

a. 对   **b.** 错（比赛在城市公园的湖上举行。）

c. 对   **d.** 错（每队十人。）   **e.** 对   **f.** 对

5 Writing

Ask students to analyse each item and first find the three major elements in the Chinese sentence structure (time, place and action). Then they should decide whether the rest of the items are adjectives, adverbs or part of a compound word and place them with one of the three main elements. Lastly, they should try to put everything into the correct order.

Answers

a. 中学毕业以后哥哥打算／哥哥打算中学毕业以后去英国的牛津大学留学。

b. 他希望去那里学习数学专业。

c. 牛津城里不仅有世界一流的牛津大学，还有一座座古老的建筑。

d. 这座城市每年都吸引了成千上万的游客。

e. 这些游客们来自世界各地。

6 Speaking

Walk around the classroom and listen to students' conversations. Provide support as necessary.

 Encourage students to elaborate on their answers. For example, they could add in their reasoning to question 2 and question 3. They could analyse the academic conditions in different countries and how they have affected their decision. They could also give more details about the university they plan to attend in the future, such as its location, student demographic and anything special.

Sample answers

a. 我是理科A班的学生。

b. 我擅长数学、物理和化学科目。我最喜欢电脑和应用数学。

c. 我打算到大学读电脑科技专业。

d. 我想去美国留学。

e. 我希望去麻省理工学院留学。

7 Writing

Remind students to read the instructions for the writing carefully. In this case, the instruction says 应该 (should); therefore, students must cover all bullet points.

Sample writing

英国人口共有六千五百多万人，首都是伦敦。全年温和多雨。最传统的节日是圣诞节，在外工作读书的人都会赶回家过圣诞，一起吃大餐并且交换礼物。英国的餐桌礼仪繁多，例如：不同的食物有不同的餐具，进餐时不打嗝或大声说话。

脸书和推特都是英国很受欢迎的社交网站。

Further differentiation

In groups, students give a presentation on their nation's sense of humour. Humour is notoriously difficult to translate. However, give students this challenging task and see if they can make the rest of the class laugh.

 Ask students to show photos or pictures and explain what makes their nation laugh.

 Ask students to compare the senses of humour of two different nations and work out what makes each nation laugh.

Assessment suggestion

 Show students the video *5分钟看完BBC纪录片《中国新年》，英国人在中国过春节——电影小镇* [00:00–05:45], produced by the BBC. Ask them the following questions (answers and timings of clips shown in brackets):

Q1: 中国很大, 所以, 影片中提到的的第一个场景特色是? (人, 满屏幕的人 [00:59])

Q2: 中国很大, 人很多, 春节期间的交通运输, 堪称世界奇观, 称之为? (春运 [01:02])

Q3: 春节期间, 数百万人涌出北京, 回家过年, 造成北京拥堵, 交通部统计总共有多人次? (32亿人次 [01:38])

Q4: 春节期间, 火车站帮助旅客搬行李的人叫什么? (小红帽 [02:02])

Prior knowledge

By Unit 12 your students should have learned all the vocabulary and grammar essential for their examinations. They should have developed a routine in class and in their home study. Remind students that it is essential to know all the vocabulary. Encourage them to make good use of flashcards; Quizlet provides a helpful system of flashcards along with games for students to use. The website mdbg.net provides useful information about characters and phrases, including radicals, number of strokes and writing sequence, etc.

This is a synoptic unit, so no explicit homework suggestions are given. Teachers can use their discretion and utilise some of the assessments as homework if required.

 You may need to help students build up their vocabulary unit by unit by making good use of the grammar patterns in Unit 13. Combining these will enable them to use the language at a conversational level, if not at least a basic level. If writing the new words is too difficult, make sure they can at least recognise them visually and aurally. Ask them to revisit their previous homework, and make sure all their previous mistakes have been rectified and understood. You may need to give them some one-on-one tutorials.

 In addition to making sure students have a solid knowledge of the learned vocabulary and grammar patterns, you may set them more challenging tasks. For example, reading Chinese newspapers and watching Chinese dramas is an easy way to improve pronunciation and fluency. Encourage them to use more complex sentence patterns and develop more logical and critical thinking in Chinese, which will take their language skills up to an advanced level.

12.1 叔叔结婚了 Uncle is getting married

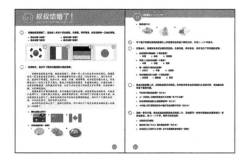

This lesson consolidates what students have learned in:

- Lessons 1.8, 11.3: attending a special event
- Lessons 3.1–3.4: food from around the world
- Lessons 7.3–7.4, 10.2: countries and continents

Icebreaker activity

 Show students the video 侨委会宏观家族 台湾喜饼学问多 [00:00–01:59], produced by 侨委会台湾宏观电视. Ask them the following questions (answers and timings of clips shown in brackets):

Q1: 中国人结婚送喜饼给亲友起缘于哪一朝代? (三国时代 [0:29])

Q2: 喜饼大致分为哪两种? (中式大饼和西式盒装饼 [0:47])

Q3: 为什么送喜饼习惯送六的倍数? (双双对对, 吉祥如意 [1:10])

Lesson activities

1   **Listening**

Students should recognise the flags and know the country names, so this should be fairly straightforward.

Transcript

a. A: 你来自哪个国家?

B: 我来自日本。

A: 他来自哪个国家?

b. A: 你来自哪个国家?

B: 我来自法国。

A: 她来自哪个国家?

c. A: 你来自哪个国家？

B: 我来自韩国。

A: 他来自哪个国家？

d. A: 你来自哪个国家？

B: 我来自德国。

A: 她来自哪个国家？

Answers

a. iv **b.** ii **c.** i **d.** iii

 Ask students if they know any other ways to say "I come from...".

2   Reading

Students need to recognise what each image is representing and find the relevant points in the text. The vocabulary required is about nationalities and food.

Answers

a. ii **b.** i **c.** iii

3   Writing

Remind students of the structures for "favourite" and "least favourite". For further practice, they can use this structure to make sentences with things other than food.

Sample writing

在汤姆叔叔婚礼上，我最想吃的菜是水煮鱼，最不想吃的是酸辣汤。

 Ask students to give reasons for their statements.

4  Listening

Tell students that the recording is about Chinese food; however, the questions focus on continents.

Transcript

弟弟：今天的菜来自不同的国家，种类真多，我吃得真开心。对了，哥哥，你刚才吃了什么菜？

汤姆：我刚刚吃了中国的酸辣汤。你知道吗，弟弟，中国的酸辣汤特别有名，特别辣，特别好吃。

弟弟：对，我也喜欢中国的菜。我也很喜欢中国这个国家，我还知道中国是欧洲最大的国家呢！

汤姆：才不是呢！中国在亚洲。中国是亚洲最大的国家，它的人口也是亚洲最多的，所以菜式也特别多。爸爸妈妈今天吃的水煮鱼这道菜就是中国有名的菜。

弟弟：听爸爸妈妈说，他们今天也吃了加拿大羊肉。哥哥，我记得地理老师上课说过加拿大在南美洲，对不对？

汤姆：弟弟，加拿大不在南美洲，它在北美洲。你上课不专心，回去要跟你的地理老师好好学习学习！

Answers

a. ii **b.** i **c.** iii **d.** ii

5  Speaking

Walk around the classroom and listen to students' conversations. Provide additional support if necessary.

Sample answers

a. 平时我常吃中餐，因为我觉得中餐比西餐好吃。

b. 上一次我和家人去了一家米其林餐厅吃饭庆祝，吃了很多美味的法国美食。

c. 如果朋友要外出吃饭庆祝，我一定会推荐这家餐厅，因为这家餐厅不仅菜好吃，而且餐厅的布置很高雅。

d. 今天晚上我打算带你们去一家中餐厅吃饭，他们做的北京烤鸭特别好吃。

6  Writing

Revise letter structure, greetings and sign-offs with students. Make sure they understand which tenses are needed to answer the questions (past/future).

Sample answer

叔叔您好，

非常感谢您邀请我们一家参加您的婚宴。

昨天的宴会特别热闹，来了很多客人。我们吃了很多美食，每一道菜都非常可口，水煮鱼很辣很够味，澳洲牛肉很鲜美。

下个月十八日爸爸妈妈要庆祝结婚周年，要在家里举行宴会，希望叔叔婶婶都能够来。 敬祝

安康！

小华敬上 7月25日

 Ask if students know other expressions of thanks.

Further differentiation

 Students carry out research to find out what are some common presents guests bring to weddings, and make a list.

 Students give reasons to explain why certain presents are suitable as wedding gifts.

Assessment suggestion

Ask students to write a diary entry about a special occasion such as a wedding or special anniversary celebration where they have eaten something special.

12.2 去医院看奶奶 Visiting grandma in hospital

This lesson consolidates what students have learned in:

- Lessons 3.5–3.6: health and wellbeing

- Lessons 6.5–6.6: locations and directions

- Lesson 7.7: public transport

Lesson activities

1   Reading

Here students need to recognise what part of speech the missing word is likely to be. They should read the paragraph first to get the full context and note there are more answer options than are needed.

Answers

a. 重感冒 b. 暖和 c. 发烧 d. 天气

2   Listening

Students may need a quick recap on vocabulary relating to illnesses and ailments before doing this activity.

Transcript

男医生：您好。您怎么啦?

奶奶：你好，医生，我头疼得厉害。

男医生：什么时候开始不舒服的?

奶奶：今天早上开始不舒服的。

男医生：我给您量一下体温。有39.5度，发烧了。来嘴巴张开，我看看。喉咙也有点儿发炎了。我给您开点儿药。等会儿去药房取药，回家吃了应该就没事儿了。

奶奶：谢谢医生。

男医生：放心，没什么大问题。回去多喝水，好好休息，多喝点儿粥。

奶奶：谢谢。哦，请问医生这药是饭前吃还是饭后吃?

男医生：记得在饭前吃，千万别饭后吃。

奶奶：好的，谢谢医生。

Answers

a. 头疼得厉害、发烧、喉咙发炎 b. 去药房取药

c. 多喝水、好好休息、多喝点粥 d. 在饭前吃药

 Ask students if they can pick up any specific commands given by the doctor in the recording (e.g. 记得在饭前吃, 千万别饭后吃).

3  Reading

Tell students that the focus here is on the journey to the hospital. Students should be looking for information on tickets, types of transport and the name of the bus stop.

You may also use the reading passages in Activities 1 and 3 to revisit the key language features used when relating a story (connecting words, sequence of events, etc.).

Answers

a. 奶奶还是觉得不舒服。 **b.** 因为他听爸爸说，来回票比较便宜。 **c.** 因为前方的铁路出了小事故，通知说铁路上出现了两头牛。 **d.** 他在美术馆附近下了车。

4  Listening

Students may benefit from a quick recap on numbers, compass points, directions, names of public places, etc.

Transcript

小文：很抱歉，打扰您。我迷路了。我想去郊区医院，但是我不知道怎么走。请问医院离这儿远吗？

女路人：郊区医院吗？医院离这儿有点儿远。

小文：医院怎么走？

女路人：这儿的附近有一个动物园，医院在动物园的北边。顺着动物园方向一直走，你会看到一个十字路口，在十字路口向北走一千米就会看到医院了。

小文：谢谢您！

女路人：不用客气！

Answers

a. iii **b.** iii **c.** iii

5  Speaking

Tell students that this role-play requires talking about how they feel, and go over some useful expressions.

Sample answers

a. 我今天觉得还是有点不舒服。

b. 我不喜欢住院，医院总是没有家里好。

c. 医院的饮食很不好吃，我一点也不习惯。

d. 出院以后，我要直接到中国餐厅去吃北京烤鸭。

6 Speaking

This activity focuses on asking for/giving directions. It may be helpful to look at the hospital layout first with the students, and revise basic directional phrases.

Sample answers

a. 从病房下楼梯到一楼左转就可以到药房。

b. 办公室在病房两侧。

c. 从医院大门进去一直直走就会看到食堂。

7 Writing

Remind students that they are writing a thank-you card. Depending on the status of the writer and receiver, they need to consider whether 你 or 您 is more appropriate.

Sample writing

陈医生您好，

非常感谢您的医治，我恢复得很好，头不疼了，烧也退了，不过觉得有点累。我现在每天都喝八杯水，晚上很早就睡觉。我以后外出也会注意保暖。

DP For extra practice, turn the sample writing passage into a true-or-false or comprehension activity.

Further differentiation

 Students should write an email to their friend, declining their birthday party invitation due to a sudden illness.

 Students write a short paragraph about whether or not the use of medication is always better than resting.

Assessment suggestion

Students make a list of 5 things they should avoid doing to stay healthy.

12.3 考试前的准备 Preparing for school exams

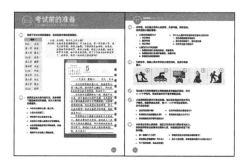

This lesson consolidates what students have learned in:

- Lessons 2.4–2.5: daily routines, school life
- Lessons 3.7–3.8: work–life balance

Lesson activities

1 📖 Reading

Before the activity, revise vocabulary for school subjects and times with students.

Answers

a. 八点二十分   **b.** 英文   **c.** 休息   **d.** 三   **e.** 数学

f. 午休   **g.** 放学   **h.** 三   **i.** 二十

2 📖 Reading

This diary entry is about a school day. Make sure students back up their answers with reasons as most of the statements are false.

Answers

a. 错 (他错们没有一起上学。)   **b.** 错 (本杰明迟到了，因为他睡过头了。)   **c.** 对   **d.** 错 (老师教他们用中文写课程表。)   **e.** 错 (他觉得学中文真没意思。)   **f.** 对

3 🔊 Listening

Tell students that the recording is about how to keep healthy around exam time. They need to listen for reasons, as two of the questions are "why" questions.

Transcript

本杰明：心美，你的中文考试准备得怎么样?

心美：还好啦，本杰明。不过我觉得考试压力很大。

本杰明：我也是，我不喜欢中文，考试压力特别大，所以这几天我每天都吃快餐，吃完之后特别开心。

心美：我最近都不吃快餐。因为考试快到了，我不想生病，我想保持身体健康，所以我特别注意自己的饮食。我不吃快餐，因为这些食物大多是油炸的，热量很高，不健康。我会吃大量的水果和蔬菜，我也会喝我最喜欢的果汁。

本杰明：你真注意饮食。我应该向你学习。

Answers

a. i   **b.** ii   **c.** i

4 🔊 Listening

It would be a good idea to revise activity/hobby vocabulary with students before this activity.

Transcript

本杰明：喂，心美，除了注意饮食之外，你在考试前还会做什么?

心美：啊，本杰明，我会做运动。我常常去我家附近的健身房跑步，我也会去游泳馆游泳。我还喜欢和朋友一起去爬山和参加舞蹈班。

本杰明：你的生活习惯真好。我应该向你学习。我从明天开始也要多做运动，少玩网上游戏。

Answers

心美考试前会做的活动是：**a.** 在健身房跑步 **b.** 去游泳馆游泳 **d.** 参加舞蹈社 **e.** 爬山

5 ✏️ Writing

Begin by discussing healthy activities with students, focusing on why they are healthy.

Sample writing

保持身体健康的运动很多，例如：游泳、跑步、网球、拳击、举重等等。我最喜欢举重，因为举重可以锻炼肌肉。我最不喜欢跑步，因为跑步会流很多汗。

6   Writing

If necessary, remind students how to voice their views and opinions, and to back them up with reasoning.

> **Sample writing**
>
> 志军你好，
>
> 我刚刚收到中文考试成绩，这次考试实在太难了！我的成绩刚刚好及格六十分，我觉得还不错，因为有很多人都不及格。我觉得考试的压力太大了，所以考试前我每天都去跑步减压。我觉得心美最用功，她每次考试都是一百分，她常常帮助我学习中文。
>
> 本杰明

7   Speaking

Revise frequency versus duration, and the structure "should...more". Then ask students to complete the dialogue in pairs.

> **Sample answers**
>
> **a.** 我每天一般睡四到五个小时。
>
> **b.** 我每天都花六小时做功课和温习。
>
> **c.** 我觉得这样不太健康，我觉得我应该睡多一点。
>
> **d.** 压力大的时候，我通常喜欢弹钢琴或是看影片来减少压力。
>
> **e.** 为了保持健康，我会多做运动并且吃健康的食物。

Further differentiation

 Students write an email to their parents, who are on holiday abroad, about their exam results.

 Students write an article on "effective exam techniques" for the school magazine.

Assessment suggestion

In small groups, students plan and act out a short sketch about how students feel the night before the day of their big exam. Use the worksheet "Planning a short sketch" to make notes. You may assess students' verbal and/or script-writing skills.

12.4 我们毕业了！ We are graduating!

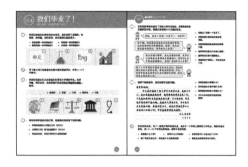

This lesson consolidates what students have learned in:

* Lessons 2.1–2.4: school subjects and exams
* Lesson 8.5: plans for university
* Unit 9: future employment plans and CV writing

Lesson activities

1   Listening

Make sure students know the subject each picture represents. You may also take this opportunity to revise complements of degree: v + 得 + adj.

> **Transcript**
>
> **a.** A: 安吉拉，这次你哪一科考得最好？
>
> B: 我英文考了98分。英文是我考得最好的一科。
>
> A: 安吉拉哪一科考得最好？
>
> **b.** A: 阿俊，这次你哪一科考得最好？
>
> B: 我化学考得最好。化学是我最喜欢的科目。
>
> A: 阿俊哪一科考得最好？
>
> **c.** A: 尼玛，这次你哪一科考得最好？
>
> B: 我英文考得不错，但我中文比英文的成绩更好。
>
> A: 尼玛哪一科考得最好？
>
> **d.** A: 天伟，这次你哪一科考得最好？
>
> B: 应该是地理考得最好吧！不，我记错了，应该是经济。
>
> A: 天伟哪一科考得最好？

> **Answers**
>
> **a.** iii **b.** ii **c.** i **d.** iv

2   Writing

Discuss some typical reasons for liking/not liking different subjects before students write their sentence.

> **Sample writing**
>
> 我最喜欢英国文学，最不喜欢经济，因为我的数学不好。

3   Listening

Begin by revising careers vocabulary and ensure students know which profession each picture represents.

> **Transcript**
>
> **a.** 我是安吉拉，我从小就对历史特别感兴趣，这次我考得不错，可以在大学选择读历史。
>
> **b.** 我是阿俊。我想将来当一名医生，为病人治病，我想在大学读医科。
>
> **c.** 我是天伟，妈妈想我读法律，但我想读工程，我想将来当一名工程师。
>
> **d.** 我是尼玛，我的中文和英文都考得很好，我的语文特别好，虽然爸爸想我读医科，但我想在大学读法律。
>
> **e.** 我是子敏，我从小就喜欢玩电脑，我对网络特别感兴趣，我想读计算机学。

> **Answers**
>
> **a.** iv **b.** v **c.** i **d.** iii **e.** ii

4   Speaking

Tell students that they will need to use the future tense for this dialogue, and revise how to do this if needed.

> **Sample answers**
>
> **a.** 我将来想做发明家，因为我想发明新的东西，帮助人们解决许多生活上的困难。
>
> **b.** 我的工作可以在国内也可以在国外，但是我想在一个风景美丽的海岛工作。
>
> **c.** 如果有时间，我还打算多学一些电脑技能。

5  Reading

Make sure students read the rubric and are aware that they just need to find the three correct statements here.

> **Answers**
>
> The three correct statements are a, b, c.

6  Reading

Remind students to note the key words in the questions, so they have a focus when reading the text.

> **Answers**
>
> **a.** 安吉拉想在大学读历史。
>
> **b.** 安吉拉现在在高中读文科。
>
> **c.** 妈妈想安吉拉在大学读法律。
>
> **d.** 安吉拉希望妈妈尊重她的决定。

7   Writing

Students may need to be reminded how to write a more formal email before completing this task.

> **Sample writing**
>
> 张先生您好，
>
> 我是A＋大学的应届毕业生，我想应征贵公司新闻主播的工作。在大学求学期间的暑假，我分别在BBC和CNN有短期的工作经验。我的个性认真，擅长分析和解决难题，我觉得我很适合这份工作。除了专业知识以外，我还能流利地说五种语言：英语、汉语、法语、德语和西班牙语。
>
> 我期望很快能够收到您的回复。敬祝
>
> 秋安！
>
> 安吉拉敬上

> **Further differentiation**
>
> Students write a paragraph about their dream job.
>
> Students write a paragraph about whether they would prefer a dream job with a low salary or a well-paid job they do not like.

Assessment suggestion

Students write a paragraph describing where they see themselves 10 years after their school graduation. Encourage them to write not just about their careers but also about their home and personal lives, using vocabulary they have learned in previous units.

12.5 参加自行车比赛的一天
A day at the cycling race

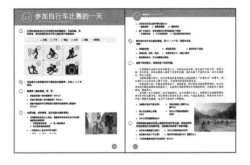

This lesson consolidates what students have learned in:

- Lessons 1.6–1.7: hobbies
- Lessons 3.7–3.8: physical and mental wellbeing
- Lesson 4.9: reading public signs
- Lessons 6.1–6.4: weather
- Lesson 8.4: volunteering

Lesson activities

 **1** **Listening**

Revise hobbies vocabulary, and go through the pictures to ensure students know what hobby each represents.

Transcript

a. 我是天伟。我有很多兴趣爱好，以前我喜欢画画和唱歌，现在我比较喜欢做运动，我最喜欢骑自行车。

b. 我是丁卡。我从小就对摄影特别感兴趣，爸爸最近才买了一部新的相机送给我，我特别高兴。

c. 我是劳拉，我很多朋友都喜欢玩游戏机，但我不喜欢，我最喜欢画画。

d. 我是小文，我和天伟一样都喜欢做运动，我最喜欢爬山。

e. 我是约翰，我也喜欢做运动，我喜欢跑步，但是我不喜欢爬山。

f. 我是尼玛，我喜欢做运动，但是我更喜欢唱歌，我觉得唱歌特别有趣。

Answers

a. ii **b.** vi **c.** i **d.** iii **e.** iv **f.** v

 **2** **Writing**

The 喜欢/不喜欢 structure should be very familiar by now, but provide a template if needed.

Sample writing

我是心心，我喜欢滑雪、拳击和旅游。我不喜欢跑步、唱歌和跳舞。

3 **Speaking**

Students must include their reasoning here, so remind them of the ways to do this.

Sample answers

a. 我最喜欢的爱好是滑雪，因为我觉得滑雪可以一方面运动，另一方面亲近大自然。

b. 我最不喜欢的运动是拳击，因为我觉得拳击太危险了！

c. 我觉得跑步和滑雪都可以帮助我们保持身体健康和心情愉快。

4 **Listening**

Revise good causes and volunteering vocabulary with students before playing the recording.

Transcript

a. 天伟：我想参加社区义工活动，帮忙举办社区自行车比赛，我要先和学校的体育老师联络。

女同学：天伟要先和谁联络？

b. 天伟：昨天一共有20人想参加自行车比赛，今天多了5人，现在一共有25人参加比赛。

女同学：一共有多少人想参加自行车比赛？

c. 天伟：我是天伟，在自行车比赛活动中，因为人很多，我会帮忙放警告标牌。

女同学：天伟在自行车比赛活动中帮忙做什么？

d. 女同学：学校的体育老师告诉我，是天伟、小文和娜依玛一起帮忙计划和组织自行车比赛的。

男同学：除了天伟之外，还有谁负责计划和组织这个活动？

Answers

a. i **b.** ii **c.** ii **d.** ii

5  Writing

Encourage students to include artwork in their posters, but remind them to focus on communicating information and using their language skills.

Sample writing

约克春季自行车比赛

活动目的：自行车运动不仅可以促进健康，更是节能减排、保护环境的最佳方式。本次比赛全程20公里，途经约克市多个景点，欢迎大家踊跃报名参加。

活动日期：3月23日

活动时间：9:00am–5:00pm

活动地点：约克

活动名额：50名

线上报名：www.cycleinyork.exmaple.com

负责人：大海

报名费用：20英镑 (膳宿自理)

报名截止：2月1日

6 Reading

As this is a longer reading text, you may want students to read through and discuss it as a class or in pairs before answering the questions on their own.

Answers

a. 比赛那天的天气有点冷，没有太阳，阴天多云。

b. 参赛的人都穿了外套和长裤，也戴了手套和头盔。

c. 路上左边标牌上写着"注意安全"的警告。

d. 子敏发觉钱包丢了，所以想给警察打电话。

e. 天伟很高兴因为他帮助了别人。

Language and culture

Chinese abbreviations: on many occasions four-character phrases are shortened to two characters; for example: 参加比赛 → 参赛.

Here are some more examples:

环境保护→环保 台湾大学→台大

北京大学→北大 流行感冒→流感

7 Speaking

Remind students that they will be talking about an event that happened in the past. Discuss what kind of structures/vocabulary they might need to use.

Sample answers

a. 自行车比赛在公园举行。

b. 我喜欢骑自行车因为骑自行车有益健康而且非常环保。

c. 我在比赛中不小心从自行车上摔下来，天伟是义工带我去急诊室看医生。到了急诊室，我发现我的钱包不见了，心里很着急，正想打电话给警察，但是还好天伟告诉我说他捡到了我的钱包。我很高兴。

d. 骑自行车的时候要注意保暖，戴手套和头盔，还要注意交通标志，遵守交通规则。

e. 下次我还想参加自行车比赛，因为我喜欢支持这项又环保又健康的活动。

Further differentiation

Using the worksheet "My favourite sport" (on the CD-ROM), have students carry out a survey in their neighbourhood to find out which are the most popular sports among their friends and family.

 Students write a few statements to summarise which sports are most and least popular.

 Students explain any trends they see in the data they have gathered.

Assessment suggestion

Students write a paragraph on whether they think it is more exciting to play a sport or to watch it on television, giving their reasons.

12.6 让我们一起去做义工 Let's volunteer

This lesson consolidates what students have learned in:

- Lessons 1.1–1.4: introducing yourself
- Lessons 5.6–5.7: shopping and money
- Lesson 4.3: Spring Festival
- Lessons 8.2, 8.4: volunteering

Lesson activities

1 🔊 Listening

As these are short-answer questions, encourage students to jot down notes as they listen.

Transcript

黄老师：李老师，学校附近有没有银行？我需要去一趟银行。

李老师：有，在学校大门对面的百货商店就有一家银行。黄老师，你想去银行做什么？

黄老师：哦，我想去银行取钱，我身上没有现金了。我打算带学生在春节时去老人院，我们想买一些年糕给那儿的老人吃。

李老师：我和你一起去吧。我正好要去银行存钱，我身上的现金太多了。

Answers

a. 在学校大门对面的百货商店

b. 一些年糕

c. 李老师要去银行存钱，因为他身上的现金太多了。

2 📖 Reading

Revise floor levels and the different departments/areas in a store to refresh students' memories.

Answers

a. ii b. iv c. iii d. i e. vi f. v

3 🗨 Speaking

Advise students to refer to the floor directory in Activity 2 to complete this dialogue.

Answers

a. 银行在百货商店的五楼。

b. 肚子饿了可以去一楼食品区吃东西。

c. 买钢笔应该去三楼文具部。

d. 停车场在地下一层。

4 🔊 Listening

Tell students this is an interview so they should focus mainly on Teacher Huang's responses for the answers.

Transcript

男记者：黄老师，您是第一次来这家百货商店吗？

黄老师：是的，我第一次来这儿。我身边的这位李老师就来过很多次了。

男记者：您觉得这个百货商店怎么样？

黄老师：我觉得这是一个购物天堂。特别是这个月有大减价，很多商店都在打折。

男记者：您买了一些什么东西？

黄老师：我买了一些年糕，打算和我的学生一起送给老人院的老人们吃。

男记者：您和您的学生们真好！您们还打算去老人院做什么？

黄老师：谢谢！我和我的学生会到老人院拜年。学生们会跟老人聊天和给他们讲故事。

男记者：谢谢您接受采访。

Answers

a. i b. i c. iii

5  Reading

Make sure students are aware that there are more options in column B than they will need. Encourage them to underline in pencil the key words in column A, and then find the same key words in the text to help them.

Answers

a. ii **b.** iii **c.** iv **d.** v

6  Speaking

Point out the use of 您 in the questions, as they are directed at an elderly person. For the response to question a, prompt students to use a date that makes sense.

Sample answers

a. 我是1930年出生，我的生日是1月10日。

b. 我是在爱丁堡出生的。

c. 我在很多地方住过：英国、法国、意大利、日本，还有中国。

d. 我有很多爱好。年轻的时候，我喜欢滑雪、打网球。现在我喜欢散步、下棋和看电影。

7  Writing

Remind students they are writing a text message, so they should keep it as concise as possible.

Sample writing

春节期间我们要探访老人院！班上有二十人会参加，五人不参加。大海和我负责联络，我们会联络老人院的院长，安排活动。

Further differentiation

 Ask students to make a list of 5 benefits of volunteering.

 Ask students to write a short essay on "Can volunteering help you get a job?"

Assessment suggestion

 Show students the video 台湾高中生前进史瓦济兰从事国际志工服务 [00:00–01:30]. Then ask them to answer the following questions (answers and timings of clips shown in brackets):

Q1: 主角人物年纪多大？ (16岁[0:24])

Q2: 这段志工服务影片主要是支援哪一个国家？ (史瓦济兰 [0:40])

Q3: 史瓦济兰正饱受什么的摧残? (贫穷、饥饿、爱滋病[1:20])

12.7 在博物馆的一天 A day at the museum

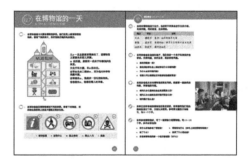

This lesson consolidates what students have learned in:

- Lessons 6.5–6.6: directions
- Lesson 6.8: environmental issues
- Lesson 4.9: reading public signs
- Lessons 5.5, 7.5: culture and traditions from around the world

Lesson activities

1  Reading

Revise the vocabulary for different areas in a museum with students. Write out the possible answers on the board for students to choose from.

Answers

a. 大门 **b.** 自然环境厅 **c.** 办公室 **d.** 地球科学厅

e. 纪念商品店 **f.** 餐厅

2 📖 Reading

The signs themselves should be relatively straightforward for students to understand. Remind them of the "commanding" tone used on some (禁止......, 请勿......, etc.).

Answers

a. ii b. iv c. iii d. i e. v

3 🔊 Listening

Encourage students to look at the text first and try to guess what might be missing; i.e. dates, places. This will give them a focus when they listen to the recording.

Transcript

a. 日本的樱花节是春季的节日，一般是在三月到四月之间。

b. 泰国的泼水节是在每年的四月十三日到十五日之间，它也是泰国的新年。

c. 巴西里约的狂欢节是世界上最著名的，通常在每年的二月举行。

Answers

a. 三月　b. 四月　c. 新年　d. 巴西　e. 二月

4 🔊 Listening

Tell students that they will hear a speech about the environment. Encourage them to take notes while listening.

Transcript

大家好！我姓陈，是一位中学地理老师。今天我很高兴能被博物馆邀请来讲关于环境保护的话题。

我看到这儿有很多我们学校的学生，相信同学们都应该在上地理课的时候学过水灾、旱灾、空气污染、酸雨、全球暖化这些环境问题吧！

因为人类一直在破坏自然环境，所以才会有这些问题。作为人类的一份子，我们每一个人都有责任。

为了保护环境，我们学校环保小组将会举办一些社区环保活动，活动从下个月开始，有兴趣的话可以上博物馆的网站看最新的消息。

谢谢！

Answers

a. 中学地理。

b. 水灾、旱灾、空气污染、酸雨、全球暖化等等环境问题。

c. 因为人类一直在破坏自然环境，所以才会有环境问题。

d. 博物馆的网站有最新的消息。

5 💬 Speaking

Revise giving directions, including "go up/down one level", and ensure students refer to the map in Activity 1 before practising this dialogue in pairs. Encourage them to make notes, as they will be helpful for the next exercise.

Sample answers

a. 从办公室下一层楼，纪念品商店就在右手边。

b. 从办公室上一层楼，四楼整层都是自然环境厅。

c. 从办公室下两层楼，餐厅在博物馆一楼，大门的左边。

6 ✏️ Writing

If students made notes when completing Activity 5, they will be able to make use of them here.

Sample writing

从办公室上一层楼，四楼整层都是自然环境厅。

从办公室下一层楼，纪念品商店就在右手边。下两层楼，餐厅就在博物馆一楼，大门的左边。

7 ✏️ Writing

Remind students that they are writing a blog post (so it should be informal), and as it is about a past event, they need to use the past tense.

Sample writing

上个周末我跟爸爸一起去了博物馆，博物馆里有自然环境厅、文化厅、地球科学厅、餐厅，还有纪念商品店。我每个厅都去参观了，还到纪念商品店买了一个漂亮的包包给妈妈。我觉得地球科学厅最有趣，在里面可以玩到许多很有意思的科学游戏。

Further differentiation

Students write a review of a sightseeing trip they have been on recently (to any kind of tourist attraction).

 Students can write about two things they did there.

 Students can compare their visit with another place they have been to elsewhere.

Assessment suggestion

 Show students the video 台北故宫博物院--国宝总动员 [00:00–02:00], produced by NPM 国立故宫博物院. Then ask them the following questions (answers and timings of clips shown in brackets):

Q1: 影片一开始的三个国宝级的文物主角是哪三个？(婴儿枕、玉辟邪、玉鸭 [00:45])

Q2: 这部影片主要是描述什么？(描述三个主角如何寻找从翠玉白菜上飞走的螽斯的整个历程 [01:35])

Q3: 根据影片剧情，是哪一个主角抓走了翠玉白菜上的螽斯？(婴儿枕 [01:45])

12.8 我们搬家了！ We have moved!

This lesson consolidates what students have learned in:

- Lessons 2.6–2.7: furniture and layout of new home
- Lessons 5.1–5.4, 5.8: comparing old and new home environments
- Lessons 7.3, 7.4, 10.2: countries and continents

Lesson activities

1 Reading

Revise housing vocabulary and, as a class, spot the differences between the two houses.

> **Answer**
>
> Picture A is the correct answer.

2 Reading

Revise local area vocabulary and locations before asking students to complete this activity. Remember not to tell them it is a speech, as that is the answer to the first question!

> **Answers**
>
> **a.** ii **b.** i, iv, vii

3  Listening

Prompt students to take notes as they listen because they will need to write short answers for this activity.

> **Transcript**
>
> 日晴：哈里你好。你的家乡在哪儿？
>
> 哈里：日晴你好。我的家乡在加拿大的温哥华。
>
> 日晴：你喜欢温哥华吗？
>
> 哈里：我很喜欢。我觉得温哥华是北美洲最棒的城市之一，因为那里除了有很多设施外，还有美丽的自然景色。它在加拿大的西边，城市中心不但有很多公园和博物馆，而且周边还有山、森林和海洋等等。
>
> 日晴：你觉得温哥华是一个什么样的地方？
>
> 哈里：我觉得它是一个多元文化的地方。在这里居住着来自世界各地的人。这里也有北美洲第二大的唐人街，是一个重要的华人聚居地。我觉得温哥华市是一个十分有意思的城市。
>
> 日晴：我希望有一天能去温哥华看看！哈里，希望你喜欢在上海的新生活。
>
> 哈里：谢谢！

Answers

a. 哈里的家乡在加拿大的温哥华。

b. 温哥华在加拿大的西边。

c. 温哥华的周边有山、森林和海洋。

d. 因为温哥华居住着来自世界各地的人。

4 🗨 Speaking

Make sure all students know how to say the name of their home town in Chinese before starting this activity.

Sample answers

a. 我的家乡在英国中部的斯特拉福镇。它是一个又美丽又古老的小镇。

b. 家乡的镇中心有许多古老的建筑，周边有河流、小山和黄石灰石三种地理景观。

c. 我喜欢我的家乡，因为无论是人文或自然景观都非常迷人。

5 🔊 Listening

Revise furniture vocabulary and all the corresponding measure words, as well as location structures (房间里有一张书桌 /书桌在房间里), before students listen to the recording.

Transcript

露西：哈里，我知道你最近搬到上海了，听说你的新房间特别大，那你房间里有什么家具？

哈里：是啊，露西！我的房间里有一台电视机、一张大床，还有一张书桌和一把椅子。电脑、台灯和电话都放在书桌上面。我还有一个大衣柜。

露西：真好！房间的衣柜有镜子吗？有多少面？

哈里：一面也没有！为什么衣柜要有镜子？

露西：我就是喜欢在换衣服的时候照镜子！所以我的房间有两面大镜子。你上次来我家没看到吗？

Answers

a. i **b.** i **c.** ii

6 ✏ Writing

You may ask students to listen to the Activity 5 recording again and take notes before they start their writing.

Sample writing

哈里的新房间特别大，里面有很多家具，例如一台电视机、一张大床、一张书桌和一把椅子。书桌上面还有电脑、台灯和电话。阿里的房间里还有一个大衣柜，但是却没有一面镜子。

7 ✏ Writing

Remind students that for this activity they are pretending to be Harry describing where he lives.

Sample writing

彼得，你好！

我最近搬了家，住在上海市内一个小区。那儿有很多良好的设施。小区里面有一个运动中心，里面有健身房、舞蹈室还有网球场。小区的绿化工作也做得很好，因为有专人负责。小区里有很多树，四季有不同的花开着，还有一大片草坪。小区的附近就是一个地铁站，交通非常方便。我很喜欢我的小区。有空来找我吧！

哈里

Further differentiation

Have a class discussion about students' dream homes.

 Students use simple sentences to describe the location of their dream home, and how they would furnish it.

 Encourage students to give reasons for their answers.

Assessment suggestion

Students write an advertisement listing their house on a letting website.

12.9 开派对 It's party time!

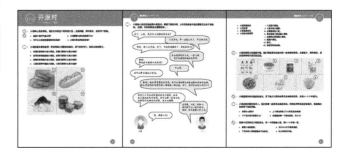

This lesson consolidates what students have learned in:

- Lesson 1.8: invitations
- Lesson 1.9: planning activities
- Lessons 3.1–3.4: food and drink

Lesson activities

1  Listening and writing

Encourage students to take notes while they listen as they will need to write their own answers.

> **Transcript**
>
> 小明：心美，这个周末你有什么打算？
>
> 心美：我没什么好的计划啊，小明。你想做什么？
>
> 小明：我上网看了天气预报，星期六天气不错，天气很暖和，但也不太热，应该不会下雨，要不要来我家玩？
>
> 心美：开派对吗？
>
> 小明：对，我刚搬家，打算开一个派对庆祝一下。
>
> 心美：好啊！我最喜欢开派对，谢谢邀请。还有谁会来？
>
> 小明：志军、汤姆、米娜都来。我还问了其他朋友，有一些人没回复我。
>
> 心美：人多才好玩。小明，你邀请苏菲了吗？
>
> 小明：哎呀，我本来打算邀请她的，但是我不小心给忘了。我一会儿就发短信去邀请她。
>
> 心美：真是的！

> **Answers**
>
> a. 星期六天气不错，天气很暖和，但也不太热，应该不会下雨。
>
> b. 小明请心美去他家参加他的派对。
>
> c. 他不小心给忘了！
>
> d. 他打算发短信去邀请她。

2 📖 Reading

As students just need to pick out the food item in the sentences, this activity should be quite straightforward. If they struggle, revise party food vocabulary with them.

> **Answers**
>
> **a.** i **b.** ii **c.** iii **d.** iv

3 📖 Reading

You could ask students to read the dialogue aloud in pairs before working together to match the sentences.

> **Answers**
>
> **a.** iii **b.** v **c.** vi **d.** viii

4  Listening

Make sure students know the vocabulary for all the items in the pictures before listening to the recording. The focus is on the items that the brother *needs to buy*.

> **Transcript**
>
> 明天是周末，弟弟要开派对。他叫我帮他买一些食物和饮料。
>
> 嗯，买什么好呢？小明喜欢吃草莓蛋糕和冰淇淋，就买这两样吧！
>
> 他们都应该喜欢喝茶和果汁，这些家里都有，就不用买了。
>
> 小明说他的好朋友心美喜欢喝可乐，我应该去买几瓶。

> **Answers**
>
> b, c, f

5 ✏️ Writing

Revise which measure words should be used for different foods/containers.

> **Sample writing**
>
> 小明邀请我去他家参加派对，我打算带一盘炒米粉、一个蛋糕和一打汽水去他家，因为这些都是我爱吃的东西和爱喝的饮料。

6 💬 Speaking

Advise students to pay attention to the different tenses used in this dialogue.

Sample answers

a. 我的爱好很多，我喜欢旅行也喜欢看电影。

b. 上个周末我去看了一场很有意思的电影。

c. 下个周末我打算跟一个好朋友去巴黎玩。

d. 我喜欢外出旅游的周末，因为出去旅游可以看看不同的风景，体会不同的风俗。

7 ✎ Writing

Revise how to apologise in Chinese, along with how to give an explanation.

Sample writing

小明你好，

非常感谢你邀请我去参加你的派对，很抱歉我不能去，因为今天是我妈妈的生日，我们家人也为她举行派对。下次你若再邀请我，我一定会参加。再一次跟你说对不起。 苏菲

Further differentiation

Tell students the school is holding a China Day party to celebrate the Chinese National Day.

 Students write a list of things they need to prepare for the party.

 Students write a passage in the school magazine to promote China Day.

Assessment suggestion

Tell students to imagine the school is organising a tea party for a VIP from China. Students should design a detailed itinerary to show what should happen on the day.

12.10 上网一族 We are the online generation

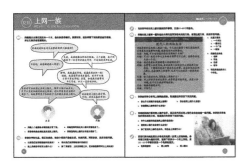

This lesson consolidates what students have learned in:

- Lesson 2.9: comparing old and new technology
- Lesson 11.9: communication and social networking

Lesson activities

1 📖 Reading

You could ask students to read the dialogue aloud in pairs. Remind them they need to give their reasoning for any statements that are false.

Answers

a. 对   **b.** 对   **c.** 错 (她常用手机和说中文的朋友在网上聊天。)   **d.** 对

2 🔊 Listening

Revise technology vocabulary, and encourage students to take notes while they listen to the recording.

Transcript

大家好，我是苏菲，今天我会给大家介绍现代智能生活。

自从互联网开始流行以后，它给我们的生活带来了很多变化。以前，我们要写信和寄信给国外的朋友，长途电话费也十分贵。

有了互联网以后，现在我们想联系国外朋友的时候，可以用电脑通过电子邮件和朋友们联系，也可以跟他们在网上聊天，又快又方便。

上网可以做很多事情。如果我们有能连上网络的手机，我们可以随时上社交网站，给朋友发短信，不用打电话。想买东西的时候，我们可以在网上购物，东西都比较便宜，买到的东西很快就会送到家里。

我们还可以玩网络游戏和使用网上银行业务。我就常常和朋友一起玩网络游戏。我爸爸他经常使用网上银行业务，不用去银行排队，真方便！

今天我的演讲就到这儿，谢谢大家。

Answers

a. 以前我们用写信、寄信和打长途电话跟国外的朋友联络。

b. 现在有了互联网，可以用电子邮件或是网上聊天跟海外的朋友联络。

c. 连上网络的手机可以随时上社交网站，给朋友发短信，网上购物等等。

d. 网上还可以玩网络游戏，使用网上银行业务。

3 Writing

As a class, discuss what people do online. Students then write about the four things they enjoy most.

> **Sample writing**
>
> 我平时喜欢在网上收发电子邮件，使用脸书看看朋友的近况，用Skype跟朋友聊天，也在网上看一些我喜欢的影片。

4 Reading

Remember not to tell students that this is an interview, because that is the answer to question a.

> **Answers**
>
> **a.** i   **b.** ii
>
> **c.** 1）社交网站－跟家人朋友保持联系，网上聊天
>
>   2）增长见闻－阅读网上新闻
>
>   3）娱乐生活－看网络电视，上网听歌

5 Speaking

Before the activity, revise vocabulary related to shopping in general, as well as online shopping. Remind students how to use 好处 (and 坏处) in a sentence.

> **Sample answers**
>
> **a.** 我一年前开始在网上购物。
>
> **b.** 我会在网上买书、文具、电器和日常用品。
>
> **c.** 我觉得网上购物有许多好处：节省外出的时间，可以快速找到商品并且通过比价找到最好的价钱。

6 Speaking

Discuss the advantages of online banking, and what else people can do online. If students don't know how online banking works, maybe you can talk about how banks promote their online banking facilities.

> **Sample answers**
>
> **a.** 我大概五年前开始使用网上银行业务。
>
> **b.** 使用网上银行业务可以节省许多去银行排队等候的时间，有效率地处理许多银行业务。
>
> **c.** 除了使用网上银行业务，我还会上网工作，例如网上编辑文件等等。

7 Writing

Remind students to use their answers from Activities 5 and 6 to write about what they do online.

> **Sample writing**
>
> 我们全家都非常喜欢网上购物，因为我们都不爱出门到市中心跟一堆人挤着买东西。我每次去市中心买东西回来都会头痛。我爸爸爱在网上买电脑和各种音响零件，妈妈喜欢在网上买衣服和首饰，哥哥喜欢买书和游戏，我最爱在网上买电子用品和网上音乐。我们全家都在网上买圣诞节礼物。

> **Further differentiation**
>
> Students design a poster contrasting a world with smart technology and a world without.
>
> Students write a short paragraph, imagining how technology will change the way we live in 30 years' time.

> **Assessment suggestion**
>
> In small groups, students use the worksheet "Planning a short sketch" to prepare a short sketch on the pros and cons of online shopping. You may assess them on their verbal and/or script-writing skills.

13 语法复习
GRAMMAR UNIT

Unit 1

Grammar focus 1.1

正在

Answers

a. 我回家的时候，妈妈正在做饭。

b. 对不起，我正在做功课，不能出去踢足球。

c. 别走了，外面正在下雨呢!

Grammar focus 1.2

除了…… 以外，还

Answers

a. 本杰明除了又高又帅以外，还很聪明。

b. 他除了喜欢打篮球以外，还喜欢听音乐。

c. 我除了喜欢玩电子游戏以外，还喜欢和宠物玩。

Grammar focus 1.3

是……的

Answers

a. 莉莉是从美国来的。

b. 马克是从五岁时开始打网球的。

c. 她是在中国学会了打篮球的。

Grammar focus 1.5

1 量词

Measure words

Measure words are almost an alien concept to English speakers, so it takes time and practice to grasp them. Elementary learners may use 个 for all nouns, but intermediate and advanced learners should use a great variety of measure words to show their Chinese linguistic skills.

There are two types of measure words:

1. Noun classifiers, such as 一本书、两支笔、三把椅子、四张嘴、五盘菜.

2. Verb quantifiers, such as 看一下、读两遍、去三趟.

Common mistakes

- Not using measure words: 我有一妹妹。✗

- Using the wrong measure words: 妈妈有一条头发，爸爸带着一把眼镜。✗

Answers

a. 我们家里养了两只绿色的鸟。

b. 她家的农场里有三匹马。

c. 我以后想养一只白色的小猫。

2 看上去

Answers

a. 他看上去瘦了。

b. 米娜的新衣看上去太漂亮了。

c. 朋友做的饭菜看上去好吃极了。

3 给

Answers

a. 爷爷(或外公)给我们做了一顿晚餐。

b. 她给我唱了一首歌。

c. 他给他的儿子买了两条金鱼。

Grammar focus 1.6

1 了

The two main uses of 了

1. An action has been completed → 了 comes after the action verb:

   我吃了两碗饭。

   她喝了三杯咖啡。

2. A condition has changed → 了 comes at the end of the sentence:

   弟弟长高了。

   奶奶变胖了。

Common mistakes

- Adding 了 after 是. 是 is a static verb, not an action verb, and should not be followed by 了:
  她是了老师。✗

- Adding 了 unnecessarily:

  你明天去不去了学校? ✗
  你明天去不去学校? ✓

  从我家走了十分钟就到学校。✗
  从我家走十分钟就到学校。✓

- Confusing 了 with 得:

  我们玩了很开心。✗
  我们玩得很开心。✓

  他工作了很卖力。✗
  他工作得很卖力。✓

- Mistaking 了 as past tense, when in fact 了 can be present, past or future tense:

  我等了三个小时。(present or past)

  昨天哥哥去了电影院。(past)

  爸爸明天就回家了。(future)

Answers

a. 生日那天他收了很多礼物。

b. 他们今年秋天去了中国的北京。

c. 去年冬天我和同学们在日本滑了雪。

d. 上个周末我和好朋友一起看了电影。

2 最

Sample answers

a. 周末我最喜欢看电影。　b. 我觉得滑雪最好玩。

c. 在我们家哥哥最高。

3 不

不会 vs. 不能

我不会说中文。I don't speak Chinese. (I am not capable of speaking Chinese.)

这里都是英国朋友，我不能说中文。There are lots of English friends here, I cannot speak Chinese. (I am capable of speaking Chinese but I will not as a courtesy to my English friends.)

我不想看到他，明天我不会来。I don't want to see him and I won't come tomorrow. (It's a subjective decision.)

我最近很忙，明天我不能来。I have been very busy recently and I won't come tomorrow. (It's a objective decision.)

Do not confuse 不 with 没 (see Grammar Focus 2.7, page 186 for more information).

Answers

a. 这个周末爸爸不去郊外拍照了。

b. 今天他有很多作业所以不看电视了。

c. 她因为唱得不好听所以不唱歌了。

Grammar focus 1.7

完

Answers

a. 做完作业以后，她看了一会儿电视。

b. 他想画完画以后去河边钓鱼。

c. 逛完街以后，米娜去音乐厅看了一场音乐会。

Grammar focus 1.8

1 要

Answers

a. 明年夏天我们要去香港看爷爷奶奶。

b. 这个周末她要和家人去看音乐会。

2 Verb–object compounds

These are also called separable verbs (离合词). They are compound verbs that can be separated, such as:

帮忙／帮了忙／帮过忙

结婚／结了婚／结过婚

吃饭／吃了饭／吃过饭

见面／见了面／见过面

Common mistakes

- Following verb-object compounds with an object:

  他结婚了一位美国小姐。✗
  他跟一位美国小姐结婚了。✓

  我喜欢我的学校，因为我可以见面我的同学。✗
  我喜欢我的学校，因为我可以跟我的同学见面。✓

Answers

a. 他们在山上看美丽的风景。

b. 放学以后我和同学一起打了网球。
(No change; this sentence is correct!)

c. 爷爷经常周末去河边钓鱼。

d. 他的爱好是踢足球。

e. 他们一边吃东西，一边聊天，聊得很开心。
(No change; this sentence is correct!)

3　吧

Other uses of 吧

1. to make a request or give an order:

   我看我们先找家旅馆吧。

   你走吧！我不想再见到你！

2. to speculate or guess:

   她四十多岁了吧？

   来这儿喝咖啡的人一定很多吧？

3. to show approval:

   好吧！我们明天早上10点见。

   你喜欢就拿去吧！

4. to indicate pauses in sentences:

   举例来说吧，喜欢看科幻小说的人大都是男生。

   拿我来说吧，我每天至少喝五杯咖啡。

Answers

a. 买完东西后，我们去看电影吧！

b. 放学后我们去打篮球吧！

Grammar focus 1.9

了 (used with 快／快要／要)

Answers

a. A: 现在几点了？

   B: 现在八点十五分。我们要快点走。我们快要迟到了！

b. A: 圣诞节快到了，儿子要回国了。

   B: 我们一起去机场接他吧。

c. A: 天快黑了。我们回家好吗？

   B: 好的，我们走吧。

Unit 2

Grammar focus 2.2

1　也

Answers

a. 我喜欢读德语，也喜欢读中文。／我喜欢读中文，也喜欢读德语。

b. 她觉得生物课有趣，她的好朋友也觉得生物很有意思。

c. 他昨天考了化学，也考了数学。／他昨天考了数学，也考了化学。

2　很

Answers

a. 我觉得德语作业很难。

b. 我觉得新校园很漂亮。

c. 她很想去美国上大学。

Grammar focus 2.3

1　……先……，然后……

Common mistakes

- Not putting 先 before the verb:

  吃完饭以后，我先七点半坐公共汽车上雷丁中心。✗

  吃完饭以后，七点半我先坐公共汽车上雷丁中心。✓

Answers

a. 我们先参观了礼堂，然后去看了教室。

b. 放学以后，他通常先做作业，然后去外面玩。

c. 上体育课的时候，我们先跑了十分钟步，然后踢了二十分钟的足球。

2　因为

Sample answers

a. 我喜欢吃中国菜，因为中国菜很好吃。

b. 我不喜欢吃薯条，因为薯条的热量太高了。

Grammar focus 2.4

1 比 ...... (更)   **2** 最

> **Answers**
>
> **a.** 小文的英语说得不错，但是米娜的英语说得更好。   **b.** 我们学校的设施比他们学校好。
> **c.** 苏菲中文考试考得最好。

Grammar focus 2.5

1 之前   **2** 之后

> **Answers**
>
> **a.** 美术课之前是中文课 。   **b.** 午休之前是历史课。
> **c.** 英文课之后是经济课。

Grammar focus 2.6

1 ......在哪儿?   **2** ...... 在......

> **Common mistakes**
>
> • Putting 是 before 在:
>   厨房是在浴室旁边。✗
>   厨房在浴室旁边。✓

> **Answers**
>
> **a.** 我的卧室在楼上。   **b.** 我们的客厅和书房在楼下。
> **c.** 房子前面有一个小花园。   **d.** 房子后面有一个大花园。
> **e.** 车库在房子的旁边。

Grammar focus 2.7

1 的   **2** 有   **3** 没有

> **Answers**
>
> **a.** 这栋房子没有车库。   **b.** 我的卧室旁边是浴室。
> **c.** 那个有五间卧室的房子真大!
> **d.** 夏天的时候，因为没有空调，我的房间很热。

For more on using 没(有), see Grammar focus 10.7.

Grammar focus 2.8

1 多少   **2** 什么时候

> **Answers**
>
> **a.** 什么时候   **b.** 多少   **c.** 多少
> **d.** 什么时候   **e.** 多少

Grammar focus 2.9

1 给

> **Answers**
>
> **a.** 他给他弟弟写信。   **b.** 姐姐给我发电邮。
> **c.** 心美给陈明复习功课。

2 的时候

> **Answers**
>
> **a.** 陈明五岁的时候开始学中文。
> **b.** 志军十岁的时候开始学上网。

Unit 3

Grammar focus 3.2

1 经常／常常

> **Answers**
>
> **a.** 我们晚餐经常吃米饭、蔬菜和一些肉。
> **b.** 周末的时候我常常跟朋友一起去逛街。
> **c.** 他们通常在星期六晚上看电影。

2 通常

> **Answers**
>
> **a.** 她们家通常是爸爸做饭。
> **b.** 杰明家通常吃西餐。
> **c.** 星期五晚上妈妈通常做中餐。
> **d.** 下雨天他通常会在家里尝试做蛋糕。

Grammar focus 3.3

1 量词

Answers

a. 碗　　b. 杯　　c. 杯; 包／块

d. 壶　　e. 双　　f. 瓶

2 您和你

Answers

a. 您　　b. 你　　c. 您　　d. 你

Grammar focus 3.5

地

Answers

a. 儿子很慢地走路。　　b. 他很认真地学做饭。

c. 她很流利地说中文。

Grammar focus 3.6

得

Answers

a. 中文老师经常说: 你们要好好得学外语, 认真得做外语作业。

b. 兔子可以跑得很快。

c. 公园里有很多高高的树, 美丽的花。

d. 海伦生病时, 妈妈每天给她做鸡汤喝, 让她好好休息, 这样就好得快一点。

e. 因为弟弟吃太多甜的东西, 所以他的牙齿不太好。

f. 喝汤的时候, 一定要轻轻地喝, 千万不要发出很大的声音, 因为那样很没有礼貌。

Grammar focus 3.7

应该

Answers

a. 天冷了, 你应该穿件外套。

b. 为了健康, 我们应该多吃蔬菜水果。

c. 好学生应该多读书少上网。

Grammar focus 3.8

为了

Answers

a. 为了有健康的身体, 我们除了应该有好的饮食, 还应该经常运动。

b. 为了让自己在跑步比赛前放松, 不紧张, 杰西卡会听一会儿音乐。

c. 为了考试考得好, 他学习很认真。

Unit 4

Grammar focus 4.2

......月......日/号

Sample answers

a. 今天是一月二十八日。

b. 我的生日是五月十六日。

c. 七月一号开始放暑假。

Grammar focus 4.3

1 把

Changing the focus of a statement

把 changes the focus of a statement and emphasises the verb after it:

他喝了三杯茶。→ He drank three cups of tea.
(This is a normal statement.)

他把三杯茶喝了。→ He had drunk the three cups of tea.
(This emphasises the "drinking".)

Common mistakes

- Using the 把 pattern unnecessarily:

  他昨天在饭馆里把晚饭吃。✗
  他昨天在饭馆里吃了晚饭。✓

Answers

a. 爸爸把车子修理好了。

b. 老师把这一课教完了。

c. 我把房间打扫干净了。

2 们

Answers

a. 长辈们　　b. 男孩　　c. 同学

Grammar focus 4.4

1 例如

Answers

a. 我很喜欢吃春节的食物,例如饺子、汤圆和年糕。

b. 中国有很多节日,例如春节、中秋节和端午节。

c. 妈妈经常做运动,例如骑自行车、游泳和打网球。

2 呢／吗

Use of 吗

1. to create yes/no questions (added to direct statements):

   你是学生吗?

   你吃牛肉吗?

   NB: The pattern verb + not verb also creates yes/no questions without using 吗:

   你是不是学生?

   你吃不吃牛肉?

Common mistakes

- Combining the two question patterns above together:

  你是不是学生吗? ✗

  你吃不吃牛肉吗? ✗

  Instruct students to use one pattern or the other for yes/no questions.

Uses of 呢

1. to show progressive action:

   外面正下雪呢!

   她正在看书呢。

2. to express things about to happen (used at the end of a sentence):

   彼得还没结婚呢,婚礼是在下个星期。

3. to express praise, exaggeration, or disdain (used at the end of a statement):

   中文可难学呢!

   他很矮呢!

4. to add a pause:

   我呢,明年才要去中国。

   颜色呢,我最喜欢紫色。

5. to function as a tag question:

   我喜欢吃宫保鸡丁,你呢?

   我弹古筝,你呢? 你弹什么乐器?

Answers

a. 吗　　b. 呢　　c. 吗　　d. 吗

Grammar focus 4.5

1 和

2 一起

Answers

a. 和　　b. 一起　　c. 和　　d. 和; 一起

Grammar focus 4.6

1 不用

Note: 不用 is also often added before certain stative verbs to form idioms (e.g. 不用谢 or 不用客气, both meaning "you're welcome", 不用担心 "no worries").

Sample answers

a. 明天是星期天,我不用上学。

b. 我带了手机,不用借你的手机发电子邮件。

2 有没有

Sample answers

a. 你有没有地图?　　b. 你有没有行程表?

c. 你有没有机票?

Grammar focus 4.7

1 虽然／但是

Sample answers

a. 大卫虽然努力温习了，但是他考试还是不及格。

b. 心美虽然是中国人，但是她的英文说得很好。

2 不多／不少

Sample answers

我家的房间不多。 房间里的家具不少。

花园里的花朵不少。 客厅里的装饰品不多。

Grammar focus 4.8

1 不但……而且／还……

Sample answers

a. 妹妹不但会唱中文歌，还会跳中国舞。

b. 安娜不但会说中文，还会写毛笔字。

2 都

Answers

a. 我们都要订有游泳池的旅馆。

b. 我朋友和我两人都想去看中国的长城。

c. 住在那家旅馆的时候，他们都去了健身房。

Grammar focus 4.9

1 大概／可能／好像

Answers

a. 妈妈好像在书房。 **b.** 陈明大概一米七高。

c. 心美可能喜欢台湾吧。 **d.** 明天好像会下雨。

2 因为……所以……

Answers

a. 小华因为丢了钱包，所以很不高兴。

b. 因为是春节，所以孩子们穿红色的衣服。

Unit 5

Grammar focus 5.1

的

Answers

a. 这是我姐姐的公寓。Correct!

b. 这是我的朋友电脑。→这是我朋友的电脑。

c. 他们家在北京的郊区。Correct!

d. 城市的中心有好几家很不错的美术馆。Correct!

Grammar focus 5.2

动词的重叠

Verbs that cannot be duplicated

1. verbs expressing mental status: 喜欢、讨厌、爱、恨

2. verbs expressing development and change: 开始、结束

3. verbs expressing existence, belonging and judgment: 在、是、有

4. verbs already in progression:

   我正在跑跑步。✗
   我正在跑步／我想跑跑步。✓

   她正在看看电视。✗
   她正在看电视／她想看看电视。✓

Answers

a. 逛逛 **b.** 尝尝 **c.** 走走

d. 来来往往 **e.** 吃吃；喝喝；聊聊

Grammar focus 5.3

第

Answers

a. 这座城市是英国第二受欢迎的旅游城市。

b. 黄河是中国第二长的河。

c. 这座建筑是伦敦的第一高楼。

Grammar focus 5.4

得

> **Answers**
>
> **a.** 到最近的超市开车得二十分钟。
>
> **b.** 今年春节我得回家看看我的父亲和母亲了。
>
> **c.** 我们得带她女儿去医院看看病了。

Grammar focus 5.5

的

> **Answers**
>
> **a.** 美丽的地方　　　　　　**b.** 安静的图书馆
>
> **c.** 古老的小镇　　　　　　**d.** 现代的建筑
>
> **e.** 热闹的街道

Grammar focus 5.7

1 Money expressions in Chinese

> **Answers**
>
> **a.** 三十欧元　　　　　　　**b.** 八英镑
>
> **c.** 两百块人民币　　　　　**d.** 四百美元

2 两 and 二

See 7.3 for practice activities.

Grammar focus 5.8

就

> **Answers**
>
> **a.** 妈妈刚刚做完晚饭，爸爸就到家了。
>
> **b.** 那个小区就在城市的中心，很方便。
>
> **c.** 她刚从中国回来，就又要去英国了。

Grammar focus 5.9

希望

> **Answers**
>
> **a.** 她希望未来到新加坡读书。
>
> **b.** 我小的时候希望当篮球运动员。
>
> **c.** 他希望有一天能够住在上海。
>
> **d.** 我希望每一天都开心。

Unit 6

Grammar focus 6.2

1 昨天／今天／明天

> **Answers**
>
> **a.** 昨天他游了泳。　　　　**b.** 今天我要读书。
>
> **c.** 今天天气很好，我们要去爬山。
>
> **d.** 明天是星期天，我会去看奶奶。
>
> **e.** 明天我要跟爸爸一起吃晚餐。

2 在 + location

> **Common mistakes**
>
> • Using 在 unnecessarily:
>
> 　我们住在巴黎在希尔顿饭店。✗
>
> 　我们住在巴黎的希尔顿饭店。✓

> **Answers**
>
> **a.** 阿里在家中玩电脑游戏。
>
> **b.** 心美在百货商店买东西。
>
> **c.** 小明放学后在球场上踢足球。

Note: 在 is also a verb, so it can be negated using 不 (e.g. 我不在家 I'm not at home).

Grammar focus 6.3

1 根据

> **Answers**
>
> **a.** 根据天气预报，下星期会下雨。
>
> **b.** 根据老师的要求，志军完成了功课。
>
> **c.** 根据姐姐的建议，这家餐厅的食物味道最好。

2 星期（一至六）；周末（星期六、星期日）

> **Sample answers**
>
> 今天是星期一，我放学后要弹钢琴。
>
> 今天是星期二，我有两堂中文课。
>
> 今天是星期三，我放学后有社团活动。
>
> 今天是星期四，我下午有体育课。
>
> 今天是星期五，我中午十二点就放学了。
>
> 星期六不用上学，我常常跟家人去看电影。
>
> 星期日放假，我在家看电视。

Grammar focus 6.4

1 Measure words for items of clothing

Answers

a. 一件衣服　**b.**　一条围巾　**c.**　一件雨衣

d. 一条裤子　**e.**　一双袜子

2 会

Answers

a. 明天会起雾。　　　　**b.**　下星期一我会打网球。

c. 星期五爸爸妈妈不会在家。

Grammar focus 6.5

1 从

Answers

a. 从学校到机场要多长时间？从学校到机场坐大巴车要三小时。

b. 从学校到心美的家要多长时间？从学校到心美的家要走二十分钟。

c. 从台湾到北京要多长时间？从台湾到北京坐飞机要三小时。

2 往

Answers

a. 往前边走五分钟，你就可以到食堂。

b. 往博物馆方向坐一站地铁，就到百货商店。

c. 往南边骑车，半个小时就到森林公园。

Grammar focus 6.6

1 怎么

Sample answers

a. 学校怎么走？　**b.**　机场怎么走？

2 这儿／那儿

Answers

a. 这儿是市区最好的旅馆。

b. 根据地图，动物园就在这儿。

c. 世界最长的河流就在那儿。

d. 北京最古老的建筑就在那儿。

Grammar focus 6.7

什么

Answers

a. Q: 动物园里有什么动物？

　　A: 动物园里有熊猫、老虎和猴子。

b. Q: 运动中心里有什么设施？

　　A: 运动中心里有游泳池、健身房和篮球场。

Grammar focus 6.8

将／将会／将要

Answers

a. 明天同学们将要参加动物园一日游。

b. 飞机将会在十五分钟以后降落。

c. 心美和我将会去汤姆的生日聚会。

Grammar focus 6.9

1 Duplication of single-word stative verbs

Answers

a. 胖胖的　**b.**　高高的　**c.**　急急地　**d.**　慢慢地

2 只有

Answers

a. 在我们家只有妈妈会开车。In our family, only mum can drive.

b. 在我们班里只有我去过南美洲。In our class, only I have visited South America.

c. 那么多朋友里面只有杰克是素食者。Among all my friends, only Jack is a vegetarian.

d. 到法国旅游时只有大卫要签证。When travelling to France, only David had to apply for a visa.

Unit 7

Grammar focus 7.2

是……的

> **Sample answers**
>
> **a.** 我们是去年认识的。
>
> **b.** 我是和家人一起去马来西亚的。
>
> **c.** 我们是坐飞机去马来西亚的。
>
> **d.** 我是来香港工作的。

Grammar focus 7.3

二 and 两

> **Common mistakes**
>
> 他今年二岁。✗   他今年两岁。✓
>
> 他今年二十两岁。✗   他今年二十二岁。✓

> **Answers**
>
> **a.** 第二次   **b.** 两件毛衣   **c.** 二楼
>
> **d.** 两个小时   **e.** 十二月二号

Grammar focus 7.5

最好

Note: In the context of 你/他/她最好 + action, it does not mean You/He/She are/is the best at doing something!

> **Sample answers**
>
> **a.** 你最好坐美国航空公司的飞机，因为座椅比较舒服。
>
> **b.** 你最好多穿衣服多休息。
>
> **c.** 你最好秋天去，因为秋天天气最好。
>
> **d.** 你最好多带几件暖和的衣服。

Grammar focus 7.6

着

> **Answers**
>
> **a.** 她看着火车慢慢地远去。
>
> **b.** 孩子们都安静地听着。
>
> **c.** 他们一边吃着，一边聊着。
>
> **d.** 最近小美忙着准备去澳大利亚留学。

Grammar focus 7.7

更喜欢

> **Answers**
>
> **a.** I like flying to Spain, but I prefer taking the ferry because I can walk around freely.
>
> **b.** I like autumn because of the variety of colours, but I prefer the cold winter because I love skiing.
>
> **c.** I like old towns, but I like beautiful and tranquil villages even more because I like uncrowded places.

Grammar focus 7.8

忙不忙

> **Common mistakes**
>
> • Including both characters of a two-character stative verb:
>
> 你舒服不舒服? ✗
>
> 你舒不舒服? ✓

> **Answers**
>
> **a.** 快不快   **b.** 多不多   **c.** 满不满意
>
> **d.** 舒不舒服   **e.** 方不方便

Note the different ways of asking the same question using 不 and 吗:

• 你舒不舒服? and 你舒服吗? both mean "Are you comfortable/well?"

• 你不舒服吗? means "Aren't you well?" or "Are you unwell?"

Grammar focus 7.9

被

Note: in this context, 被 and 给 are interchangeable.

> **Answers**
>
> **a.** 我的书被妈妈拿走了。
>
> **b.** 小美的护照被机场工作人员找到了。
>
> **c.** 巧克力被她吃完了。

Unit 8

Grammar focus 8.2

1 试一试

NB: This pattern is similar to Grammar focus 5.2 "Duplicated verbs". The same rules apply.

Answers

a. 听一听 **b.** 尝一尝 **c.** 聊一聊 **d.** 用一用

2 学......学了

Answers

a. 我做义工做了三年。

b. 弟弟上网上了一个上午。

c. 姐姐听音乐听了一小时。

Grammar focus 8.3

1 坐......去

Answers

a. 我坐飞机去日本。 **b.** 我走路去学校。

c. 我骑自行车去植物园。 **d.** 我坐船去马来西亚。

2 住在

Answers

a. 心美住在大学宿舍。 **b.** 我住在上海的市区。

c. 小华和父母一起住在广州的郊区。

Grammar focus 8.4

几

- 几 is normally used when referring to numbers below 10:

  你有几个兄弟姐妹? 我有一个妹妹还有一个弟弟。

- 多少 can be used for any number:

  你的学校有多少学生? 我的学校有五百个学生。

Answers

a. 问: 你学中文学了几年?

b. 问: 你家有几个人?

c. 问: 你参加过几次社区活动?

Grammar focus 8.5

1 不......吗?

See 7.8 for more ways of asking questions.

Answers

a. 你不打算在暑假里做义工吗?

b. 你不想读医科吗? **c.** 你不喜欢外出吃饭吗?

2 为什么......?

Answers

a. 问: 你为什么要学中文?

b. 问: 为什么中学生做兼职工作?

c. 问: 你为什么申请那所大学?

Grammar focus 8.6

1 如果......, 就......

Answers

a. 如果今天天气好, 我们就踢足球。

b. 如果有地图, 你就不会谜路。

c. 如果下雨, 就不外出。

d. 如果妈妈没有煮饭, 我们就去外面吃饭吧。

2 只要......, 就......

Answers

a. 只要努力读书, 你就能得到好成绩。

b. 只要认真准备, 你面试就会顺利。

c. 只要肯努力, 我就有可能成功。

d. 只要经常练习, 你的汉语就会进步。

Grammar focus 8.7

1 要是......, 就......

Answers

a. 要是今天下雨, 你就要带雨伞。

b. 要是带了雨伞, 我就不会被淋湿。

c. 要是在家不能上网, 我就会做一些户外活动。

2 或者

Sample answers

a. 周末的时候，哥哥喜欢读书或者画画。

b. 我们家的晚饭一般吃意大利菜或者中国菜。

c. 明年暑假，我可能会去台湾或者北京旅行。

Grammar focus 8.8

1 第一、二、三

Answers

a. 高铁有三个好处：第一，价钱比飞机便宜。第二，速度很快。第三，火车的座位比飞机舒服。

b. 打游戏有三个坏处：第一，影响学习。第二，对眼睛不好。第三，影响你和家人的关系。

c. 我有三个优点：第一，我很聪明。第二，我热爱生活。第三，我心地善良。

2 只

Answers

a. 我妹妹只有三岁。 b. 我只有一个弟弟。

c. 我只会唱歌，不会跳舞。／我只会跳舞，不会唱歌。

Grammar focus 8.9

1 为了……而……

Answers

a. 我为了考第一名而努力读书。

b. 妈妈为了照顾家人而不做全职工作了。
(This is correct!)

c. 他为了提高汉语水平而每天学40个汉字 。

d. 爸爸为了给家人好的生活而努力工作。(This is correct!)

2 一边……一边……

Answers

a. 吃东西 b. 做功课 c. 驾驶

Unit 9

Grammar focus 9.3

很，比较，十分

Answers

a. 很吸引人 b. 比较无聊 c. 十分有礼貌

d. 很快乐 e. 十分流利

Grammar focus 9.4

过

Remind students 过 is added to a verb to describe a completed experience or process that is not continuing.

Answers

丽亚是一个英国大学生，是我的网友。她对中国文化感兴趣。她不仅学过汉语，还来过中国旅游。她爬过万里长城，参观过北京的故宫，还吃过"全聚德"北京烤鸭。她还坐过中国高铁。我的这个英国网友做过很多有意思的事情。

Grammar focus 9.6

是

是 is used for linking two noun phrases that are connected by a shared context.

Common mistakes

- Treating 是 as the English verb "to be", and linking it unnecessarily with stative verbs:

  哥哥是很高。✗   玛莉是很漂亮。✗

Sample answers

a. 空档年对很多年轻人来说是很好的经验。

b. 在空档年旅行是了解不同文化的好方式。

c. 在社区做义工是获取工作经验的好方法。

Grammar focus 9.7

刚刚

Sample answers

a. 她刚刚做完工作实习。

b. 爸爸刚刚到超级市场。 c. 飞机刚刚起飞。

Grammar focus 9.8

1 得

In the Grammar focus formula, the stative verb/verb phrase following 得 is also known as a complement. It provides additional meaning to the verb.

Answers

a. 马可学汉语学得很快。　**b.** 飞机飞得越来越高。

c. 心美说英语说得比我流利。

2 趟

Answers

a. 这一趟中国之旅需要两个星期。

b. 地铁每十分钟开出一趟。

c. 睡前他喝了很多水，所以晚上上了三趟卫生间。

Grammar focus 9.9

还是

Answers

a. 问：你晚上想吃中国菜还是法国菜？

b. 问：你想读新闻还是历史专业？

c. 问：你要买单程票还是来回票？

Unit 10

Grammar focus 10.2

1 差不多

Answers

a. 陈明和志军的身高差不多。

b. 中国和印度的人口差不多。

c. 日本和英国的气候差不多。

2 比......一点儿

Answers

a. 他比我高一点儿。

b. 中文语法比写汉字难一点儿。

c. 去广州坐飞机比坐高铁快一点儿。

Grammar focus 10.3

1 Omitting 的

Answers

a. 我房间有一张书桌。　**b.** 我爸爸是医生。

c. 国庆节时她姐姐去了新加坡度假。

2 别

Answers

a. 别说了，我知道做什么！

b. 别赶了，火车已经开走了！

c. 现在别吃薯片了，我们待会儿要吃大餐。

Grammar focus 10.4

一些

Answers

a. 他给朋友买了一些糖果当纪念品。

b. 爬山的时候，你最好带一些食物和水。

c. 上星期购物的时候，我花了一些零用钱。

Grammar focus 10.5

1 左右

Answers

a. 到最近的地铁站要往前走大约三百米左右。

b. 这次到欧洲跟团旅游的人数有大约八十人左右。

c. 明天去郊游要大约十点左右出发。

2 不 + stative verb

Refer to Grammar focus 10.7 for more on when to use 不 and 没(有).

Answers

a. 美美说普通话说得很不错。

b. 在商场里购物的人不少。

c. 我觉得这次考试的问题不难。

Grammar focus 10.6

1 谁

Answers

a. 问：你要找谁？

b. 问：刚才和你说话的人是谁？

c. 问：你想邀请谁参加生日聚会？

2 哎呀

Sample answers

a. 哎呀，我赶不上飞机了！

b. 哎呀，我忘了带毛巾和牙膏！

c. 哎呀，我的钱包不见了！

Grammar focus 10.7

1 Using 不 and 没(有)

不 and 没 are the most frequently used negative adverbs. The distinction between these two does not rely on the timing. The best way to distinguish them is:

- 不 negates subjective views

- 没 negates ownership, objective facts and experiences.

Common mistakes

- Confusing 不 and 没:

  大伟昨天身体不舒服，只好没上课。✗
  大伟昨天身体不舒服，只好不上课。✓

  来北京以前，她没有会说汉语。✗
  来北京以前，她不会说汉语。✓

  我小的时候，对体育课没感兴趣。✗
  我小的时候，对体育课不感兴趣。✓

  今天早上起床太晚，我不吃早餐。✗
  今天早上起床太晚，我没吃早餐。✓

Answers

1. 不   2. 没有   3. 不   4. 没有

2 到底

Answers

a. 我们到底去看电影还是去逛街呢？

b. 你到底想怎么样？

c. 我们去上海到底是坐飞机还是坐高铁？

Grammar focus 10.8

米，吨

Answers

a. 这座教学楼有六层楼，总共有十八米高。
(This is correct!)

b. 这个建筑有差不多三百米高。

c. 在今天的体育课上他跑了五千米。

d. 非洲大象是陆地上最大的动物，体重可以有五吨重。(This is correct!)

Grammar focus 10.9

1 到

Answers

a. 五点半我到家。／我五点半到家。

b. 请到体育馆找李老师报名。

c. 今天我们要到郊外的山上种树。

2 ……既……也

Answers

a. 我们既去过日本也去过美国。

b. 小明既爱看中文书也爱看英文书。

c. 中国的四川省既有许许多多的历史古迹也有众多奇特的自然风景。

Unit 11

Grammar focus 11.3

又……又

Answers

a. iii   **b.** v   **c.** iv   **d.** ii   **e.** i